DIGITAL VISUAL EFFECTS
IN CINEMA

DIGITAL VISUAL EFFECTS
IN CINEMA

{ The Seduction of Reality }

STEPHEN PRINCE

RUTGERS UNIVERSITY PRESS

NEW BRUNSWICK, NEW JERSEY, AND LONDON

Library of Congress Cataloging-in-Publication Data

Prince, Stephen.
   Digital visual effects in cinema : the seduction of reality / Stephen Prince.
       p.   cm.
   Includes bibliographical references and index.
   ISBN 978–0–8135–5185–2 (hardcover : alk. paper) — ISBN 978–0–8135–5186–9
   (pbk. : alk. paper)
   1.   Motion picture industry—Technological innovations. 2   Motion pictures—
   Aesthetics.   3. Digital cinematography.   4. Cinematography—Special
   effects.   5. Cinematography—Technological innovations.   I. Title.
PN1995.9.T43P75 2012
778.5'3—dc22

                                                                2011012787

A British Cataloging-in-Publication record for this book is available from the British
Library.

Visit our Web site: http://rutgerspress. rutgers. edu

Manufactured in the United States of America
Typesetting: BookType

For my parents

CONTENTS

ACKNOWLEDGMENTS

I have had the opportunity and pleasure to work out some of the ideas in these pages at the 2010 conferences of the Society for Cognitive Study of the Moving Image and the Society for Cinema and Media Studies. Speaking invitations to Lund University in Sweden and the University of Copenhagen in Denmark afforded me with additional opportunities to develop the material. I thank Eric Hedling and Johannes Riis for their hospitality and to the lively audiences in Lund and Copenhagen.

VFX industry journalist Joe Fordham, who has written about visual effects for more than a decade in the pages of *Cinefex* magazine, graciously read through the manuscript and offered keen insights on digital aesthetics and the effects industry and corrected a few infelicities of expression. Joe's good cheer is complimented by his fine taste in cinema. I extend a heartfelt thanks to Joe for his invaluable assistance.

Paul Harrill brought a digital filmmaker's perspective to chapter 2. He kindly read the material on digital cinematography, corrected some gaffes, and pointed me in the right direction regarding some key topics. Paul's appreciation for the interplay between aesthetics and technology was a great help to me in parsing this material.

Patricia Raun read chapter 3 from the standpoint of a professional actor, and she kindly took time from her schedule to give me a working actor's perspective on performance in the digital domain and how this differs from what an actor creates and contributes in live theater. Thank you, Patty.

Some of the material in chapter 1 was previously published as "Through the Looking Glass: Philosophical Toys and Digital Visual Effects," *Projections* 4:2 (Winter 2010). I thank *Projections'* editor Ira Konigsberg for his permission to use that material here.

I thank also Leslie Mitchner, who loved the idea for the book from the start. Leslie is a great editor and someone with whom it is always a pleasure to work.

DIGITAL VISUAL EFFECTS
IN CINEMA

Introduction
Beyond Spectacle

Avatar, Alice in Wonderland, Iron Man, The Lord of the Rings—these are the kinds of movies that people think of when the subject of "special effects" comes up. The blue Na'vi of the planet Pandora, flying atop giant winged beasts; the diminutive Alice tumbling into a 3D wonderland; a superhero in an iron suit; wizards and Orcs battling for Middle-earth—in these story situations, filmmakers use visual effects to open doors onto imaginary lands and characters. Indeed, common wisdom holds that "special effects" take movies far away from realistic characters, situations, and locations. According to our customary way of thinking about cinema, this dichotomy in film, between the real and the fantastic, is nothing new. The progenitors of cinema included Auguste and Louis Lumière, who filmed actualities, slices of life that were portraits of everyday events, and Georges Méliès, a magician who made movies about fabulous trips to the moon or to the bottom of the sea. Again, according to conventional wisdom, "special effects" belong to the domain of fantasy that Méliès helped to establish rather than to the actuality-based lineage of the Lumières. As we shall see, however, "special effects" are more profoundly connected with cinema than conventional wisdom supposes.

At a recent cinema studies conference in Los Angeles, a colleague asked me what I was working on. When I told her it was a book about digital visual effects, she exclaimed, "Oh, I hate those movies!" For her as for many people, visual effects call to mind gaudy spectacle, overstuffed blockbusters, or action adventure fantasies catering to young audiences. Visual effects are sometimes viewed as having taken over Hollywood blockbusters and overwhelmed good storytelling. Yet scholarly thinking about cinema has been relatively slow to grasp the important and myriad roles that visual effects perform beyond those associated with spectacle. Dan North writes that visual effects are "a mistreated and misunderstood field in film studies."[1] He notes that disparagement of visual effects often involves "a condescending presumption of a correct function for cinema, and a miscalculation of the viewer's ability to discriminate."[2] Cinema, according to a predominant model, is a photographic medium oriented toward live action in which filmmakers arrange performers and events before the camera during production, with the camera used as a recording mechanism to capture an accurate facsimile of what has been placed before it. Even when filmmakers use their cameras in this fashion, setting up a shot imposes a frame upon the action. Editorial and rhetorical decisions must be made about what to include and what to exclude, producing a manufactured world upon the screen. Visual effects merely provide a more overt kind of construction. Moreover, movies such as *Avatar* (2009) and *Toy Story 3* (2010) are not very compatible with a film medium conceived in terms of photographic facsimiles and the sobriety of a realist aesthetic—they are stylized in overtly artificial ways, and they emphasize visual effects.

I suggest throughout this book that photographic models of cinema—those that attribute the medium's properties to a base in photography—provide an insufficient account of the ways that cinema operates in a narrative mode and as a medium amalgamating different image types and categories. Visual effects are not live action, and they are not created as an element photographed on the set with actors during production. Furthermore, they are not a peripheral element of cinema but a core feature, essential to its operation as a narrative medium. *Citizen Kane* (1941) would not exist were it not for the optical printer. Visual effects can be used to create spectacle, but more often they work in subtle, nonspectacular ways.

I will have much to say about the compatibility of visual effects with cinematic realism. Indeed, in numerous ways visual effects provide filmmakers with avenues toward realism, provided the category of realism is expanded from the precondition of live-action filming and image spaces that are created and treated holistically. Major traditions of realism—such as Italian neorealism or Dogme 95—emphasized live action and sought to attain a realist design by severely limiting the inflections of style. Shooting on location, using nonprofessional actors, avoiding highly inflected editing, cinematography, or production design—these methods aimed to return cinema to a threshold of articulation that eliminated or reduced the ornamentations of style in the interests of respecting something true about the characters or places being dramatized. Visual effects go in the other direction, away from live action and toward images that are highly designed and that can depart in many ways from camera reality. Nevertheless, as I show, they open pathways for the attainment of realist designs just as they afford ways of designing fantasy worlds and situations that are patently unrealistic. We cannot understand visual effects unless we overcome the dichotomy in our thinking represented by Méliès and Lumière.

Pursuing the relation of realism and visual effects raises issues of indexical meaning, since photographic indexicality is a commonly accepted basis for realism in cinema. Digital images are said to lack indexical value, but, as I show in several contexts, this claim is not tenable. I examine issues of indexical meaning throughout the coming chapters and show how compatible such meaning is with digital visual effects. A caveat, however, is in order. I wish to acknowledge at the outset that I am concerned with cinema in a narrative mode but not in the context of documentary. Questions of photographic truth are relevant to documentary in ways they are not for fiction film, and issues of indexical meaning have a different inflection in documentary than they do in fiction. Documentary is an assertive mode. It states to viewers that some situation or event exists. Fiction does not inherently do so. Some of the attributes of indexical meaning that I examine with regard to visual effects would provide an insufficient basis for the photographic veridicality that one often looks for in documentary. In this book I am strictly concerned with cinema in a narrative and mainly a fictional mode.

The reader will have noticed by now that I am avoiding the term "special effects." For reasons that I explain, it makes little sense to write or talk about "special effects" in contemporary film. Except in a limited sense, the era of special effects is over. The industry continues to use the term, but it now designates mechanical and practical effects, such as explosions or stunts involving car wrecks. Everything else is known as visual effects. The first Academy Awards ceremony bestowed an honorary plaque to *Wings* (1927) for its flying sequences, honoring what were then termed Best Engineering Effects. From 1939 to 1962, the industry awarded Oscars in a Special Effects category that also included sound effects. In 1963, Special Effects and Sound Effects were split into separate Oscar categories, and then in 1964 the Special Effects category was renamed Special Visual Effects. The term "special" was dropped in 1972, making the category Visual Effects. In popular parlance people continue to use the old terminology of special effects, but visual effects operate more broadly and can be understood as creating the kind of fantasy characters and situations that special effects once designated, as well as performing numerous other roles and functions beyond this. Thus the distinction between the terms is nontrivial; they designate different historical periods. In one period, visual effects were "special" because they were regarded as tricks supplementing live-action cinematography—set extensions achieved with hanging miniatures or matte paintings, live actors married with stop-motion puppetry via matte-and-counter-matte systems.

They were special, too, because the joins were generally visible between the elements comprising the effect, and this made boundaries between live-action cinematography and composited shots clear. Optical printers in that era were within the province of post-production, blending footage of visual elements that had already been photographed and usually exhibiting a generational loss of image quality in the composites. In today's era, digital effects are not solely a post-production endeavor, and visual effects can blend seamlessly with live action so that clear boundaries between the domains often do not exist. The title character in *The Curious Case of Benjamin Button* (2008) is a visual effect as well as a live actor's performance. The same is true of the Na'vi in *Avatar*. Virtual environments found in *Changeling* (2008), *Master and Commander* (2003), and *Zodiac* (2007) are indistinguishable from real locations. On *Avatar*, James Cameron directed his actors as their digital characters in the digital environments of Pandora. As with the dichotomy of Lumière and Méliès, the disjunction proposed by "special effects"—that effects stand apart from the normative body of live-action filming—does not characterize contemporary film. Visual effects are coextensive with narrative film, and digital tools have made them more expressive, persuasive, and immersive.

While I will have occasion to discuss visual effects during the analog era, this book is not a history of effects technologies. It concentrates on the period from the mid-1980s to the present. In 1982, *Star Trek II: The Wrath of Khan* and *Tron* showed audiences and other filmmakers the contributions that digital imaging could make to narrative, and a transformation in film production and its expressive capabilities soon followed, as digital imaging tools permeated all phases of filmmaking. Since then, much of the writing on the transition from analog to digital imaging has sounded an anxious tone, posing crises of form and function and meaning. By eroding the indexical basis of photography (in its photo-chemical mode), digital images are said to undermine the reality status of cinematic images, rendering viewers doubtful about the credibility of all cinematic images. As a result, some observers report a techno-nostalgia for the older analog forms, apparent in the use of digital elements to emulate such photographic features as motion blur, grain, and the response curves characteristic of particular film stocks. My account strikes a different tone, however. I do not believe that the transition from analog methods of imaging to digital ones represents a break either stylistically or epistemologically. Instead, I emphasize the ways that visual effects in narrative film maintain a continuity of design structures and formal functions from the analog era to the digital one. Digital visual effects build on stylistic traditions established by filmmakers in earlier generations even while providing new and more powerful tools to accomplish these ends.

This latter point is most important. In the analog era, optical printers provided a way of joining image elements which themselves remained unchanged. The printers merely photographed them on top of one another as layers. Digital visual effects are composited as layers, but all components of every layer are susceptible to being changed and tweaked, whether they are a live-action element or a computer-created one. Thus at the point of compositing and rendering, the image layers are infinitely adjustable. This makes it possible to exactly match the lighting on live actors and digital sets and to have organic and synthetic components interact convincingly. The perceptual cues that optical printing could never exactly replicate across image layers are easily finessed in a digital composite. Digital composites thereby achieve much higher levels of perceptual realism than optical printing could ever attain. I explore the expressive possibilities that digital tools have given filmmakers and explicate these with reference to what could be accomplished using analog methods.

Chapter 1 provides some necessary background, tracing the history of computer graphics and its intersection with motion pictures. Ivan Sutherland's development of the Sketchpad graphical user interface, the transition from vector to raster graphics, the design of early 8- and 24-bit paint systems, algorithms for modeling and texturing objects in computer space, and the migration of computer graphics engineers from the New York Institute of Technology to Lucasfilm—these developments furnish the prehistory for understanding what digital imaging brought to the movies. Art and science intersected; the computer scientists who wrote the algorithms were also artists interested in exploring the imagination and taking a mathematical route into wonderland. After a slow debut, in spite of being showcased in such prominent films as *The Abyss* (1989) and *Terminator 2* (1991), digital effects came of age in *Jurassic Park* (1993), the film that, more than any other, sped their adoption throughout the industry.

Jurassic Park conjoins analog and digital effects technologies. The dinosaurs are portrayed using a blend of animatronic models, old-fashioned man-in-a-monster-suit theatrics, and digital animation. The latter generated the film's extraordinary buzz of publicity and intrigued audiences with cinema's enduring promise to show viewers things they hadn't seen before. Compared with the animatronics and the suited performers, the digital dinosaurs are more supple, their movements more complex and nuanced, and they interact with the live actors in more active and spatially convincing ways. They give different and often better performances as digital characters than as an animatronic or an actor-in-a-suit. I explore these differences as a means of explicating some of the expressive possibilities that the new toolset offered filmmakers. The credibility of the film's effects enabled Steven Spielberg to linger on effects shots that in earlier generations of film would have been much briefer. In previous eras, filmmakers often needed to cut away from effects images lest viewers have a chance to study them at length and in ways that revealed the seams. The relative seamlessness of digital effects images made possible an expansion of screen time devoted to fantastical elements. This capability raised anew the enduring issues in cinema involving the relation of spectacle and narrative, and I explore the place of digital imaging in a cinema of attractions.

Chapter 2 examines digital methods of lighting and color and the ways these have changed production processes and the role of the cinematographer. Compared with optical printing, digital compositing offers finer-grade controls over image elements, and many adjustments of light and color can be performed during a multipass render. *Spider Man 2* (2004) and *King Kong* (2005) furnish illuminating examples. Digital lighting may use local or global illumination approaches, and the aesthetic functions of digital light are assessed through a discussion of the ways that Pixar artists illuminated food in *Ratatouille* (2007). In the photochemical era, Hazeltine printing lights enabled filmmakers to fine-tune color levels, but digital intermediates today provide expanded methods of color control and have taken cinematography much closer to painting, as well as transformed the cinematographer's role in production. The impact of digital intermediates is assessed through discussion of the color design in *Flags of Our Fathers* (2006) and other films. Shooting on high-definition video opens new expressive possibilities in terms of how the image light curve is handled, which Michael Mann pursued in *Collateral* (2004), *Miami Vice* (2006), and *Public Enemies* (2009), as did David Fincher in *Zodiac*, *The Curious Case of Benjamin Button*, and *The Social Network* (2010). I assess the results of their experiments in relation to issues of image resolution in analog and digital eras. Using digital light and color, filmmakers have created alternative optical domains to camera-reality as established in traditional methods of celluloid-based imaging. I conclude the chapter by examining striking examples in *Speed Racer* (2008), *300* (2006), *WALL-E* (2008), and *Children of Men* (2006).

Chapter 3 analyzes modes of performance in the digital realm. Enduring anxieties about synthespians replacing real actors have tended to obscure the ways that digital imaging provides expanded opportunities for actors to play types of characters and to inhabit situations and environments that were foreclosed to them in the analog era. Actors may be present in a digital world in three ways. They can be composited with digital animation. They can give a performance that is motion captured and turned into digital animation. And, third, the animator who creates a digital character performs as an actor. The chapter examines each of these conditions through coverage of *WALL-E, Beowulf* (2007), *Alien Resurrection* (1997), *The Wolfman* (2010), *The Polar Express* (2004), *The Lord of the Rings*, and other films. Also discussed in this chapter is the persistent phenomenon of the uncanny valley—the unease in viewers provoked by failures of photorealism in digital characters. Film scholars have tended to discuss "the uncanny" in terms of Freud's essay and associated psychoanalytic concepts.[3] But the core of the problem as a practical impediment to crafting photorealistic digital characters lies in the biologically programmed reflex in human beings to search faces for ecologically valid information pertaining to a person's feelings, thoughts, and intentions. Marker-based motion-capture systems do not generate enough facial data to satisfy this deep-level, hard-wired impulse in viewers. The digital faces generated using such methods have been found wanting. The chapter shows why such films as *Final Fantasy* (2001) and *The Polar Express* fall into the uncanny valley and how *The Curious Case of Benjamin Button* successfully avoided it.

Chapter 4 examines digital visual environments—sets, locations, and landscapes—and the ways these can be orchestrated to convey narrative meaning. Digital environments blend such disparate image sources as live action and animation, still and moving photographic images, paintings in 2D and 3D, and objects modeled in computer space and textured with photographic or painted details. Fashioning screen environments is the work of production design, employing a blend of miniature models, full- and partial-scale sets, matte paintings, real locations, and other sources for image compositing such as rear-screen projection during the classical studio era (or front-screen projection in more recent years). In that period, the studio backlot furnished sets, streets, props, and locales needed for simulating story situations. These substituted for on-location filming. The digital era has established several areas of continuity with existing traditions of production design. The digital backlot today sees computer-designed environments substituting for on-location filming and is a clear successor to the studio-crafted locales of previous decades. Miniatures and matte paintings remain essential ingredients of production design, although today miniatures may be previsualized in digital terms before construction. Matte paintings exist in 2D, 2½D, and 3D formats, depending on whether they are planar, a texture wrapping on digital geometry, or painted and animated additions to a fully dimensional digital environment. The chapter explores the areas of continuity and convergence between production design in the analog and digital eras. Case studies include comparison of the methods used to create nautical environments in two adventure films about naval warfare, *The Sea Hawk* (1940) and *Master and Commander* (2003). Both are dry-dock movies, shot in the studio and not on location at sea, and the differences in their ability to create a virtual environment on screen tell us much about the expressive capabilities of the analog and digital tools used in creating them.

A continuing theme across the chapters is the idea that the digital toolbox affords filmmakers ways of crafting more persuasive and convincing effects, blending live action and synthetic image elements into scenes that have greater perceptual credibility than what optical printing in the analog era permitted. Thus digital effects are more sensually immersive than their analog counterparts; lighting is organic and consistent across the layers of an image blend, and scene action can be staged with much greater Z-axis articulation than in the analog era, when the image planes on which live action, miniatures, and stop-motion puppetry were filmed remained visibly separate. Chapter 5 explores the immersive appeals of digital effects, not by the familiar route of connecting them to notions of spectacle or spectacular entertainment, but in terms of the ways that digital tools expand the amount of visual information that can be obtained and then manipulated inside the image. I show how methods of photogrammetry, image-based lighting, and HDRi (high dynamic range images) create new forms of indexicality within cinema. Image-based lighting, for example, enables filmmakers to light a digital environment or character with the same light sources and values as found in a real location or set with live actors. It provides a means of bridging the two domains, an ongoing requisite of effects work. The shift from planar cinema, with its image projected onto a flat viewing surface, to stereoscopic cinema represents a significant move toward greater visual immersion for the viewer. Although stereoscopic cinema has existed in one form or another from the inception of the medium, celluloid film provided a flawed basis on which to construct it, and stereoscopy never established itself as an accepted feature of popular film. Digital stereoscopic projection solved the key problems that beset celluloid, and today 3D cinema is a flourishing medium. It is also potentially the most far-reaching of the digital effects technologies examined in this book because, properly used, it elicits a different aesthetic configuration of the medium. Shooting and editing for stereoscopy requires a distinct approach from filmmakers to what is needed in planar cinema. The chapter concludes by examining the aesthetics of stereoscopic cinema.

Digital methods have given filmmakers a new set of tools to manipulate images. Filmmakers have been manipulating images for more than a century, and in this respect little in cinema has changed. Although I use the terms CG and CGI for "computer-generated" and "computer-generated images" because these have become standard descriptors, they remain very poor designators. "Computer-generated" implies that a computer created the image, which clearly is a false condition. Computers carry out the tasks they are given, and images are crafted as always by users, many of whom are disciplined and keenly imaginative artists. When I use the term CG, therefore, it should not be taken as a descriptor of coldly manipulative, soulless, mechanical imaging processes, which is one of the contexts in which digital imaging is sometimes understood.

My intent is not to practice extensive critical exegesis of themes in movies that employ digital effects. Much fine work is being done in that regard. Kristen Whissel's account of the use of Massive software to generate hordes of thousands in movies such as *The Lord of the Rings*, *Troy* (2004), and *I, Robot* (2004) is a compelling interpretation of this visual trope.[4] She shows how the digital multitude functions as a harbinger of apocalypse in these films, its infinitude proffering a visual sign of social transformation from the individual to the collective. While I engage in an extensive amount of aesthetic analysis in this book, I am less interested in extrapolating social or psychological themes from groups of movies that employ visual effects than in providing an account of what filmmakers are doing, what toolsets they have available, how these relate to earlier traditions of visual effects, and how the era of digital imaging in cinema connects with and departs from the photochemical medium that has been the traditional format. My work is thus a formalist and aesthetic and theoretical analysis of imaging tools rather than an exegesis of macroscopic thematic issues. What the digital era has altered and brought forth in new forms are imaging tools. A first task for scholars is to contemplate these tools, understand them, and connect them with filmmaking across the century and beyond, during which moviemakers have crafted synthetic image blends to stand in for worlds, characters, and story situations.

James Cameron described his efforts on *Avatar* as "the seduction of reality," meaning that he wanted to create an experience so detailed and textured that audiences could surrender completely to it.[5] Visual effects always have been a seduction of reality, more so today than ever before. This seduction is not predicated upon an impulse to betray or abandon reality but rather to beguile it so as to draw close, study and emulate it, and even transcend it. Examining cinema's landscapes through the digital looking glass shows us the medium's enduring characteristics, its continuing strengths and its appeals and challenges to some of our orthodox assumptions of what cinema is. Numbers have transformed and enlivened pictures. Digital methods bridge the analog era while taking viewers to new thresholds of optical experience. The themes enunciated by digital effects movies are perhaps less important in drawing viewers to them than are the new optical domains on display. These new visual designs are the subject of this book, along with a fan's speculations about their appeal.

CHAPTER 1

Through the Looking Glass

The digital era in cinema challenges our understanding of the medium and not simply because of the shift to electronics from celluloid. It challenges us to think anew about the nature of realism in cinema and about the conjunction between art and science, as these domains collaborate in the design and use of technologies that make possible the creation of a new class of images, ones that have a transformative effect on existing media and offer viewers opportunities to enter new optical domains. As Barbara Maria Stafford points out, visual technologies are "tools for transformation and revelation [and] expand human consciousness."[1] Digital tools are merely the latest instance in a long history of imaging technologies that have been designed to take viewers through a looking glass into domains of novel perceptual experience. As Scott Bukatman notes, "The special effects of contemporary cinema are . . . a more recent manifestation of optical, spectacular technologies that created immersive, overwhelming, and apparently immediate sensory experiences."[2] For centuries, optical technologies have offered art and science a productive meeting place, and digital applications exemplify this relationship. Digital visual effects come to us by way of the phenakistiscope. Nothing ever happens for the first time in film history, and we can learn about contemporary imaging modes by keeping in mind the bridge between art and science that gave birth to the movies. This will enable us to chart a different investigative direction into digital cinema than more familiar ones that equate visual effects with the provision of spectacle and that regard effects as being mostly incompatible with realism.

Before taking up these topics, I offer in this chapter some necessary historical and theoretical background. I begin by examining the arrival of cinema's digital era by tracing the development of computer graphics and their application to cinema, paying particular attention to the achievements

Visual effects often are equated with eye-popping spectacle, but digital tools have enlarged domains in which effects operate and have enabled filmmakers to achieve greater levels of realism in representing a world on screen. *The Mask* (1994, New Line Cinema). Frame enlargement.

in *Jurassic Park* (1993), the film that unequivocally demonstrated for Hollywood the benefits of computer-based imaging in narrative filmmaking. I then explore the union of art and science in cinema's prehistory and its relevance for understanding digital visual effects as more than spectacle. I conclude by examining the complexity of viewer response to pictorial illusion in ways that inflect the construction of visual effects.

The Development of Computer Graphics

If the 1990s were the takeoff years for digital effects in cinema (the "wonder years," in Michelle Pierson's terminology),[3] the foundations for the new generation of images appearing in *Terminator 2* (1991), *Death Becomes Her* (1992), *Jurassic Park*, and *Forrest Gump* (1994) were established in the 1960s and 1970s at a series of industry and academic research labs, including MIT, Harvard, Ohio State University, the University of Utah, Xerox Palo Alto Research Center, Bell Labs, Lawrence Livermore National Laboratory, and the New York Institute of Technology (NYIT). The period saw a burgeoning interest among academics and industry professionals in engineering, electronics, and computer science to extend the computer's capabilities, using them to draw, paint, model solid objects, and even make films.

The research generated numerous academic papers and dissertations, and in 1974 the area's professional interest group, SIGGRAPH (Special Interest Group on Computer Graphics, as it was then called), held its first conference. As many of the algorithms and procedures basic to computer imaging were developed, the available computer memory and its prohibitive cost meant that implementing these breakthroughs in a high-resolution medium like cinema remained years away. Computational power, however, was not the only constraint. The behavior of natural phenomena needed research and study from the standpoint of computer modeling. As a 1983 SIGGRAPH round-table on the simulation of natural phenomena noted, "Most items in nature, trees, clouds, fire and comets being some examples, have not been displayed realistically in computer graphics. . . . Previous attempts at realism have dealt with the appearance of the surfaces being modeled, in terms of their illumination or relief. . . . However, it appears that natural phenomena will require more research into the fundamental way things occur in nature, and in terms of computer graphics, their representation will build on previous work, but will still require new modeling techniques."[4] Modeling reality in the computer in perceptually convincing pictorial forms proved to be quite difficult.

The high cost of computing and such "lack of understanding of the intricacies of the picture-generating software that would be needed for an effective computer graphics system" impeded progress.[5] But as the cost of memory plummeted, the introduction of powerful small computers on a workstation model made it possible to take computer graphics to high resolution and pictorially complex domains. Thus it is in the early 1980s that computer graphics and feature filmmaking begin to intersect in major and substantial ways, although Hollywood was slow to adopt digital imagery in this period. By contrast, computer-generated imagery was more plentiful on broadcast television, where it appeared in advertising and as corporate logos. Corporate advertising budgets could afford the cost-per-minute expenditures that made short CGI effects feasible; Hollywood as yet could not. Moreover, film was more unforgiving of digital artifacts than the low-resolution medium of television. Digitally animated artwork graced the opening of *Entertainment Tonight* in 1983 and ABC's Winter Olympics coverage the following year, and flying logos appeared on the nightly network newscasts and broadcasts of National Football League games.

Fully functional electronic computers date to the ENIAC (Electronic Numerical Integrator and Computer) in 1946, designed and developed by the U.S. Army during World War II for use in ballistics research. Military contracting provided a powerful incentive for the initial research on digital computing. The Whirlwind, developed for the U.S. Navy in 1951 and adopted in a later version by the Air Force in its SAGE air defense program, was the first digital computer that displayed real-time graphics on an oscilloscope screen. Data entry was interactive. Using a light pen, Air Force personnel could input instructions to the computer to track specific aircraft, making it the first interactive computer graphics system.

Although the initial developments in high-power computing occurred in a military and industrial context, the potential to use computers for aesthetic ends swiftly emerged. As programming languages such as FORTRAN (1954) and BASIC (1964) enabled computers to perform an increasing variety of tasks, artists as well as mathematicians and engineers were drawn to the idea of creating graphics via computer. Charles Csuri, a computer scientist at Ohio State University, predicted that art and science would draw closer together. "The frontiers of knowledge in computer research offer a glimpse into the future role of the artist. . . . The computer, which handles fantastic amounts of data for processing, brings the artist close to the scientist. Both can now use the same disciplines and knowledge in different ways."[6] Wayne Carlson points out that the difference in this early period between artists and scientists drawn to the computer's graphic capabilities "was blurry at best."[7] Beginning in 1950, Ben Laposky, for example, a mathematician and artist, used cathode ray oscilloscopes to create abstract visual designs he called Oscillons. Bell Labs developed a computer animation system in 1963 and used it to produce films by avant-garde filmmaker Stan VanDerBeek. John Whitney, another cinema artist, embraced digital imaging. After making a series of experimental films in the 1940s, Whitney began to build what he termed mechanical drawing machines, assembled from discarded military hardware, to create and photograph abstract patterns of motion. In 1957 he rebuilt an army surplus mechanical (nondigital) computer that had been used in an anti-aircraft gun system so that he could use it to control a camera (thus taking a major step along the path to motion-control cinematography). He used it to mechanically orbit a strip of film negative displaying the number 1961 and filmed these orbits frame by frame, graphically transforming the numbers into abstract shapes and creating streaks of colored light in a film entitled *Catalog* (1961). Saul Bass used Whitney's machine in designing the title sequence to Hitchcock's *Vertigo* (1958), which featured Oscillon-type imagery, and Whitney created titles for the *Bob Hope Television Show*, *The Dinah Shore Show* and MGM's Doris Day movie *The Glass Bottom Boat* (1966). Whitney believed that computers offered a revolution in the visual arts, the possibility of creating a "liquid architecture," one in which computer manipulation of motion patterns could enable him to find visual equivalents for the dynamic harmonic structures of music. He wrote about this objective in his book *Digital Harmony*, where he observed that the graphic domain enabled by computers would be of historic proportions. "Before us lies an optical domain which may prove to be quite as vast as the historic world of music."[8]

Michael Noll, who created digital art for Bell Labs in the early 1960s, published a paper in 1967 boldly entitled "The Digital Computer as a Creative Medium" in which he observed, "Composers, film animators, and graphic artists have become interested in the application of computers in their creative endeavors."[9] "This is not to say that the traditional artistic media will be swept away," he predicted, quite presciently, "but they will undoubtedly be influenced by this new active medium. The introduction of photography—the new medium of the last century—helped to drive painting away from representation, but it did not drive out painting. What the new creative computer medium will do to all of the art forms—painting, writing, dance, music, movies—should be exciting to observe."[10]

Computer graphics began with the work of Ivan Sutherland, a doctoral student at MIT, who, for his dissertation, created in 1963 a program and associated hardware called Sketchpad. It employed a graphical user interface (GUI) and a light pen to enable simple line drawing on a cathode ray tube. In his 1963 paper "Sketchpad: A Man-Machine Graphical Communication System," Sutherland wrote, "The Sketchpad system makes it possible for a man and a computer to converse rapidly through the medium of line drawings. Heretofore, most interaction between man and computers has been slowed down by the need to reduce all communication to written statements that can be typed. . . . The Sketchpad system, by eliminating typed statements (except for legends) in favor of line drawings, opens up a new area of man-machine communication."[11]

Sketchpad treated pictures as a nested hierarchy of structures, enabling the user to manipulate portions of an image, including such now-standard commands as copying, moving, resizing, rotating, and zooming. Intended as a tool for creating engineering drawings (and thus a predecessor of CAD/CAM or computer-assisted-design/manufacturing systems, the first of which, DAC-1, debuted in 1964 as a joint effort of General Motors and IBM), it employed vector graphics, a system for creating geometrical forms by storing the information about them as mathematical formulae, a method compatible with the restricted memory capabilities of the period. Vector systems draw simple lines rather than carrying out complex operations directly on pixels (the smallest picture unit of a digital image or display), as do raster displays. Sutherland aimed to move toward a raster-based graphics system where pictorial manipulations could be performed on pixels themselves. (Raster scanning was the technology employed on standard television CRTs. The barrier it presented to computer imaging was the memory necessary for storing an entire screen's worth of pixel information.) In 1968 he joined David Evans at the University of Utah, where they formed a computer graphics department sustained by a $5 million grant from the Department of Defense's Advanced Research Projects Agency (ARPA). ARPA wanted them to develop a flight simulator for pilot training, but this required raster graphics in order to represent landscape surfaces. The primitive lines supplied by vector graphics were insufficient for displaying the tonal and textural detail needed for landscape representation. A raster system required both enough memory (what soon would be called a frame buffer) to store the pixel information and also programs for manipulating it, which didn't yet exist. Research at Utah, therefore, went into working toward raster graphics with a usable frame buffer and into creating, modeling, and lighting 3D objects in computer space. By the end of the 1960s, it was possible to build wireframe models in the computer and subject them to transformations and rotations. Subsequent research in the 1970s went toward developing the surface-level algorithms necessary for representing textures, tones, shadows, and highlights.

With Evans, Sutherland also formed the company Evans & Sutherland (E&S), which contracted with the Defense Department to build computer simulators for airplanes and ships. By 1974 E&S was marketing a commercial frame buffer following the development in 1972 by Xerox researcher Richard Shoup of a system he called "picture memory," an early iteration of frame buffering. Initial computer paint systems also developed in this period, enabling artists to work directly on pixels. At Xerox, Shoup created "Superpaint," the first 8-bit paint system.[12] Digital images derive from pixels, and each pixel has three components or channels—red, green, blue—determining color intensity. Bit depth measures the amount of color resolution contained in a computer image according to the number of bits assigned to each component. (A bit comprises the binary distinction 0 or 1.) An 8-bit system can display 256 colors.

Breakthroughs at MIT in the 1960s included Steven Coons's work on "surface patches," a formulation for representing curved surfaces as found on the hull of a ship or fuselage of an airplane. Curves were a problem for wireframe models of objects because these were built in the computer using polygons, simple, closed plane shapes that had hard edges and vertices. Polygons were not very accurate in representing curved surfaces. Coons's formulation of surface patches enabled the representation of more complex shapes than polygons afforded, and he envisioned his mathematical formulae as a means for enhancing the artistic potential of computer design by removing "almost entirely the need for the designer to be an analytic geometer." The computer would assume the geometric calculations and number crunching "and leave the user free to be a sculptor assisted by an exquisitely skillful mechanical slave."[13] Lawrence Roberts solved a critical issue in the machine replication of 3D visual data by creating an algorithm for hiding the occluded surfaces in computer-built objects. His program enabled a computer to "process a photograph into a line drawing, transform the line drawing into a three-dimensional representation and, finally, display the three-dimensional structure with all the hidden lines removed, from any point of view."[14] Thus the final 2D display would have hidden surfaces concealed from the viewer's line of sight, a necessary achievement in representing an observer's field of vision.

Developments like hiding occluded surfaces required the accumulation of complex knowledge about dimensional transformation; to appreciate this, one needs to consider the differences between painting on a 2D surface and computer modeling. The painter creates an illusion of depth, but the suggested recession of objects doesn't truly exist because the canvas is a flat surface. The painter creates an impression of 3D space, but the computer artist must create that space. The computer artist must define and then control true three-dimensional relationships and be able to translate that information accurately to the terms of a 2D viewing surface. This is no simple task, and its challenges help explain why the algorithms for a realistic representation of space in computer images were relatively slow in coming. Robert Rivlin perceptively expressed the problem this way: "For the artist, a three-dimensional object or landscape portrayed on a two-dimensional surface merely has to look real. But a model in the computer database must, for all intents and purposes, actually simulate the properties of a three-dimensional object in nature. The single view of an object in a painting or drawing is not enough for an interactive three-dimensional computer-graphics display."[15] The latter must allow for any view possible within three-dimensional space, with the appropriate transformations, such as surface occlusion relative to the viewing angle.

As these modeling achievements were occurring at Utah, MIT, Xerox, and elsewhere, entrepreneur Alexander Schure, who had financed and launched NYIT in 1955, added a Computer Graphics Laboratory to pursue applications to film. Interested in making animated movies, Shure wanted to find ways of using computers to ameliorate problems that existed in traditional cel animation, such as the labor-intensive process of animating all frames instead of simply the keyframes (with a computer handling the rest).

Schure recruited a team of computer graphics specialists, some from the program at Utah, to research methods of digital animation that could be employed to produce a feature-length film. One of the Utah graduates, Edwin Catmull, had already created a short 3D animation—*Hand* (1973)—by using his own hand as a source for 3D modeling. As noted, solid objects in computers were beset by the hard edges and sharp corners that derived from the underlying polygons used to make them, and Catmull's research extended Coons's methods for smoothing edges and surfaces. Catmull developed algorithms generating curved parallelograms assembled in patches or clusters to quickly build smooth, curved surfaces on an object, and he also helped implement the process of wrapping textures onto a geometric model (texture mapping). (Catmull's work and career exemplify the intersection of science and art manifest by the research in computer graphics. He went on to become president of Pixar Animation Studios.) The NYIT researchers examined basic problems of lighting and texturing that needed solving in order to produce real-looking images from objects modeled in the computer.

Recognizing that computer imaging needed the ability to capture translucent surfaces, Catmull and Alvy Ray Smith, another researcher at NYIT, developed the alpha channel, which specifies an object's degree of opacity. In addition to the red, blue, and green channels, the fourth, alpha, channel describes not how colorful a pixel is but how transparent it is. In 1977, Smith had designed the first 24-bit paint system, capable of generating 16 million colors. Adding a fourth component or channel raised a 24-bit image to a 32-bit image. Although this required more computing power, manipulations of opacity or translucence enabled animators to make huge strides forward in their abilities to mimic the behavior of light and its interactions with solid, gaseous, and liquid objects. The alpha channel, for example, helped make possible the convincing interactions of actress Mary Elizabeth Mastrantonio with the liquid pseudopod in *The Abyss* (1989), especially during that moment when her character pokes the liquid creature with a finger. Made of seawater, the pseudopod is translucent, and the viewer sees the character's finger inside the creature, whose pixels have been rendered as semi-transparent. Beyond giving computer graphics a stronger perceptual anchoring in the physical behavior of light, the alpha channel gave filmmakers another benefit. It provided an effective mechanism for matte extraction since it can be used to generate high-contrast images. Matte extraction has been an essential element of optical (and now digital) compositing throughout the history of cinema, and the alpha channel provided a new tool to augment existing means of pulling mattes.

Computer Graphics Meets Hollywood

At mid-decade the research developing around computer animation inter-sected with feature filmmaking. Working at the graphics company Triple-I (Information International, Inc.), John Whitney Jr. created 2D graphics for *Westworld* (1973) in scenes representing an android's electronic viewpoint. In *Future World* (1976), Triple-I created footage of a digitized Peter Fonda along with footage of Edwin Catmull's hand from his student film. The footage appeared on a monitor in the background of a shot. These debuts did not jolt Hollywood. Few even seemed to notice. But two powerful Hollywood figures—George Lucas and Francis Coppola—had a keen interest in using digital tools to simplify the labor and extend the creative possibilities of film-making, and, as Mark Rubin shows in *Droidmaker*, his history of Lucas's role in digitizing Hollywood, they pursued their interests in ways that altered the industry. Coppola's visions were grander and more epic than Lucas's, but his methods also were more scattershot and left less of a legacy. Lucas funded the systematic research that led to the eye-popping CGI with which he became forever after associated, an ironic outcome given his original intentions. Instead of funding research with its delayed gratifications, Coppola wanted to explore immediate applications of video and computers to filmmaking. He edited *Apocalypse Now* (1979) on videotape, for example, but then found he had no reliable way of translating his edits to film because of the different frame rates that operated in each medium. Lucas was uninterested in digital tools as a means to create special effects; he wanted to streamline film editing by removing the tedium of recording and tracking edge numbers in order to find shots. A computer could keep track of edge numbers more efficiently, and the random access permitted by a nonlinear system could speed the process of finding shots in the mass of footage. Coppola's approach was freewheeling. While it generated useful tools, such as the process of video assist that he used on *One from the Heart* (1982), it didn't have the lasting power that an institutional presence can achieve. Lucas, by contrast, had a company, and he was willing to fund a program of pure research focusing on digital applications in film production. He recruited Edwin Catmull from NYIT in 1978 to start a computer graphics program at Lucasfilm, which eventually grew into the company's Computer Development Division, which, years later, became Pixar.

Lucas had three objectives in funding the research. These were to develop a nonlinear editing system, a complementary system for digitally processing and mixing sound, and a digital film printer to replace existing optical printers. There was no point in developing computer graphics for film unless the results could be scanned onto film for exhibition. This was the objective that a digital film printer would achieve.

Lucas's pursuit of nonlinear editing eventually yielded the EditDroid at mid-decade, a random access (but analog, not digital) method using laserdiscs as the storage medium for raw footage. It was similar to the CMX 600, which had been marketed in the early 1970s to broadcasters, employing a computer interface and stacks of videodiscs containing dubs of videotape. CBS used a CMX in 1971 to edit a made-for-television movie. But EditDroid never had a commercial future because by 1988 Avid and EMC2 digital nonlinear editing systems came on the market, followed by Lightworks. In 1991 Adobe released its Premiere digital editor to the consumer market. In just a few more years digital editing held a significant and established place in Hollywood's post-production processes, making editing the first domain to go digital and be accepted by the industry as a professional standard.

Lucasfilm had a working ASP (Audio Signal Processor) by 1982, and although film sound remained analog until 1990 (when *Dick Tracy* became the first film released with a digital soundtrack), Lucasfilm used the ASP to create multichannel effects for *Return of the Jedi* (1983) and to mix sound digitally. The digital film printer and its associated computer and graphics projects evolved into Pixar (a name coined as a sexy version of pixel). Pixar officials wanted to pursue animated films, but Lucas did not. As their creative interests diverged, the companies parted ways, with Lucasfilm selling Pixar to Steve Jobs for $5 million in 1986. The chief graphics personnel left Lucasfilm to go with the new company, where they pioneered digitally animated feature films beginning with *Toy Story* (1995). But Pixar's first animated short, *The Adventures of Andre and Wally B* (1984), was made at Lucasfilm. It premiered at that year's SIGGRAPH conference and was notable for containing a convincing rendition of motion blur, an element of photorealism that digital animators had long sought. Shortly after the break with Lucasfilm, Pixar released a software package that became widely used throughout the computer graphics industry. RenderMan performed a comprehensive set of calculations that were needed in rendering—lighting, texturing, and adding other 3D effects—to wireframe models. The software calculated the physical properties of the digital set, its distances and layout, the positioning of digital characters, and the virtual camera along with its focal length, and then added appropriate lighting effects and shadows. RenderMan helped create the shimmery T-1000 robot in *Terminator 2*, penguins in *Batman Returns* (1992), the ballroom in *Beauty and the Beast* (1991), and dinosaurs in *Jurassic Park*.[16]

For his part, after the break with Pixar, Lucas continued to push the digital boundaries of cinema by shooting the next set of *Star Wars* movies on high definition video. *The Phantom Menace* (1999) was shot partly on film because high-speed HD video needed for effects work wasn't yet viable.[17] Lucas persuaded Sony to build a customized hi-def camera for his needs, and, using the Sony HDW-F900, Lucas shot all of episode two in the second trilogy, *Attack of the Clones* (2002), in digital format. He used an improved version of Sony's camera on the next installment, *Revenge of the Sith* (2005). Panavision introduced its own digital camera in 2004, the Genesis, capable of accommodating Panavision's standard line of 35mm film lenses. *Superman Returns* (2006), *Flyboys* (2006), *Apocalypto* (2006), and many other films have been shot with the Genesis. Lucas did not singlehandedly move feature cinematography into a digital realm, however. Cinematographer John Bailey had already shot *The Anniversary Party* (2001) on digital video, and methods of digitally grading film images to adjust color and other tonal values were employed on *Pleasantville* (1998) and *O Brother, Where Art Thou?* (2000). But Lucas and his company were the powerhouse, and his efforts in taking cinematography in a digital direction helped to establish digital image capture as a professional industry standard. Other major filmmakers swiftly identified themselves with digital image capture. Prominent among these have been David Fincher (*Zodiac, The Curious Case of Benjamin Button*) and Michael Mann (*Collateral, Public Enemies*).

Although digital effects were not part of George Lucas's original vision, the effects created by the artists at ILM became widely identified with the filmmaker and his company as its primary product and influence on cinema at large. In light of this popular legacy, interestingly, Lucas was relatively slow to incorporate digital effects into his own films. *Star Wars* (1977) included a brief 3D computer graphic visualizing the planned attack on the Death Star. (Other computer screens in the film displaying graphics were animated by hand. The innovative computer work on *Star Wars* lay not in digital effects but in motion-control cinematography. A computer-controlled camera made multiple, exactly repeatable passes, photographing a model numerous times to create the layers of elements needed for an effects shot.) On *The Empire Strikes Back* (1980), ILM explored a relationship with competitor Triple-I under which the latter was to furnish a 3D computer animation of an X-wing fighter. But ILM demurred, the effects shot was never used, and the film contained no computer graphics. The sequel, *Return of the Jedi*, used only a small amount of digital animation to simulate graphics displays. By contrast, during this period the major digital effects showcases were in films made by other production companies, some of which ILM worked on as a contractor. Chief among these was Paramount Pictures' *Star Trek II: The Wrath of Khan* (1982), whose "Genesis sequence" was the era's great industry eye-opener, showing what digital imaging could do for cinema. It contained the first application in a theatrical film of a digital paint system, a newly created 32-bit (four channel) program.[18] In the sixty-second sequence, a Genesis probe missile fired at a dead planet revivifies it. A wave of fire sweeps across the planet, leading to a lush rebirthing process on a global scale. Previous instances of digital graphics, as used in *Star Wars*, *Future World*, or 1981's *Looker*, did not aim to simulate a photographic or an organic reality. They looked like what they were—schematic computer images—and functioned in the scenes as what they were—primitive images displayed on computer monitors that the characters in the scene were viewing. (The Genesis sequence is also viewed by characters in the scene on a monitor, but it does not resemble primitive vector graphics.)

The Genesis sequence is cinema's first attempt to simulate properties of organic matter in a photographically convincing manner, one not intended to look like a computer graphic, as did the applications in earlier films. The sequence broke ground by using two relatively new modeling procedures—particle systems and fractal geometry. The sequence included such difficult-to-animate objects as fire, sparks, smoke, and clouds, and these were treated as particle systems, dynamic aggregates manifesting their own behavioral laws, spawning (or spreading in the case of fire) at a known rate and subject to the influence of wind and gravity. This was a different approach than the standard used to animate solid objects, which involved building polygon models and then texturing them. William Reeves, the Lucasfilm animator who created the wave of fire, explained the concept of particle systems in a paper prepared for the Association of Computing Machinery. He noted that "fuzzy" objects—clouds, smoke, water, fire—had proven difficult to model using existing techniques. "These 'fuzzy' objects do not have smooth, well-defined, and shiny surfaces; instead their surfaces are irregular, complex, and ill defined. We are interested in their dynamic and fluid changes in shape and appearance."[19] The method did not use fixed surface elements to define objects but rather clouds of particles, a particle being simply a point in three-dimensional computer space that changes over time in its size, coloring, and transparency. The particle system is fluid, not static, with new particles born and old ones dying. The laws governing an object's shape and behavior are not fixed and deterministic. They are stochastic, that is, a degree of randomness is included. This gives the particle system the appearance of being alive, dynamic. Treating the particles as point light sources enabled elaborate painting effects. "When many particles covered a pixel, as was the case near the center and base of each explosion, the red component was quickly clamped at full intensity and the green component increased to a point where the resulting color was orange and even yellow. Thus, the heart of the explosion had a hot yellow-orange glow which faded off to shades of red elsewhere.... The rate at which a particle's color changed simulated the cooling of a glowing piece of some hypothetical material."[20]

In addition to fire, the sequence also displayed convincing representations of the organic features of the Genesis planet, such as forests and mountains. These were built as fractals using stochastic processes, drawing on the skills of Loren Carpenter, a member of Lucasfilm's computer group working on the sequence but formerly a Boeing employee who had used computers to make aircraft drawings and graphics for flight simulators. Lucasfilm hired him after he presented an animated film using fractal modeling at the 1980 SIGGRAPH Conference. Entitled *Vol Libre*, Carpenter's film showed traveling aerial views of mountains and valleys, with appropriately scaled object resolutions changing according to camera distance. As Carpenter wrote in his SIGGRAPH paper, "Fractals are a class of highly irregular shapes that have myriad counterparts in the real world, such as islands, river networks, turbulence, and snowflakes."[21] He noted that fractal sets are self-similar. "Self-similarity refers to the property of a form that remains unaltered through changes in scale."Because each part of a fractal is structurally like the others, they can be recursively subdivided to change scale or to create new objects. Introducing a degree of randomness into the structures enables the artist to simulate an organic look by making edges and shapes appear rough and irregular. Carpenter had been inspired by Benoit Mandelbrot's book *The Fractal Geometry of Nature*, in which the mathematician argued that these formulas organized many organic, natural forms. (*Cinefex* writer Joe Fordham points out that when Mandelbrot passed away, computer graphics artists mourned him as "one of their founding fathers.")[22] In another paper, Carpenter and his coauthors wrote, "The importance of the stochastic properties of the real world will lead to greatly increased flexibility in the modeling techniques used in computer graphics."[23] In *Vol Libre* he showed that fractals and stochastic modeling had a key place in computer animation. The Genesis sequence brought this application to a much wider audience than had *Vol Libre*, and it was the first stand-alone, all-digital sequence to appear in a feature film.

A few months after *The Wrath of Khan* opened, Disney released *Tron*, the second prominent industry feature to showcase computer graphics. The film portrays a computer specialist who is bodily transported into the digital world of a mainframe computer, where he has a series of adventures in a tyrannical electronic world. The cleverest sequence in the film occurs during this transporting. As Kevin Flynn (Jeff Bridges) is scanned into the computer, he is converted into a wireframe model composed of a series of polygons, reversing the sequence by which computer graphics generate solid objects that begin as polygon models. Triple-I and several other companies (not including Lucasfilm) created the digital effects, which were more plentiful than in any previous film—fifteen minutes of all-digital imagery and an additional twenty-five minutes composited with live action. Unlike the Genesis sequence in *The Wrath of Khan*, however, the effects do not emulate photorealism or an organic world. Because the narrative premise is that the hero is inside a computer, the landscapes are meant to look electronic rather than natural. The viewer is intended to see that they are not real. Thus, they lack texturing and modeled lighting and look like vector graphics, composed of hard, clear, geometrically simple lines instead of analog surfaces. This look was probably unappealing to a wide audience in comparison with the kind of photorealism that computer graphics in cinema have generally aimed to emulate. Although the film's box office performance was not poor, critical reviews were tepid and the industry perceived the film as a failure. At least, that is, initially. *Tron* gained a cult following in the decades after its release, one sufficiently devoted to the film that Disney produced a sequel, *Tron: Legacy* (2010), whose 3D digital design softened the hard and unappealing vector graphics-look of the original and used the art of motion capture that had matured during the intervening years.

Hollywood continued exploring digital effects in feature films but without the boxoffice success that could be galvanizing and industry-changing. *The Last Starfighter* (1984) featured twenty minutes of CGI, and a human being was digitally animated for a brief effect in *The Young Sherlock Holmes* (1985). The level of image control achieved in the watery pseudopod crossed thresholds in digital animation, but *The Abyss* performed poorly at the domestic box office. Digital effects remained expensive, and no film had yet demonstrated conclusively that the artistic results of such expense could in themselves command wide popular appeal.

Spielberg's Dinosaurs

Terminator 2 was the first blockbuster to carry extensive digital effects. Its global box office was just over $500 million, and in its wake numerous films began utilizing computer graphics. Sometimes this was for showy ends, as in the outré contortions (a turned-around head, a giant hole in the chest) visited upon Meryl Streep's character in *Death Becomes Her* (1992), but in other cases, such as the Clint Eastwood thriller *In the Line of Fire* (1993), crowd-augmentation effects were unobtrusive and dramatically realistic. While the early 1990s saw an uptick in the use of computer graphics in feature films,

Terminator 2 (1991, Carolco Pictures) was the first blockbuster to feature extensive digital effects, but it was Steven Spielberg's *Jurassic Park* (1993) that galvanized the industry. Frame enlargement.

it was *Jurassic Park* in 1993 that demonstrated their dramatic and economic potential more vividly than any previous film. It met with a smashing box office reception. The film's global gross was nearly $1 billion. Partly this was attributable to the enduring popularity of dinosaurs, which have a long history in fantasy films, going back at least to Willis O'Brien's work on *The Lost World* (1925), where stop-motion animation brought miniature puppets to life. With his unerring commercial instincts, Steven Spielberg tapped into this enduring fascination.

But the film's digital aura also worked in its favor. A carefully orchestrated marketing campaign promoted the film's use of digital images and promised viewers they would see dinosaurs that were more vivid and lifelike than any they had seen before in the movies. This aura was enticing, alluring—it promised viewers a radically new experience, and dinosaurs were the perfect vehicle for launching an era of unprecedentedly vivid visual effects. Such promises, of course, can backfire if a film does not follow through. But *Jurassic Park* did honor its claim to give audiences a radically new experience. Its dinosaurs were remarkably vivid, and if the storyline in the film seemed a bit mechanical and the characters relatively lacking in psychological depth, the main objective held just fine, which was to engineer a series of narrative situations that would place the characters in jeopardy from prehistoric beasts. Movies like this tend to be about one thing—run from the dinosaurs!—and *Jurassic Park* contained enough such scenes to adequately deliver its goods.

Its mix of visual effects technologies made *Jurassic Park* a perfect film to usher in a new era of electronic imaging capabilities. It is an appropriately transitional film because it mixes old and new in expert and exhilarating ways. Although it is now and forever branded as a CGI film, there are only about fifty computer graphics shots in the movie. Critics and scholars tend to describe the film as if every dinosaur seen on screen came out of a computer, but most scenes involving dinosaurs feature a blend of traditional effects elements and digital ones. In this respect, the film runs counter to claims that digital technology will drive out more traditional effects tools. Voicing anxieties in the film industry that were prevalent in the period of the early 2000s, Michelle Pierson wrote that "the techniques of visual effects animation are being lost to CGI."[24] She continued, "The concern for many people trained in the techniques of makeup and prosthetics, model making, and animatronics was that the demand for this type of workmanship would simply disappear altogether should CGI ever prove capable of stimulating the materiality of physical effects effectively enough to meet with audiences' approval."[25]

To date, this kind of wholesale change has not occurred. CGI happily coexists with the traditional techniques of cinema—models, stop motion, animatronics, location filming—as *Coraline* (2009), *The Lord of the Rings* trilogy, and *Inception* (2010) demonstrate. Designing *Inception*, director Christopher Nolan stressed the value of on-location filming and practical effects accomplished in-camera and with physical sets and props. These were extended with digital tools. Real locations with actors Leonardo DiCaprio and Ellen Page included Paris streets, which were then treated digitally for a spectacular scene in which the urban environment folds up into a cube containing the actors. Nolan wanted to achieve a tactile realism and felt that only by blending physical stunts and effects with digital ones could he attain this objective.[26] Tangible benefits derive from staging things in-camera and enabling the actors to perform on location or to interact with a puppet. The emotional connection in *E.T.: The Extra-Terrestrial* (1982) between the children Elliott (Henry Thomas) and Gertie (Drew Barrymore) and their diminutive alien visitor was enriched by having the puppet on set where the child actors could interact with it. *Cinefex* writer Fordham points to another example: "I think Teddy in *A.I. Artificial Intelligence* (2001) is a more recent candidate to prove that there is still a place for practical puppets on a movie set. They made a couple of full CG versions for wide ambulatory shots, but he was brilliantly and perfectly realized by the Stan Winston team, and I would not conceive of him being done any other way today—he was supposed to be a ratty-looking but super-sophisticated mechanical bear, and I think it would have just felt wrong if he'd been done entirely as CG."[27] Despite the hype generated by *Jurassic Park*'s digital dinosaurs, they share time with animatronic models. Indeed, a significant measure of the film's artistry is its canny and often imperceptible blend of diverse effects technologies.[28] Only two scenes in the film feature all-digital

Digital tools have not replaced physical props and models in the creation of effects images. Christopher Nolan used digital tools as extensions of real locations and physical stunts throughout *Inception* (2010, Warner Bros.). Frame enlargement.

work—when paleontologists Alan Grant (Sam Neill) and Ellie Sattler (Laura Dern) see a brachiosaurus in the film's first sequence showing dinosaurs and a subsequent scene later in the film when a stampeding herd of gallimimus surrounds Grant and the children, Tim (Joseph Mazzello) and Lex (Ariana Richards). That scene ends with the giant T-Rex gobbling up a gallimimus. An extended sequence of digital animation comes at the end of the film when the T-Rex attacks two velociraptors in the park's Visitor's Center, but it is preceded by shots of the raptors menacing Grant, Sattler, and the kids that are done with animatronic models. Every other dinosaur scene in the film is done either with animatronics only or as a blend of shots featuring animatronics and CGI.

Spielberg originally planned for the film to be done with full-size robotic dinosaurs and stop-motion puppets, but this proved unfeasible. He then envisioned a blend of animatronic models designed by the Stan Winston Studio and Go-Motion puppetry designed by Phil Tippett. Animatronic models are built with motors and cables and pulleys so they can simulate character behavior. One of the most striking of these models is the ailing triceratops that Grant and Sattler find lying on its side. The model was twenty-five feet long and constructed of plywood, covered with clay and foam latex skin modeled to simulate the detailing and texturing of actual triceratops skin. The model was built with eyes that blinked, a jaw and tongue that moved, and an expandable rib cage to simulate breathing. The artistry is extraordinary, and the illusion that it creates of an ailing triceratops is overwhelmingly persuasive, so much so that many of the film's viewers may have believed it to be a digital effect. By contrast, the animatronic T-Rex was modeled in sections—separate models for a head and for legs to be used in shots featuring partial views of the creature. A huge twenty-foot-tall model was constructed for a few shots used in a nighttime attack sequence.

For a long while, Phil Tippett and other animators at ILM had been experimenting with methods of introducing motion blur into stop-motion puppetry. These methods eventually earned the name Go-Motion. Motion blur is an artifact of the camera's way of seeing. Motion pictures capture a moving subject as a series of still frame photographs, each of which freezes the action, blurring the image to a degree that depends on the camera's shutter speed. As used in films like *King Kong* (1933), stop-motion animation lacked motion blur because puppets were filmed in stationary positions, then reanimated and filmed again in a stationary position. The absence of motion blur was a giveaway that the animated puppets and the live actors in a composited shot had not been filmed at the same time or inhabited the same space. ILM's interest in correcting this facet of stop-motion animation was sustained and intense. On *Star Wars*, computer-driven motion control cameras executed moves around stationary models of spaceships and filmed them a frame at a time, capturing motion blur because the camera was moving when its shutter was open. On *The Empire Strikes Back*, the wooly tauntans were filmed as miniature puppets that were moved slightly during stop-frame filming to produce a simulation of motion blur. Phil Tippett worked on these scenes and also on those in *Dragonslayer* (1981), where a more elaborate, computer-controlled mechanism was used to move the puppet during filming. Spielberg had planned to use Go-Motion puppetry for *Jurassic Park*, but ILM, which had been retained by the production to create and animate the gallimimus sequence, ran tests indicating that digital motion blur could be effectively applied to standard stop-motion animation; further tests suggested that a full-scale CG dinosaur could be built in the computer with the requisite personality and behavioral nuances to give a compelling performance. (Fordham points out that Tippett "saw ILM's first test and said 'I am extinct.' Spielberg put the line in his film and recruited Phil to oversee the performance of CGI dinosaurs.")[29] The gallimimus sequence had been planned for digital animation because it involved aggregate herd behavior and simple crowd replication of the sort already demonstrated in other films. But a digital character, made of skin and bone and blood, giving a performance as the T-Rex and the raptors do was another thing entirely. Computers had been very good at depicting hard and/or shiny surfaces, like the T-1000 terminator or the pseudopod. An organic character performance digitally created was something new, but Spielberg was impressed with the ILM tests and boldly decided to dispense with plans for Go-Motion and instead do everything with Stan Winston's models and ILM's computer graphics. Tippett remained on the production to oversee the animated performances of the CG dinosaurs. His animators used a digital input device that translated hand-animated puppet moves to a computer model that would be used for a CG creature. The digital input device (or "dino-input-device") was a robust way of connecting traditional effects techniques with CGI. Anything that could not be done live on the set using the animatronics would be done digitally. In practice, this often meant that elaborate, complicated, or fast full-body dinosaur movements would be digital, while the models would be used for partial views of a creature, as when the T-Rex head comes into frame or the raptor feet come down in close-up on the park's kitchen floor.

The film's blending of these methods is extraordinary and subtle, even across back-to-back shots that switch from a sculpted model to a digital creature. The T-Rex attack on two park vehicles is one of the film's major set-pieces, and Spielberg films much of the action from the viewpoint of characters trapped in the vehicles as the monster threatens them. The T-Rex appears first as a Stan Winston animatronic, a partial body model. The head rises into view above the foliage surrounding the park's electrified fence. Then it vanishes back into the jungle, and when the T-Rex next appears, it does so as a digital creature seen full body, breaking through the fence and striding between the two vehicles. Spielberg cuts to a close-up of Grant and Ian Malcolm (Jeff Goldblum) in one vehicle looking off-frame, then cuts to another view inside the vehicle as the digital T-Rex stalks past the front of the

The dinosaurs in *Jurassic Park* (1993, Universal Pictures) are a brilliant blend of animatronic models and digital animation. Frame enlargement.

car, moving in a serpentine manner from head to tail. When it next appears, we again see it outside the windows of Grant and Malcolm's vehicle, but this time in a single shot that blends an animatronic model and a digital rendition of the character. Its head looms into view—the animatronic model—and as its attention is drawn to a flashlight in the other, distant vehicle, Spielberg moves the camera closer to the windshield.

The camera move accomplishes two things. It draws our attention to the flashlight in the distant vehicle where Lex in a panic has turned it on, and it causes the animatronic to move off-frame, making possible the switch. After a beat, the digital dinosaur stalks into frame as a full-body creature and moves toward the other vehicle. Spielberg cuts to Lex in terror holding her flashlight and then to a low-angle framing of her as the animatronic T-Rex head looms outside her car. In the space of three shots, Spielberg has introduced an animatronic model, then gone to a digital version of the creature, and then returned to the animatronic. Later in the sequence, Malcolm distracts the T-Rex with a flare, and as Spielberg tracks backward, Malcolm runs toward the moving camera with an enraged digital dinosaur thundering after him. Spielberg cuts to a park employee, Martin (Donald Gennaro), who has taken refuge from the attack in a restroom. A reverse-angle cut shows the animatronic head bursting into the restroom, and then a wider framing shows Martin seated on a toilet with the full-body digital T-Rex snarling at him. As this shot continues without a cutaway, the T-Rex snatches him off the toilet and gobbles him up. The action doesn't just blend live action and digital, as did the earlier shot where Spielberg switches from an animatronic model to a digital T-Rex within the same frame. They connect—the digital creature "eats" the live actor. The illusion was created by painting the actor out of the frame and replacing him with a digital character as the dinosaur's jaws engulf him.

Subliminal transitions between effects modes also distinguish a subsequent scene where two raptors stalk the children in one of the park's kitchens. The complexities of operating the animatronic puppets meant that whenever the two raptors appeared together in a shot, they couldn't both be models. As Winston observed, "We were always using either one puppet and one man in a suit, or two men in suits. We never had two puppets working simultaneously. That would have been too complicated because of the number of puppeteers it took to operate them."[30] The scene begins with one raptor standing in the doorway, portrayed by a man in a raptor suit. After a cutaway to the children, a second raptor appears in the doorway and both enter the kitchen. These were digital dinosaurs, and here as elsewhere key differences in the representation enable a viewer who wishes to do so to distinguish the digital from the nondigital dinosaurs. The digital raptors, and the digital T-Rex in his shots, move more fluidly, have a more extensive bodily articulation through movement, show a more complicated repertoire of responses, and react to stimuli faster than do the animatronic puppets or the actors in monster suits. The digital dinosaurs move in full-body shots, unlike the puppets, which are glimpsed in partial views, and the staging is composed more aggressively along the Z-axis (toward or away from the camera), as when the T-Rex chases Malcolm or kills a raptor in the last scene by thrashing it toward the camera. The sequel, *The Lost World: Jurassic Park* (1997), shows greater and more aggressive interactions between humans and dinosaurs because digital tools had advanced during the intervening years along with ILM's artistry. ILM's Dennis Muran commented that the shot designs and camera movements were conservative on the first film because everyone was a little unsure about the capabilities of the technology.[31] Camera moves in the sequel were much bolder. The round-up sequence provides vivid examples, as the camera follows dino-hunters on jeeps and motorcycles riding between, under, and through the legs of giant, galloping mamenchisaurs. The digital action is far more dynamic and visceral than what could be achieved with animatronics. Action staging occurs in and through a volume of space rather than on a plane.

Perceptual Realism

The digital animals exist only in 3D computer space and not in the world that was before the camera. The puppets, by contrast, do exist in the actual space before the camera, but they do not interact as dynamically with the actors. (Nevertheless, as noted earlier, positive benefits derive from using puppets on set with actors, chief among them being actors delivering stronger performances.) Typically, when they loom above or below or behind the actors, their movements are limited and the shots are brief because the puppets are prebuilt to move along small axes. Moreover, traditional compositing of analog effects, mixing live action with matte paintings or miniature models, required the use of stationary cameras so that the implied angles of view would match on the different image layers. Digital motion control cinematography changed this. A live-action camera can be programmed to execute the same moves as the virtual camera in computer space, and even when it isn't, a motion control artist can track the camera's move in digital space in order to build and animate a matching virtual camera. As Mark Cotta Vaz notes about the analog era, "The commandment of locking down cameras for effects photography was particularly strict in filming and compositing live action and animated elements."[32] When the T-Rex bursts through the park fence or chases Malcolm, it traverses a huge volume of space. The camera stays on the animal rather than cutting away from the digital performance, and it moves with the actor and the animated dinosaur. The depiction of space, therefore, is more dynamic, volumetric, and three-dimensional than would be possible using traditional effects techniques. Warren Buckland was sufficiently impressed by this digital ability to unify the visual space of a scene that he compared it favorably as an aesthetic of realism with the classic emphasis on deep focus that André Bazin had invoked. "We can even argue that (however paradoxical it may sound) the shots showing the humans and digital dinosaurs interacting are the digital equivalent of the long takes and deep-focus shots praised by André Bazin for their spatial density and surplus of realism, in opposition to the synthetic and unrealistic effects created by editing."[33] The new capabilities offered by digital imaging challenge scholars to rethink existing theoretical distinctions. Tom Gunning has argued forcefully that we need to move beyond the familiar dichotomies of theory: "I believe we distort our experience of films if we try to assign the effect of realism—or even the sensation of physical presence—exclusively to the photographic or confine the artificial to 'special effects.'"[34] Scott Bukatman observes as well that "a too easy historicism has tended to divide cinematic representations into naturalist and antinaturalist categories."[35]

Indeed, there are very good reasons for insisting on a critical perspective that is amenable to integrating computer graphics capabilities with aesthetic properties of realism in cinema. In an earlier essay, I identified a digital basis for realism in cinema in terms of what I called "perceptual realism," which was the replication via digital means of contextual cues designating a three-dimensional world.[36] These cues include information sources about the size and positioning of objects in space, their texturing and apparent density of detail, the behavior of light as it interacts with the physical world, principles of motion and anatomy, and the physics involved in dynamic systems such as water, clouds, and fire. Digital tools give filmmakers an unprecedented ability to replicate and emphasize these cues as a means for anchoring the scene in a perceptual reality that the viewer will find credible because it follows the same observable laws of physics as the world s/he inhabits. The referential status of the representation is less important in this conception of realism. Dinosaurs are not living beings in the age of cinema. They cannot be photographed as sentient creatures. Thus their logical status in *Jurassic Park* is as objects that are referentially false. They correspond to no reality the film's viewer could inhabit. And yet as depicted in the film they are perceptually realistic. They interact in relatively convincing ways with the live actors in a space that bonds the domains of live action and digital animation, as when the T-Rex gobbles up Martin. And because they are perceptually realistic, they are able to compel belief in the fictional world of the film in ways that traditional special effects could not accomplish. The creation of perceptual realism is a major goal of visual effects artists. Visual effects seek to persuade viewers that the effects are real within the referential terms of the story. Therefore, the more comprehensive a scene in evoking perceptual realism, the likelier it is to compel the spectator's belief. No one watching *Jurassic Park* was fooled into thinking that dinosaurs were actually alive, but because digital tools established perceptual realism with new levels of sensory detail, viewers could be sensually persuaded to believe in the fiction and to participate in the pleasures it offered. Had the film employed only traditional effects tools, this sensory persuasion would have been far less remarkable. At the same time, much of its effectiveness derives from the canny blend of CG and physical effects. As Joe Fordham points out, "It was also quite subtle, the way Spielberg used Mike Lantieri's special effects—the [CG] bronto eats the leaves from the tree-top when we first see her; Mike did that by pulling the tree and causing it to twitch. [It was] brilliantly executed when combined with the animated creature. That's why they had the strange credits on the poster: 'full motion' dinos by Dennis Muren, 'live action' dinos by Stan Winston, 'dino supervisor' Phil Tippett, and 'special dino effects' by Mike Lantieri—it was a perfect synthesis of all four."[37]

Traditional effects tools had been more limited in their ability to create perceptual realism, and augmenting them with CGI greatly enhanced the persuasive power of effects sequences. The compositing of live action, matte paintings, and miniatures in *The Lost World* (1925), *King Kong*, *The Valley of Gwangi* (1969), and other comparable creature movies was compromised by overt matte lines between the elements and by the planar rendition of space that prevented the matted creature from interacting with the live actors. Many of the jungle scenes in *King Kong* were created as multiplane projections, combinations of miniature models and sheets of glass with matte paintings on them arrayed at varying depths in the miniature set. Actors could be inserted as rear projection elements into the set. As ingenious as this design was, it kept the dramatic elements of the scene—actors, creatures, and environment—separated from one another, with little or no interaction possible. Ray Harryhausen devised an opposite system he called Dynamation.[38] As used on such films as *The Beast from 20,000 Fathoms* (1953), it utilized a split-screen matte to rear-project live action into a scene employing stop-motion puppetry. He also seized on ingenious ways of marrying live action to stop motion, as in *Jason and the Argonauts* (1963). When Jason fights the army

King Kong (1933, RKO) featured state-of-the-art composites achieved as in-camera mattes and also via optical printing. Kong as a stop-motion puppet "looks" at the live actor who has been inserted into the scene as a miniature rear projection. Frame enlargement.

of stop-motion skeletons, his sword appears to stick into them, an illusion Harryhausen created using sheets of glass in front of the puppet onto which the spear or sword emerging from its body could be painted. And yet because the stop-motion figures do not have motion blur while the live actors do, the perceptual realism of the sequence is diminished. The composited elements exhibit a perceptual disparity—limited interaction between the domains, contradictory manifestations of motion blur—working against the emergence of an organic unity of action. Under these terms, the dramatic space of the screen action becomes perceptually suspect. Digital effects promised to free cinema imagery from those problems of perceptual realism, triggering a reality-check by the moviegoer that undermined the fictional enterprise.

Perceptual realism, then, is central to understanding visual effects in cinema, the goal of effects artists, and the credibility that the effects image seeks to elicit among viewers. I have described perceptual realism in terms of the organic bonding of space between live action and digital characters as one manifestation in *Jurassic Park*. But another very significant one involves the expansion of creative possibilities for eliciting dramatic performances by digital characters. The performances by the digital dinosaurs often are more expressive than what the puppets provide. As Dennis Muran noted about the responses of the digital raptors in the kitchen scene to the sound of a falling ladle, "The foreground raptor pauses, cocks its head, then moves down quickly toward the ladle and stops absolutely on a dime. It sniffs the spoon and *quickly* jerks its head up as if it hears something. All of that action was so positive and conveyed such an attitude in the animal that it could only have been done the way we did it. The physical world would never have allowed a puppet to do that. Ten puppeteers cannot coordinate well enough to get that kind of performance."[39]

The staging of the first appearance by a dinosaur in the film is calibrated to take advantage of this potential for digitally representing performances. As park owner John Hammond (Richard Attenborough) drives Grant and Sattler through the preserve, they come upon a huge brachiosaur nibbling leaves off the tops of nearby trees. Using four moving camera shots, Spielberg provides a series of portraits of the docile, slow-moving giant as the astonished Grant and Sattler gape in awe and get out of their vehicles to walk closer. The camera movement makes the scene dynamic, but more important it connects the actors and the dinosaur, visually establishing the scene as containing a single organic space rather than different domains of live action and computer graphics. In bonding these domains, the volumetric manipulation of space in the scene is most effective and kinetic in a low-angle tracking shot that follows Grant and Sattler as they walk to a position nearly at the feet of the brachiosaur and stare upward. The extreme depth perspective in the shot vividly conveys the animal's towering size and height. In this scene as elsewhere, digital dinosaurs are rendered with finely detailed skin texture and color. The brachiosaur's skin jostles as it moves, and ILM had to figure out how to do this first-of-its-kind rendering. Muren said, "There were a lot of problems involved in creating photorealistic dinosaur skin. How do we get the light to react with it so that it has the right kind of sheen? How do we get the light to react to all the bumps on the skin? How do we create those bumps?"[40] And with the raptors and T-Rex that appeared as puppets and also in digital form, their skin had to match across their various incarnations.

The brachiosaur scene concludes with two additional shots that show a herd of the animals in the distance. All the digital shots are held leisurely on screen rather than being presented as quick glimpses. The longest lasts fourteen seconds, and this relaxed mode of presentation was essential to establishing the digital performance. Creature effects in earlier generations of film often looked quite false. King Kong is an obvious puppet, Godzilla a man in a rubber suit. To hide the fakery, filmmakers often limited the audience's views of the creature, withholding its appearance until the last moment or restricting it to a quick and fleeting appearance. Muren said, "If our sensibilities told us that we didn't want a shot to cut yet, it was great that we weren't *forced* to cut by the limitations of the technology. These shots ran and ran, giving you what your eye wanted to see, not what the filmmaker was limited to showing you."[41] This was a new kind of aesthetic freedom—the creature effects were sufficiently persuasive that filmmakers could hold on them in defiance of past conventions.

This new freedom to showcase imaginative effects accentuated an existing tension within cinema between narrative and spectacle. When a shot can run and run to show viewers what they "want to see," integrating such moments into a narrative framework requires care and attention on the part of filmmakers. Smart directors like Spielberg designed well-constructed narratives that offered appealing attractions in the form of visual effects. The aesthetic sensibility of the filmmaker counts for much in the area of visual effects as it does in other areas of film design. "I really believe the director is the most important factor in how effective digital effects can be," notes Fordham. "Spielberg is a great filmmaker; so is [David] Fincher. They appreciate and respect the power of the cinema image, so they wield it thoughtfully."[42] Predictably, some directors not as smart and accomplished as these have made the kinds of films that could be described as effects-driven. If digital tools enabled visual effects to become more assertive, some scholars felt that the results often challenged the primacy of narrative. Michelle Pierson wrote that the appearance of the brachiosaur in *Jurassic Park* stops the film's narrative so that the digital effects can be showcased at length. "The narrative all but comes to a halt, the music gradually builds, and shots of characters reacting to the appearance of the dinosaur with wonder and amazement are interspersed with long takes displaying the computer-generated brachiosaur center screen."[43] She argues that during the "wonder years" of the early nineties, digital effects broke the narrative action and were showcased in sequences that dwelled upon visual spectacle for its own sake. "These temporal and narrative breaks might be thought of as helping to establish the conditions under which spectators' willed immersion in the action—the preparedness to being carried along by the ride—is suspended long enough to direct their attention to a new kind of effects artifact."[44] In fact, considerable narrative development occurs during the brachiosaur scene—Hammond introduces Grant and Sattler to the preserve and its treasures, and he promises to tell them how he has created these dinosaurs. Geoff King is correct when he writes that the brachiosaur scene is not cut off from the narrative "for the precise reason that our contemplative gaze is motivated by that of the protagonists, getting their first stunned sight of the recreated dinosaurs, a moment loaded with narrative resonance."[45]

Narrative and Spectacle

Pierson's criticism points to an ongoing tension within the nature of cinema between narrative structure and visual effects. Aylish Wood has described this tension as "the great divide of spectacle versus narrative."[46] Critical discussion and popular culture often identify visual effects with genres like science fiction, fantasy, and action-adventure rather than taking effects as a broader category of images that are coextensive with many forms of narrative cinema. And within science fiction, action-adventure, or fantasy, effects are said to be ostentatious, attention-getting, and spectacular in ways that overwhelm narrative or halt it altogether. As Scott Bukatman writes, "What is evoked by special effects sequences is often a hallucinatory excess as narrative yields to kinetic spectatorial experience."[47] Annette Kuhn points out that "when such [special effects] displays become a prominent attraction in their own right, they tend to eclipse narrative, plot and character. The story becomes the display; and the display becomes the story."[48] Andrew Darley writes that spectacle is "the antithesis of narrative. Spectacle effectively halts motivated movement. In its purer state it exists for itself, consisting of images whose main drive is to dazzle and stimulate the eye (and by extension the other senses)."[49] Viva Paci also finds that "high-tech special effects films" undermine narrative. "These films rely on the foregrounding of visual pleasure and the almost physical participation of the viewer, as if he or she were in an amusement park. These films do not seek the viewers' attention through plot development; they capture their gaze through a 'shooting star' effect that grabs their attention—reaching out to them so to speak in their seats."[50]

Shilo T. McClean has examined the many ways in which digital effects serve the art of storytelling in contemporary film, and she argues that poorly motivated effects are better understood as reflecting deficiencies of storytelling than any characteristics that are inherent in the cinematic application of digital technology.[51] Aylish Wood maintains that even when digital effects emphasize spectacle, they still have a temporal component that generates elements of narrative.[52] Nevertheless, though popular cinema tells stories, it also attracts viewers based on its promise to show exciting and dramatic action. It always has done so. Douglas Fairbanks's swashbuckling epic *The Black Pirate* (1926) opens with a title card that is a veritable list of the exciting scenes to come—"Being an account of BUCCANEERS & the SPANISH MAIN, the *Jolly Roger*, GOLDEN GALLEONS, bleached skulls, BURIED TREASURE, the *Plank*, dirks & cutlasses, SCUTTLED SHIPS, *Marooning*, DESPERATE DEEDS, DESPERATE MEN, *and*—even on this dark soil—ROMANCE." The title card proclaims the list of attractions that the movie will offer to its viewers. Tom Gunning has argued that a cinema of attractions accounts for much of the medium's popular appeal, found in offering viewers startling visual displays that work independently of narrative. Gunning's work on the history of early film helped to establish the cinema of attractions as a core idea in the field. Objecting to what he described as the hegemony of narrative in the study of cinema, he argued in favor of a view "that sees cinema less as a way of telling stories than as a way of presenting a series of views to an audience, fascinating because of their illusory power."[53] Gunning claimed that this conception ruled cinema until around 1907 when narrative became more dominant. In a related essay, he developed the notion of an "aesthetic of astonishment" as the expressive outcome of the cinema of attractions. Visual tricks created by editing or in-camera mattes, shots of locomotives rushing toward the camera, and other abrupt or surprising views caused viewers to vacillate "between belief and incredulity."[54] Gunning elaborated, "Rather than being an involvement with narrative action or empathy with character psychology, the cinema of attractions solicits a highly conscious awareness of the film image engaging the viewer's curiosity. The spectator does not get lost in a fictional world and its drama, but remains aware of the act of looking. . . . Through a variety of formal means, the images of the cinema of attractions rush forward to meet their viewers."[55]

Gunning also claimed that the cinema of attractions never fully disappeared even after narrative became the dominant mode of popular cinema. In stressing that it "remains an essential part of popular filmmaking," he connected it with contemporary visual effects. "Clearly in some sense recent spectacle cinema has reaffirmed its roots in stimulus and carnival rides, in what might be called the Spielberg-Lucas-Coppola cinema of effects."[56] Not all film historians have accepted Gunning's claims. Charles Musser, for example, points out that many early programs of short films, cited by Gunning as attractions, in fact exhibit various modes of narrative sequencing and that a nonstop succession of shocks would have been difficult to produce and also bad showmanship: "Early films often elicited much more than astonishment—they mobilized the sophisticated viewing habits of spectators who already possessed a fluency in the realms of visual, literary, and theatrical culture."[57]

The relation between narrative and spectacle is a function of a given film's aesthetic design and the sensibilities and goals of filmmakers on a given production. Spectacle can serve narrative; it can also be a more autonomous artifact of style. There is no necessary and unchanging relation between the two. Cinema undeniably offers its viewers the pleasures that Gunning identified as those of the attraction. But it is also the case that viewers seek the pleasures offered by a well-told tale and that spectacle for its own sake, especially when poorly integrated with narrative structure or with a structure that is poorly elaborated, may be perceived as the mark of a badly made film. Viewers may nevertheless enjoy such films. Michael Bay's *Transformers* (2007) was a huge box-office hit, and, among the nearly two thousand viewer reviews on the Internet Movie Database, many say the movie was fun because the effects were great even though the script and story were perceived as poor. As Musser points out, spectators have sophisticated viewing habits, and these judgments about *Transformers* show that discriminations can be finely calibrated. In order to recognize this sophistication, we should avoid the trap that Malcolm Turvey has identified as the lure of visual skepticism. Turvey points out that "a distrust of human vision has played a foundational role in film theory." He elaborates, "It is a general, systematic doubt about normal human vision, a distrust of everyday sight. It is a belief that the standard exercise of the visual faculty is not to be trusted in some significant respect because it possesses one or more flaws."[58] The tradition of visual skepticism takes the cinema viewer as being duped by cinematic illusion and spectacle, held passively in thrall by powerful images. It can also produce other constructions of passive viewers, such as those suggesting that the experience of pictorial illusion is dependent on social conditioning and that the science and physiology of vision hold little relevance for understanding how cinema communicates and the pleasures that viewers derive from visual displays. As Jonathan Crary writes, "If it can be said there is an observer specific to the nineteenth century, or to any period, it is only as an *effect* of an irreducibly heterogeneous system of discursive, social, technological, and institutional relations. There is no observing subject prior to this continually shifting field."[59] Crary continues, "Whether perception or vision actually change is irrelevant, for they have no autonomous history. What changes are the plural forces and rules composing the field in which perception occurs." If vision is completely subordinate to social forces, then the interplay between science and cinema becomes a chimera. If vision cannot be trusted, then neither can the arts that play to its characteristics, and it becomes difficult to see viewers as being active and sophisticated. Mary Ann Doane points out that discussion of the persistence of vision in relation to cinema tends to invoke "an insistent vocabulary of deception and failure."[60]

Doane is among a group of scholars who have emphasized the connections between scientific research and the medium of cinema. Scott Curtis has written eloquently about the relationship between the modes of vision instantiated in cinematic viewing devices and in practices of medical imaging.[61] John Durham Peters has emphasized the importance of Hermann von Helmholtz's physiological studies for the history of sound film.[62] This work examines the ways that today's digital culture is, as Lauren Rabinovitz and Abraham Geil point out, a phenomenon "larger and older than the information age."[63] Indeed, cameras and other optical devices were important components used in the scientific study of vision by artists and natural philosophers and subsequently by experimental psychologists. As Lisa Cartwright notes, "Many of the techniques and instruments that contributed to the emergence of cinema were designed and used by scientists." But, she points out, in film studies, "the historical narrative quickly shifts, however, from science to popular culture."[64]

Without an emphasis upon the continuing interplay between science and popular culture, however, the operation of digital effects in cinema cannot be grasped as much beyond spectacle or attraction. Digital tools emulate properties of human vision as well as the camera's customary way of seeing things. In this regard, the application of digital tools continues a centuries-old tradition of analogizing camera and eye, and it is worth taking a moment to examine this pre-history because it provides a necessary context for understanding digital imaging tools. Visual effects belong to a long tradition of mechanically induced illusion spaces that were themselves also research tools in the development of visual science—grasping these connections and this history will enable us to move beyond the analytic template provided by notions of spectacle. In the remainder of this chapter, therefore, I recount some of this history, emphasizing the intersection of lenses, optics, and cinema with the development of scientific research into vision. In order to replicate the optical characteristics of the camera and the human eye, the digital tools used by effects artists must have an empirical grounding in this research. Digital visual effects are grounded in the science of vision at least as much as they are in the stylistics and pictorial conventions of representational images.

The Eye as an Optical Instrument

The physiologist Hermann von Helmholtz in 1868 described the eye as an optical instrument. "Regarded as an optical instrument, the eye is a camera obscura."[65] In contrast to the natural theology of the period, which extolled the perfection of human vision as an instance of divine intervention into the world, evidence of God's plan for humankind,[66] Helmholtz explicated the numerous flaws in the eye's instrumentation—chromatic and spherical aberration, lack of clarity and optical uniformity in the crystalline lens, the blind spot and other gaps in the retina. He impishly observed, "Now, it is not too much to say that if an optician wanted to sell me an instrument which had all

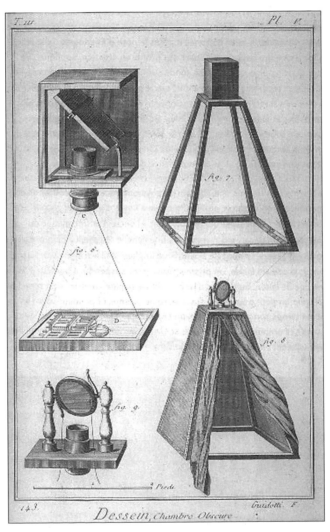

The first philosophical toy—the camera obscura, as diagrammed in Denis Diderot and Jean le Rond D'Alembert's *Encyclopédie* (1751).

these defects, I should think myself quite justified in blaming his carelessness in the strongest terms, and giving him back his instrument."[67] But he went on to point out that binocular vision enables each eye to compensate for the deficiencies in the other, providing a means of rectifying these flaws, and that the eye's speed was superior to that of a camera.

As Nicholas Wade and Stanley Finger write, "The overarching analogy that has been applied to the eye is that of the camera—both devices being capable of focusing on objects at variable distances."[68] The principles of the camera obscura—a dark chamber admitting a small amount of light to produce an upside down and reversed image on a flat surface of the scene or object outside the chamber (the image is upside down and reversed because the light rays cross as they pass through the hole)—were known in the eleventh century to the Islamic philosopher and scientist Ibn al-Haytham and were subsequently widely studied by artists, who used it as a device for tracing images, and by scientists seeking to understand optics and the eye. Leonardo da Vinci compared the eye with a camera obscura and experimented with the device, proposing the use of a translucent screen for tracing that would correct image reversal and eliminate the problem of the observer's head being in the path of the light. Da Vinci, though, could not reconcile the upside-down image captured by the camera obscura with the phenomenally correct perspectives supplied by human vision. The Venetian patrician Daniele Barbaro in 1568 used a convex lens and varying aperture sizes in a camera obscura to produce sharpened images on a sheet of paper.

Lenses were rapidly applied to the camera obscura, and, indeed, mirrors and lenses provided vital aids to the scientific study of vision and assisted in the development of what Martin Kemp has termed the science of art. The inventor of linear perspective, Brunelleschi, used a peephole and mirror device to heighten the illusion of depth in a painting he made of the Baptistry of Saint John. The viewer looked through a hole in a wooden panel at a mirror that reflected the image of the painting from the other side of the panel. By eliminating the problem that retinal disparity introduces into the perception of depth on a 2D surface, Brunelleschi's peepshow device heightened the illusion of depth perspective in the image. He even used burnished silver on part of the mirror to make sky and clouds more luminescent.[69] By analyzing the perspective geometry in Vermeer's paintings, Phillip Steadman demonstrated that Vermeer used a camera obscura to produce a series of portraits set in the same room of a house or studio.[70] Artist David Hockney has argued that "from the early fifteenth century many Western artists used optics—by which I mean mirrors and lenses (or a combination of the two)—to create living projections" as tools for producing paintings and drawings.[71]

The astronomers Tycho Brahe, Johannes Kepler, and Jesuit scholar Christopher Scheiner used camera obscuras to make solar observations. Kepler stated that the camera obscura provided a safe way to view a solar eclipse. Kepler proposed a system employing two convex lenses to correct the inverted image, and in 1611 he published *Dioptrice*, a seminal study of optics that emerged from his use of a telescope. ("Dioptrics" was the terminology in use for the study of refraction.) He also proposed an account of retinal vision whereby an image was focused on the retina as on a sheet of paper produced by a camera obscura and was then transmitted to the brain and its visual faculty. Scheiner produced diagrams of the eye and observed upside-down retinal images on the excised eyes of animals. He created a portable camera obscura, called the Pantograph, for making drawings of solar phenomena. Kepler, too, designed a portable camera obscura using a tent for the enclosure. The mathematician, linguist, and experimental scientist Athanasius Kircher also used a camera obscura for study of the sun, and he designed a picture-wheel projection device and a magic lantern projection system to exploit the properties of image formation in the eye that he had previously illustrated. The psychologist Nicholas Wade writes that "the photographic camera enabled artists to capture scenes in perspective with comparative ease, whereas scientists could consider the eye as a similar optical instrument."[72] Chromatic aberration in telescopes (color separation due to differences in the way a lens refracted light of varying wavelengths) and methods of correcting it helped to advance astronomy and pointed away from a corpuscular theory of light and toward a wave theory. The astronomer Christian Huygens, an early proponent of a wave theory, used the camera obscura, and Philip Steadman speculates that it was Huygens's father, Constantijn, who introduced Vermeer to optics.

Lenses, mirrors, and the optical devices built from them provided a technical foundation upon which the study of vision could proceed, and this conjunction between image-making devices and science gives us a different inflection to cinema's historical preconditions from what prevails in the dominant, popular narrative. That narrative regards optical devices like the thaumatrope, the phenakistiscope, and the zoetrope as toys, as diversions offered to a restless public keenly interested in visual entertainments. Historian David Cook describes them as "simple optical devices used for entertainment,"[73] and Keith Griffiths writes that they helped create "phantasmagoric illusions and performances (an aesthetic of the supernatural) for the visual entertainment of the middle classes. These parlour room and entertainment hall projections helped create the public appetite for the range of entertainment genres that would soon encompass most of the cinema and television of the future."[74]

By contrast, Wade, whose scholarship focuses on the natural history of vision, proposes that these devices be regarded as "philosophical toys"—a term commonly employed in the nineteenth century—because they served dual interests. "Philosophical instruments, like microscopes, were used to examine natural phenomena, but philosophical toys served the dual function of scientific investigation and popular amusement."[75] He suggests that the camera obscura was the first philosophical toy because of its applications to both art and science. Scientists and natural philosophers invented these optical devices to aid their inquiries into such visual phenomena as persistence of vision, stroboscopic motion, and binocular depth perception. Sir Charles Wheatstone, professor of Experimental Philosophy at King's College, defined philosophical toys as devices intended to illustrate and to popularize the principles of science. "The application of the principles of science to ornamental and amusing purposes contributes, in a great degree, to render them extensively popular; for the exhibition of striking experiments induces the observer to investigate their causes with additional interest, and enables him more permanently to remember their effects."[76] The devices originated at the hands not of carnival barkers but credentialed experimental philosophers. The optical devices helped advance experimental inquiries into vision. As Wade emphasizes, "The development of visual science was as dependent on these devices as biology had been upon the microscope."[77]

While visual persistence was an optical phenomenon that had been noted for centuries, the optical toys sharpened its study and its quantification and, via stroboscopes, connected it with the perception of apparent motion. His own investigations and experiments and those Newton carried out with color perception using prisms stimulated David Brewster to invent the kaleidoscope in 1816. He wrote, "When I discovered the development of the complementary colours, by the successive reflections of polarized light between two [glass] plates of gold and silver, the effects of the Kaleidoscope . . . were again forced upon my notice."[78] Influenced by Brewster's device and intending to illustrate visual persistence, Wheatstone created a sonic kaleidoscope in 1827 that he called the kaleidophone. He attached silver glass beads to rods which, when struck, made the beads vibrate and their reflected light to trace pleasing abstract figures in the air. Wheatstone wrote that his objective was to subject "to ocular demonstration the orbits or paths described by the points of greatest excursion in vibrating rods. . . . The entire track of each orbit is rendered simultaneously visible by causing it to be delineated by a brilliantly luminous point, and the figure being completed in less time than the duration of the visual impression, the whole orbit appears as a continuous line of light."[79] That same year, John Paris, a physician, devised the thaumatrope, a disk with drawings on each side which, when whirled, caused the drawings to be seen as one (for example, a rat inside a cage). Paris intended that the device serve a teaching function, illustrating the classics. Descriptions published in the early 1820s of stroboscopic illusions produced by counter-rotating cogwheels or by the spoke wheels of a carriage when viewed through a Venetian blind led to papers by physician Peter Mark Roget and chemist and physicist Michael Faraday analyzing the phenomena quantitatively and also to the invention of several varieties of stroboscopic disks. Faraday was a friend of Wheatstone's and was influenced by his interest in visual persistence, and his paper published in 1831 led to design applications. In 1833, after reading Faraday's paper, the Belgian scientist Joseph Plateau invented the phena-kistiscope and Simon Stampfer, a professor of geometry in Vienna, created the stroboscopic disk. Similar devices, these disks held a series of drawings on one side separated by slits. When the disk was held before a mirror and rotated, and when viewed through the slits, the drawings appeared to move. Roget claimed that he had invented a similar device a few years earlier. In 1834, using the daedaleum (aka the zoetrope), William Horner placed drawings on a horizontal wheel rather than a vertical one, making it possible for several people to view the illusion at once. Scientists and natural philosophers studied the optical phenomena produced by the disks and noted the velocity and amount of light that were needed to produce the illusion.

In addition to visual persistence, Wheatstone was intrigued by more general questions about space and depth perception. He invented the stereoscope in 1832 after noting that retinal disparities increase as the eyes converge to focus on an object very near at hand. (Brewster invented a lenticular stereoscope a few years later.) He wondered if a similar experience of depth perception could be produced using plane images instead of three-dimensional objects. "What would be the visual effect of simultaneously presenting to each eye, instead of the object itself, its projection on a plane surface as it appears to that eye?"[80] He constructed the mirrored stereoscope in order to pursue a series of experiments into binocular vision that estab-lished for the first time its role in depth perception. Visual scientists before Wheatstone had noted the existence of retinal disparity, but it had not been connected with depth perception. The stereoscope enabled Wheatstone to investigate and demonstrate this connection. His device used mirrors to reflect paired line drawings of geometric forms. Using the line drawings eliminated the presence of monocular depth cues that could have confounded the results. He mounted the mirrors onto adjustable arms that enabled him to introduce variations into retinal size and retinal disparity and degrees of convergence and accommodation as elicited by the drawings. He thus was able to study these responses as separate variables. After William Fox Talbot's negative-to-positive photographic process was invented, Wheatstone had stereoscopic daguerreotypes made for the device.

The stereoscope also pointed toward a new and strange optical domain, taking its observer through a looking glass into a disorienting world. Wheatstone varied the device to create what he called the pseudoscope, which produced conversions of relief and depth. If the pictures in the stereoscope were transposed from one eye to the other, reversing the manner in which they were meant to be viewed, or inverted in other ways, an impossible world appeared. The interior of a teacup became a solid convex body. A globe of the earth became a concave hemisphere. "A bust regarded in front becomes a deep hollow mask.... A framed picture hanging against a wall appears as if imbedded in a cavity made in the wall." A flowering shrub in front of a hedge appears behind it. "A tree standing outside a window may be brought visible within the room in which the observer is standing." These strange perceptions were as of another world operating according to different physical laws. Wheatstone wrote, "With the pseudoscope we have a glance, as it were, into another visible world, in which external objects and our internal perceptions have no longer their habitual relation with each other." This fascination with novel visual experiences held a major appeal for the computer scientists who would write the algorithms that produced digital simulations of the phenomenal world, and the new vistas offered to audiences in such films as *Jurassic Park*, *Coraline*, and *Avatar* furnish much of their appeal. Indeed, as Anne Friedberg points out, this "fascination with virtuality," with visual approxi-

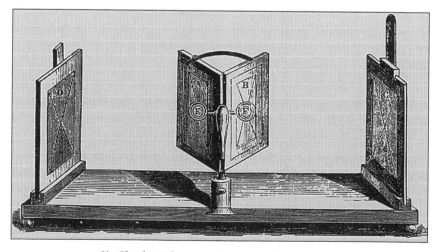

Sir Charles Wheatstone's mirrored stereoscope

mations of the real, is exerted by optical devices from the camera obscura onward as the fundamental allure of extending vision in novel ways.[81]

Whereas the pseudoscope pointed toward new aesthetic experiences, the stereoscope placed the scientific investigation of vision onto firm ground. Wade notes that the stereoscope, "perhaps more than any other instrument, ushered in the era of experimentation in vision."[82] It pointed toward the cognitive components that operate in visual perception and also to the differences between eye and camera. Accommodation—the eye's ability to shift focus between near and far—is possible because the curvature of its lens changes, becoming more extreme with nearer objects, but a camera lens doesn't change its shape. Wheatstone's stereoscope could evoke accommodation responses from viewers according to changes in the positioning of its mirrored arms, and this offered one challenge to the camera-eye analogy. Helmholtz, who used an ophthalmometer to study more precise changes in accommodation, remarked on the differences: "A photographic camera can never show near and distant objects clearly at once, nor can the eye; but the eye shows them so rapidly one after another that most people, who have not thought of how they see, do not know that there is any change at all."[83] Mechanical devices such as the camera and the camera obscura could shift focus to different parts of a scene but not with the eye's swiftness or suppleness.

Wheatstone's stereoscope made important contributions to the empirical theory of vision, associated with Helmholtz, in distinction to nativist approaches that held that visual skills such as depth perception are innate and not subject to learning. Helmholtz studied the images produced by Wheatstone's stereoscope and used them to argue forcefully for the role of mind in vision. People do not see their retinal images, he maintained. They do not perceive a world that is upside down, as are retinal images. Moreover, how are the different retinal images combined to produce a single visual field seen in depth? He maintained that depth perception is a psychological rather than a physiological process, that vision involves an interpretive act rather than a strictly physical one. "The combination of these two sensations into the single picture of the external world of which we are conscious in ordinary vision is not produced by any anatomical mechanism of sensation, but by a mental act."[84] Wheatstone's stereoscope enabled Helmholtz and others to deepen their understanding of the perceptual processes involved in vision. The relatively intimate circles through which the art and science of philosophical toys and their associated inquires were pursued is illustrated by Helmholtz's attendance at an 1881 demonstration by Eadweard Muybridge of his zoopraxiscope, a projecting phenakistoscope that he used to show his series of photographs of horses in motion.[85] The event was held at the home of Etienne-Jules Marey, a physiologist who constructed numerous instruments, including cameras and projectors, for measuring animal and human motion. Marey had invited Muybridge to show his device to the leading scientists of the time.

The upsurge of vision research in the nineteenth century was an essential condition for the invention of cinema; the boulevard amusements and fairground attractions that often are described as the medium's roots should be ranked alongside the developing science of visual perception. But, as Lisa Cartwright points out, "The prehistory of the cinema is conventionally told as a tale of early scientific experimentation marked by a break with science around 1895 with the emergence of a popular film culture and industry."[86] No such breach has occurred. Art and science commingled in the invention of cinema, as they have continued to do in the decades since, most obviously in the digital turn that the medium has taken. The new toolbox available to filmmakers enhances their abilities to create artificial realms, evident in such films as *Lord of the Rings*, *Speed Racer*, and *Avatar*. But, as we will see, it also provides new methods for establishing perceptual and indexical modes of realism.

Viewing Pictorial Illusions

I close this chapter with a brief explication of the sophisticated nature of pictorial perception and by examining one of the book's fundamental questions, namely, whether cinema is best understood as being a photographic and therefore an indexical medium. Lev Manovich describes the "general tendency of the Western screen-based representational apparatus. In this tradition, the body must be fixed in space if the viewer is to see the image at all. From Renaissance monocular perspective to modern cinema, from Kepler's camera obscura to nineteenth-century camera lucida, the body has to remain still."[87] The immobilized spectator is taken to be a passive spectator, one who is positioned and worked over by the image.

While a cinema viewer does sit still in a seat to view a film, however, paintings are typically viewed in motion, by walking around them and glancing at them from several angles. Thus the viewer of a painting is not immobilized. More important, notions of a unified gaze are misleading. There are many gazes. Human vision operates by executing multiple, rapid glances, which are termed saccades. Because the fovea (the area of the retina that produces clear and sharp vision) is small, viewers must build up their sense of an overall picture on the screen of a film or the surface of a painting by taking many visual samples. Saccadic vision is a process of directive, goal-driven visual sampling. A viewer's phenomenal experience of an organic, unified space or visual field, in fact, is derived from a kind of perceptual montage, created from scores of rapid glances at salient areas of the picture. Saccades can be as quick as 30 milliseconds.[88] And the areas are not sampled in a linear fashion. The viewer's fovea makes saccadic jumps to very different, often widely spaced areas of the image, searching for salient details—highlights, faces, bright colors, movement—that can be used in making sense of the whole. The representational space in a perspective drawing may be unified, but the viewer's gaze is not—it is restless, multiform, successive, and analytic, constructing a mental image of the representation by sampling its visual information.

Moreover, the retinal disparity (differently angled images recorded by each eye) that produces binocular vision provides clear anti-illusionist cues that the surface of a painting or film is just that, a flat surface. If the viewer moves about, then the resulting motion perspective shows that the visual surface is planar. This is why the cinema viewer remains seated and why the optimum conditions for viewing a perspective drawing are with a person standing at the point of central projection holding one eye closed, a condition that is rarely practical or practiced. Thus the illusion of three-dimensional space produced by a representational image is limited. It is further constrained by the sharply reduced exposure latitude of a camera relative to the human eye and by the fact that the plane surface of a painting or cinema screen does not evoke vergence movements by the eyes as a viewer looks at objects represented at varying depths and distances in the pictorial space. And yet despite these limitations or failures of correspondence between human vision and representational imagery, the perceptual illusion of pictorial space still claims the viewer's attention. This suggests that the nature of pictorial illusion is more complicated than skeptical critiques may stipulate and that the viewer's role is more cognitively active and self-aware than accounts of spectators lured by spectacle warrant. M. H. Pirenne has discussed the limitations of painting and photography in duplicating or mimicking natural vision. After exploring numerous differences between the abilities of the eye to handle the information contained in light and what paintings and photographs can show, he concludes, "The alleged possibility of producing a complete, perfect, imitation of visible reality is a myth. The opposite belief, namely that there are no permanent optical laws relating to human vision, and that the evolution of art must be explained entirely on subjective grounds, for instance on the basis of varying concepts or intuitions of space, is another myth."[89] He emphasizes that the pictorial illusions offered by representational images are not simple. "Their perception is a complex process because it evokes in the spectator a special kind of awareness of the painted surface itself."[90]

This complexity of perceptual response furnishes us grounds for finding an aesthetic of realism in digital cinema images and for emphasizing the spectator's role as an active and complex one. As we will see, digital imaging tools provide numerous ways of replicating the optical principles involved in vision and in seeing a material world. Moreover, such complexity furnishes us with a reason for suspecting that the emergence of digital tools of image-making is less radical, disruptive, or threatening to the nature of cinema than is often thought. A common theme found in critiques of digital imaging is that it represents a break with cinema's analog heritage. Virtually all theories of cinematic or photographic realism proceed from the idea that a photograph is an index of the object or scene before the camera, that is, the photograph is a recorded trace of those things; it is causally and existentially connected with them. As David Rodowick writes in his important study of the shift in cinema from analog to digital modes, "Comparing computer-generated images with film reaffirms that photography's principal powers are those of analogy and indexicality."[91] The model of an indexical sign derives from the work of Charles S. Peirce, who devised the triadic schema of indexical, iconic, and symbolic signs. He noted that "photographs, especially instantaneous photographs, are very instructive, because we know that in certain respects they are exactly like the objects they represent. . . . They . . . correspond point by point to nature. In that respect, then, they belong to the second class of signs, those by physical connection."[92] Writing about photography, Roland Barthes claimed that photographs, unlike every other type of image, can never be divorced from their referents. Photograph and referent "are glued together."[93] For Barthes, photographs are causally connected to their referents. The former testifies to the presence of the latter. "I call 'photographic referent' not the *optionally* real thing to which an image or sign refers but the *necessarily* real thing which has been placed before the lens without which there would be no photograph."[94] For Barthes, "Every photograph is a certificate of presence."[95]

Most famously, André Bazin based his realist aesthetic on what he regarded as the objective nature of photography, which bears the mechanical trace of its referents. In a well-known passage, he wrote, "The photographic image is the object itself, the object freed from the conditions of time and space which govern it. No matter how fuzzy, distorted, or discolored, no matter how lacking in documentary value the image may be, it shares, by virtue of the very process of its becoming, the being of the model of which it is the reproduction; it is the model."[96]

The concept of indexicality has been used to suggest that digital images might create a rupture with photographic realism. For Lev Manovich, digital images strip away the medium's analog heritage, the "deposits of reality" that photographic images carry. "Cinema emerged out of the same impulse that engendered naturalism, court stenography and wax museums. Cinema is the art of the index; it is an attempt to make art out of a footprint. . . . Cinema's identity lies in its ability to record reality."[97] This premise—that cameras record reality—suggests one reason that visual effects have tended to fall outside of theories of cinema. Visual effects are composites, artificial collages, not camera records of reality. Digital images, too, can be taken as composites. As composites or manual constructions, digital images, for Manovich, threaten to return the medium to its own prehistory, to the hand-painted and hand-animated images that flourished in the nineteenth century's optical devices. "Consequently, cinema can no longer be clearly distinguished from animation. It is no longer an indexical media technology but, rather, a subgenre of painting."Jonathan Crary finds that digital images offer a fabricated reality rather than one that has been photographically recorded. The fabricated visual spaces of the digital realm split images from a knowable, observable reality. Everything can now be faked. "Visual images no longer have any reference to the position of an observer in a 'real,' optically perceived world."[98] For Sean Cubitt, digital media pose a crisis of meaning because they seem to "sever the link between meaning and truth, meaning and reference, meaning and observation. Digital media do not refer. They communicate."[99] He continues, "The digital corresponds so closely to the emergent loss of an ideological structure to social meaning because it no longer pretends to represent the world."By this he means that digital images lack photography's indexical connection to social and physical reality. Thus they do not represent that reality in the way that photography had.

By severing photographic images from indexical referents, digital imagery is said to pose a crisis for cinema, for photography, for a knowable reality as mediated by visual culture. As I hope to show in the pages to come, however, while digital tools have opened new expressive capabilities in cinema, they have not destroyed or broken with the old. Moreover, they have created new sources of indexical meaning that were never possible with analog photography. And notions of a break with cinema's analog heritage rest on a devotion to characteristics that the medium never truly possessed as dominant features of its style or structure. Bazin, for example, stressed compositional strategies that emphasized holistic space, achieved through the staging of action in depth and in shots of long duration. Cinematic realism lay there. "Essential cinema, seen for once in its pure state, on the contrary, is to be found in straightforward photographic respect for the unity of space."[100]

Narrative cinema has rarely respected unity of space as a basis for realism—except in the constructed manner achieved by such devices as continuity editing and selective framing with the camera. Cinema is an art of the fragment, composed of slices of pictorial space created at one moment in time and picked over by filmmakers and assembled into a new organization at a subsequent point in time. Aesthetic choices inevitably inflect medium-specific characteristics. The aesthetic and social objectives of filmmakers and the contexts in which images are created and circulate influence the degrees of realism attributed to visual images far more than whether they are analog or digital. The power of a John Ford western shot in Monument Valley derives from the compositional values Ford extracts from placing tiny figures among the looming sandstone monoliths of the location. It derives as well from a viewer's sense that the location is real, that is, it exists as an authentic space outside and beyond the camera's view. Gillo Pontecorvo's ability to re-create the Algerian war for independence in so apparently authentic a fashion in *The Battle of Algiers* (1966) was due in significant measure to his practice of shooting on location with crowds of people who had experienced the very things and emotions they were reenacting. Location filming exemplifies the kind of indexical value with which realism in cinema is frequently invested, namely, the camera's ability to record images that are isomorphic with the spaces that were before the lens. Critiques of digital imaging suggest that because digital images can be invisibly manipulated, a viewer cannot trust the image or know that an authentic location is really that. But nothing precludes a filmmaker from working digitally and shooting on a real location if the authenticity of a locale is aesthetically important. Debra Granik's *Winter's Bone* (2010) was shot in winter on location in the Ozark Mountains to achieve the visual authenticity called for in the story, and the filmmakers spent two years before the shoot researching the area and scouting locations. It was shot digitally, with images captured using Red One cameras. Its aesthetic use of location makes the same claims to indexical realism as *The Battle of Algiers*.

To return to my earlier point, even when authentic locations are part of a film's aesthetic design, unity of space is most often a manufactured impression. For a key dialogue scene in which characters take a boat out on a pond to retrieve a body, Granik shot on dry land and used low camera positions to hide this fact. John Ford's cutting in *The Searchers* (1956) conjoins locations in Monument Valley that are not adjacent to one another, and he intercuts location shots with studio sets. As Lev Manovich points out, "Traditional fiction film transports us into a space—a room, a house, a city. Usually none of these exists in reality. What exists are a few fragments carefully constructed in a studio."[101] He perceptively notes that in the digital era "the problem of realism has to be studied afresh."[102] In doing so, we will find that aesthetic and stylistic practices in cinema have changed little and that the differences between analog and digital cinema do not form a stark divide.

Cinema *is* a composited medium, whether analog or digital, and this singular condition has been undervalued in our existing theories. Visual effects are at home in a composited medium, not incursions or intrusions therein. Keeping this condition in mind is fundamental to our ability to understand digital effects and the ways in which they are organic manifestations of narrative cinema's essential features. Overcoming the profilmic space—reorganizing it, reimagining it—is essential to the tradition of fiction in cinema (and also in many ways to the mode of documentary where filmmakers often feel the need to find a story and tell it). A fictional world established on screen is a synthetic creation, an amalgam of various physical continuities created in the editing along with emotional elements created by actors, editors, cinematographers, and directors that are deemed to be true to the scene as depicted. It is also an amalgam of visual effects techniques. On this basis little changes as we move from analog to digital. Thus we will need to find other bases for an aesthetic of realism than the models proposed by Bazin or derived from analogies with photography. Helmholtz's idea of vision as an interpretive act can serve us well here. As Helmholtz noted, the properties of a creative medium entail that "the artist cannot transcribe nature; he must translate her."[103] As I hope to show in the pages to come, digital tools are best understood not as applications undermining realism but as modes of translation—seductions of reality—designs for creating new extensions of realism and fictional truths. When the T-Rex gobbles Martin off the restroom toilet, the staging of the action in a single framing creates a vivid continuity of digital and live action space, prompting a new interpretive response from viewers, as does Jake Sully's stereoscopic transformation from a crippled marine to a seven-foot-tall Na'vi warrior in *Avatar*.

Rather than dismiss these juxtapositions as inconsistent with a realist aesthetic, I prefer to explore them as cinematic extensions of the senses and the imagination, extensions that are achieved through a new technology. Philip Steadman explained Vermeer's use of the camera obscura in such terms. He describes how its single, uncorrected lens fails to achieve perfect focus over a large area and transmutes the three-dimensional scene that the artist could observe with his eyes into a two-dimensional array of overlapping planes. The relative dimness of the camera's image and the translucent screen or paper onto which Vermeer traced his composition obscured detail and made objects distinguishable according to shape and tonal value, but these distinctions no longer corresponded to discriminations that the eye

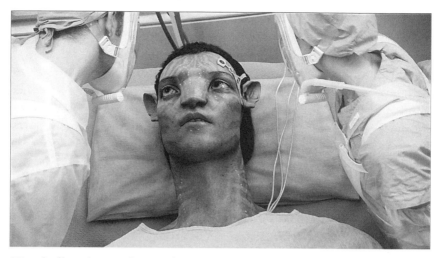

Visual effects images frequently present viewers with optical extensions of the
senses and the imagination and can be used to design wholly new worlds, as in
Avatar (2009, Twentieth Century–Fox). Frame enlargement.

would make. "It may then happen that some of these boundaries do *not* fall
at the edges of objects in the scene. Vermeer starts to paint patches of light
and colour, not fingers or bodices or violas with the forms and outlines by
which they are mentally conceived."[104] The camera obscura provided him
with a new way of seeing, disentangled from the mental habits induced by
ordinary vision, and gave Vermeer a means for achieving the strange combination of tonal clarity and dissolution of line and form that distinguishes
his late style. Steadman speculates that these aberrant visual characteristics
were exactly what intrigued Vermeer:"The camera allowed the artist to enter
a newly revealed world of optical phenomena and to explore how these
might be recorded in paint."[105]

John Whitney emphasized, "Geometry and reality are not disparate enti-
ties, one cold and impersonal, nor is the other all that lovable, of course."
The diversity of life and matter throughout the universe merely was an
expression of "the 'idiosyncrasies' of geometry."And computers opened new
possibilities for artists and scientists to capture this. "Computer geometry,
infinitely diverse, as in nature itself, constrains graphic diversity merely
as a limit of resolution," wrote Whitney. "The higher the resolution, the
greater the visual diversity."[106] To artists and scientists in earlier centuries,
the camera obscura opened up a new optical domain and made it available for study and exploration. Computer graphics and digital imaging are

doing so now. Ivan Sutherland, one of the pioneers of computer graphics, felt something of Vermeer's excitement. "A display connected to a digital computer gives us a chance to gain familiarity with concepts not realizable in the physical world," he said. "It is a looking glass into a mathematical wonderland."[107] Loren Carpenter's *Vol Libre* revolutionized computer graphics by demonstrating the power of fractals for generating animated organic forms. He had a Ph.D. but didn't want to teach. He wanted instead to see new optical worlds. "I wanted to see my imagination. And I wanted to see other people's imagination. And so in order to do that, I worked hard to give people the tools."[108] Digital images take viewers through the looking glass into new landscapes of vision unavailable to ordinary sense, enable them to peer into domains of the imagination. In the process, they have given filmmakers new methods for extending the aesthetics of cinema. The next chapters show how.

CHAPTER 2

Painting with Digital Light

Prolific Hollywood cinematographer Leon Shamroy worked for nearly a half-century and won two consecutive Oscars for cinematography. His work included such key genre pictures as *You Only Live Once* (1947), *Twelve O'Clock High* (1949), *The Snows of Kilimanjaro* (1952), *The King and I* (1956), and *Planet of the Apes* (1968). In 1947, Shamroy wrote a prescient article for *American Cinematographer* in which he predicted that the medium's future would be electronic. He envisioned an electronic camera more sensitive than present film stocks that would send its image over a cable feed to a remote storage and viewing station. Rather than waiting for dailies, the director could view the images as they were being captured, and image variables could be adjusted during production rather than afterward. "Electronic monitor screens connected into the system will make it possible to view the scene as it is being recorded. Control of contrast and color will be possible before development."[1]

Shamroy had glimpsed the future. Cinema's photochemical domain began shrinking in the 1990s as digital imaging tools reconfigured the work of filmmaking. To the public, the most visible profile assumed by these changes included startling new visual effects, as found in *Jurassic Park* (1993) and *Forrest Gump* (1994). But the changes were deeper. The shift to digital modes ended the era in which visual effects were "special," that is, were allocated to a domain of trick photography regarded as being separate from and peripheral to the main stage of production. A better term today is "visual effects," designating an expanded domain of image manipulation carried out with digital tools. This may include the creation of fantastic, attention-grabbing creatures prevalent in everyday conceptions of what a movie special effect is, but visual effects go beyond this. Most often they are subliminal and invisible to viewers, and by no means are they confined to genres like science fiction and fantasy. In 1995, the American Society of Cinematographers and Eastman Kodak sponsored a seminar examining the emerging relationships among cinematographers and digital effects artists. Speaking as a panelist at the seminar, Andrea D'Amico of Pacific Ocean Post (*What Dreams May Come* [1998]) described digital imaging as a kind of toolset offering film-makers expanded creative opportunities: "I see [digital] as a huge expansion of opportunity . . . by allowing people to do things they really couldn't do before or as easily as we can do now."[2] Visual effects encompass much more than what the term "special effects" has designated. They encompass all variety of digital manipulations carried out upon cinematic images. As cinematographer Marvin Rush emphasized, "'Digital,' or what we're calling digital, should be taken out of the realm of visual effects. We should look at digital as a concept for something besides visual effects."[3] Although Rush was advocating an entirely new terminology, his philosophical point is sound—digital imaging is about more than the creation of monsters and spectacle. In contrast with Rush, I believe the terminology of "visual effects" is suitable for creating the necessary distinction with "special effects" and for pointing to the larger domain of digital image manipulation that the present study examines. It also tracks with current terminology as employed in the industry. Audiences notice special effects. Most often they fail to notice visual effects. Greg McMurray, a visual effects supervisor at VIFX, an effects-house that has contributed work to *From Dusk to Dawn* (1996) and *Face/Off* (1997), identified two kinds of images that his company and similar firms provided to filmmakers—effects that people see because they are elaborate and fantastic and effects that no viewer notices. "I think the digital revolution has broadened that second category incredibly."[4]

While scholars, critics, and viewers have tended to see digital imaging in terms of fantasy effects—the things that people notice—filmmakers gradually came to understood that the new tools enabled cinema to incorporate important dimensions of visual realism. Neil Krepela of Boss Film (*True Lies* [1994], *Starship Troopers* [1997]) pointed to the connection between digital imaging and realism. "The effects in films are becoming more and more realistic, rather than the fantasy elements. I think this is one of the great powers of digital effects in general, that we can make things a lot more seamless and realistic and not so much 'in your face.'"[5] *Forrest Gump* may not be a film to which many viewers would attach a term like realism. Its story is a tall tale in which hero Gump (Tom Hanks) experiences numerous improbable adventures, such as meeting three U.S. presidents in scenes where actor Hanks was matted into archival footage of Presidents Kennedy, Johnson, and Nixon. These were clearly visual effects sequences, as were the Ping-Pong matches

Among the most famous of the early-generation digital effects was Lieutenant Dan's missing legs in *Forrest Gump* (1994, Paramount Pictures). Although many viewers knew this was a digital effect, it conveyed an undeniable perceptual realism. Frame enlargement.

between Gump and his Chinese opponents featuring digitally animated balls with appropriate motion blur.

But the feather drifting through city streets in the film's famous opening sequence was not a CGI element, though many viewers may have thought it so. The three Phantom F-4 jets that drop napalm in the Vietnam sequence were CGI elements, but they didn't look like such. Although most viewers probably knew that Gary Sinise's appearance without legs, playing Lieutenant Dan, a vet wounded in Vietnam, was a digital effect, this awareness did not disturb the perceptual realism of scenes in which Dan maneuvers himself, or is carried, through spaces too small, narrow, or confined for a fully limbed man to fit. The physical reality depicted in such scenes onscreen is true and cannot be perceptually denied in spite of a viewer's awareness that it is dependent on digital effects. In a pre-digital era, scenes with actors playing handicapped characters never achieved such visual credibility. Viewers always were aware that the actors had one limb tucked behind their backs or hidden below a specially constructed table or chair. (Even in *Gump*, some scenes with Lieutenant Dan were done with a trick wheelchair.) Stephen Rosenbaum, the film's graphics effects supervisor, said that "most of the effects in the film were designed to enhance reality," and Ken Ralston, another of the film's visual effects supervisors, noted that using digital methods to achieve such realism is actually harder than doing something outlandish. "The toughest thing . . . is trying to recreate reality. The more surreal an image is, the more leeway we have to fake our way through because people can't identify with it. This show was firmly based in reality."[6]

Although the feather that drifts through the opening sequence is not CGI—it is, instead, a real feather photographed and then matted into the scene, with some digital tweaks to marry the two—digital compositing enhances the scene's perceptual realism by making the join between the foreground feather and the background environment virtually imperceptible. Digital compositing, and its widespread adoption by the film industry in the 1990s, played an essential role in the developing abilities of filmmakers to enhance the realism of their visual effects and a viewer's sense of the authenticity and veracity of a scene's depicted content. I begin this chapter by examining optical and digital compositing and then consider the transformation of cinematography with the onset of digital intermediates and digital capture, and I conclude by examining attributes of the new aesthetic that these tools helped to enable.

Optical Compositing

Throughout the history of cinema, visual effects images have been composited, that is, composed of at least two elements separately created and then layered together to produce the final synthetic image. (Initial instances of combining images were accomplished using multiple exposures on original negative.) Compositing is the industry term for this process of joining image layers. The first all-digital composite performed by Industrial Light and Magic occurred in *Indiana Jones and the Last Crusade* (1989) during a scene showing the destruction of the Nazi villain Donovan, whose corpse shrivels, desiccates, and collapses into a heap of ash. Director Steven Spielberg didn't want to do the scene in the usual manner by cutting away from an actor as makeup changes are applied. "I didn't want to do a series of cutaways so the actor could be advanced in make-up. We've all seen that, and I think people have a high level of expectation with these movies."[7] As in *Jurassic Park*, he wanted to offer viewers a different kind of aesthetic. The camera, therefore, holds on Donovan as he crumbles away, and the effect was achieved using three animatronic puppet heads, each more decayed than the other. They were shot as bluescreen elements and blended using morphs, and all the main elements were digitally composited. Morphs had been introduced on *Willow* (1988) as a technique involving digital image blends, used in that film to depict a character who transforms from goat, ostrich, and turtle to tiger and then to human form. (A morph is produced by warping two images, such as a goat and an ostrich, so that pre-selected major features in each image become graphically similar. The computer then calculates the intermediate stages of transformation that will take each image through a sequence to its final warped state, reverses the sequencing for the second image and adds a dissolve to connect them.) But even though *Willow* employed morphs, the film's effects shots were finished as optical composites, one sign of the movie's transitional status. Disney was the first studio to move toward all-digital compositing. In 1989, Disney began converting traditional cel animation to an electronic format called CAPS—Computer Animation Production System—and did an all-digital composite on *The Rescuers Down Under*, continuing with the animated features *Beauty and the Beast* (1990), *Aladdin* (1991), and *The Lion King* (1993).

Prior to the digital era, compositing was performed optically. Digital methods soon put the optical printer into mothballs. (Like the veneration for vinyl records often felt by audiophiles, however, some film-based experimental filmmakers remain devoted to the optical printer for its ability to produce traditional kinds of effects.)[8] For generations, optical printers had served as the workhorses of studio effects departments. They featured an interlocked process camera and a process projector known as the printer head. Master positive footage of effects elements—models, traveling mattes, animation—were loaded into the printer head and run through and photographed frame by frame by the process camera. (A process camera is one used in the laboratory for effects work, in distinction to a production camera used to film live action.) The final composite (the finished effects shot) was gradually created by this process of rephotographing each of its components. The composite negative would have to be rewound in the process camera so that each component could be photographed. Thus an optically printed effects shot yields a dupe negative, a copy of a copy. The more elements an effects shot contained, the more elaborate this process became. Two- and four-head optical printers enabled the photographing of multiple image elements in one pass, speeding the work of compositing. Linwood Dunn, who became head of RKO's photographic effects department, designed the Acme-Dunn Special Effects Optical Printer, which was widely used throughout the studio era. In 1934 he published an article in *American Cinematographer* in which he claimed that "during the past four or five years there has not been a single production released that did not utilize the services of the optical printer to a considerable extent."[9]

Dunn gave photographic examples of numerous editing transitions created on optical printers as well as examples of using the printer to alter scenes so as to modify, correct, or extend their shots. "Almost anything in the broad spectrum of modifying a filmed scene can be done."[10] Dunn estimated that at least 50 percent of *Citizen Kane* had been optically printed. The shot where Kane appears as a tiny figure framed in a distant doorway at Xanadu after his wife Susan leaves him was composited from three elements.

Kane appears as the background element, achieved as a miniature rear projection. The midground area depicting the hallway is a matte painting, and the foreground elements—an open door and doorframe—were photographed from physical props. Dunn composited these image elements on the optical printer. It's worth noting that the matte painting included Kane's reflection on a tiled floor, and, as we will see, digital compositing offers numerous opportunities to create lighting effects that can tie image elements together.

Optical printers could create the impression of camera movement by moving the printer head toward the camera. Swinging the printer head sideways past the camera created a curtain wipe in which one moving image appears to push another off screen. Dunn used both techniques to extend camera moves in *Citizen Kane*. In the scene introducing Susan Alexander, the camera makes an elaborate move across the roof of the nightclub set (a miniature model) and through its sign (a breakaway prop), then descends toward the skylight and appears to move through the skylight and continue via a crane down to the floor below. Dunn subliminally connected the two camera moves (one on the rooftop set, the other inside the club) by moving the printer head to create optical zooms on the tail of the first shot and the head of the second and then hid the cut by creating the impression of a lightning flash. In the scene set in the Thatcher Library, an apparently unbroken camera move travels from the bust of Thatcher (a miniature model) to an inscription on its pedestal (a set), and then to a wide framing of the reporter Thompson speaking with the librarian. The miniature of Thatcher had not been filmed, and Welles decided he wanted it in the shot. Dunn supplied it and the camera move that connected it to the scene. He said, "I had a statue made—about two feet high . . . and I made a straight shot of it, and on the optical printer I made a motorised pan-down from it. Then I made a pan from the scene with the girl and I matched [the two] with a travelling split-screen."[11]

I have described the contribution of optical compositing to *Citizen Kane* in some detail in order to make the point that filmmakers routinely practice an art of elegant misdirection. The screen worlds that viewers watch tend to be constructed domains. This point can be illustrated clearly with regard to traveling mattes, a fundamental visual effects technique that digital methods have greatly facilitated. Achieved on the optical printer, traveling mattes enabled filmmakers to insert a moving foreground element over a background set, such as Superman flying over New York City. The process involved printing the foreground and background elements with a matte and counter-matte (so-called male and female mattes) in order to prevent a double-exposure that would show Superman as transparent with the city visible through him. A matte prevents this by allowing exposure in one area of the frame while blocking it in others. The male matte (aka a hold-out matte) is a length of film with an opaque area in the shape of the foreground element and is transparent everywhere else. The female matte is the reverse—transparent foreground element, all else opaque. The effect would be created on the optical printer by printing the background element with the male matte to create a shot on the composited negative of the background element (the city) with an unexposed hole corresponding to the foreground element (Superman, in this case) that will be inserted. Then the film in the process camera is rewound and the foreground element is printed with the female matte. This inserts our flying Superman onto the background and prevents additional light from hitting the background, which had been exposed on the negative during the first printing pass.

Numerous methods evolved for extracting the matted elements, most of which involved photographing the foreground action against colored screens and then printing the footage with filters or as high-contrast black and white images to generate the male and female mattes. But matting artifacts—black outlines or colored haloes around the foreground element—tended to detract from the final result, and the capability for staging action in depth was quite limited. Cameras were kept locked down to minimize problems of image registration during printing. Moreover, complex shots, like those in *Star Wars* (1977), required printing hundreds of elements, which tended to wear down the dupe negative in the printer from the stresses of running it backward and forward. Richard Edlund, who helped create the effects on *Star Wars* and *The Empire Strikes Back* (1980) and who designed sophisticated optical printers, noted that the optical approach was fundamentally flawed because too many variables affected it. "The quality of the chemical bath being used by the lab to develop film that day, voltage changes, weakening lamps, fading filters, and on and on and on. There are just so many variables that even with the best equipment in the world, a good optical composite relied partly on science and skill, and a little bit on good luck."[12] John Knoll, one of the creators of Photoshop and an ILM visual effects supervisor, said, "Some of these elements would just eventually wear out, and any problems with the B.C. [the 'black center' produced by the holdout matte] would be immediately evident. You thread them up through the optical printer enough times [that] they start getting scratches or other problems. In an optical composite if there's some flaw, and if the shot is ninety percent of the way there, there's not much you can do." By contrast, if the image is digitized, "it's putty in your hands, and you can do anything you want with it."[13]

Linwood Dunn wrote that Welles used the optical printer like a "paint brush," and Dunn looked forward to the day when "the Electronic Optical Printer" would offer filmmakers an even greater range of creativity.[14] Digital compositing is Dunn's Electronic Optical Printer, and the tools it furnishes have enabled filmmakers to actually become painters; the metaphor is no longer a poetic fancy.

Digital Compositing

Just as they have been in earlier periods, films today are an amalgamation of miniature models, matte paintings, and live action, but the digital compositing of these elements alleviates many problems that were inherent in the photochemical methods of the optical printer. Rather than using light to blend image layers by continuously rephotographing them—and thereby introducing problems of excessive grain, resolution loss, and physical damage to the image surface occasioned by running celluloid through a machine— digital compositing works by numerically transforming data according to mathematical functions called operators. A compositor has many operators available for blending image elements, which include add, subtract, multiply, and so forth. Inserting a matted object into a background merely involves adding or multiplying relevant pixels in the image sequences and introduces no visual degradation, unlike the optical printer. Creating mattes is much easier, as is blending the lighting and color values of the layered elements.

Moreover, a digital compositor can work selectively on image layers, enabling greater precision and much finer manipulation and control of the shot. Multipass compositing proceeds by rendering image layers in separate passes or operations. (Multipass compositing existed in the analog domain as well. *Return of the Jedi* [1983] was optically printed, and some of its elaborate battle scenes included more than one hundred image elements, rendered as separate passes.) Digital multipass compositing offers dramatically enhanced artistic tools. These include image channels that can be manipulated separately, such as the alpha channel (specifying pixel transparency and used for generating mattes) and the Z-depth channel, which is in grayscale and specifies where image objects are along the Z-axis. The brighter a pixel in this channel, the farther away it is from the camera. By using brightness to measure distance, the Z-channel furnishes a depth map of the shot, which can be used for 3D matte effects, enabling complex interactions amongst matted objects. A squadron of CGI jets, for example, can fly with individual planes passing in front of and behind mountains or buildings, which themselves are matted CGI objects. Z-depth matting overcomes the planar representation of space that often afflicted traditional optical compositing, and it also furnishes an effective means of establishing depth of field in a computer-generated shot. Other passes in a multipass composite will operate on layers containing lighting information. A beauty pass will build the CGI object with its greatest level of color and detail. A diffuse pass renders the diffuse light in the scene, which reflects evenly from objects according to their orientation toward the light sources. An ambient pass builds the ambient light in the environment, and an "ambient occlusion" pass is useful for generating soft shadows. A specular pass establishes the positioning and size of reflected highlights.

In *Spider-Man 2* (2004), for example, the fight scene on the elevated train between Spider-Man and the villain Doc Ock was composited using separate renders of all elements—the city background, buildings and train tracks, the train, and the characters. The compositor consulted with the cinematographer on lighting and color preferences and used beauty and multiple lighting passes to control reflections, highlights, and shadows within the scene. Reflections on the shiny train surface of passing buildings and of Spidey and Doc Ock were added as separate elements and then subjected to a diffusion pass to blur them and to a "dirt pass" to dull them down by adding a layer of grime to the outside of the train. A reflective occlusion pass served to block building reflections when the characters, fighting outside the train, come between it and the surrounding buildings. A matte pass used the RGB channels in the image to apply selective color corrections. The red channel, for example, served to isolate the train wheels. Z-depth passes created depth of field by blurring distant elements, such as the furthermost end of the train. Changes in camera exposure were added in relation to virtual camera moves relative to the light source. Grain and lens distortion were also added to blend shots across the sequence.[15]

Although the fight scene in *Spider-Man 2* is mainly CGI, digital compositing also offers great flexibility in handling live-action elements. In Peter Jackson's *King Kong* (2005), a major climax occurs when Kong saves Ann Darrow (Naomi Watts) from a hungry Tyrannosaurus Rex. The scene takes place in a rocky clearing with mountains in the distance. Its elements were composed of Watts as the live-action element filmed against bluescreen, Kong and the T-Rex as CG elements, CG foliage in the foreground, and a digital matte painting representing the distant mountains. When Watts was shot on bluescreen, the CG characters and environment had not yet been built, and the lighting on Watts failed to match what was subsequently created for the CG elements. Watts looked flat when placed against the high-contrast lighting on the CG creatures. This disparity undermined the representational realism the sequence required and provided a clear tell for viewers about the scene's artificial construction. The solution was to relight Watts as a digital figure. Matchmoving, a procedure that maps the movement of live action and a live camera to a computer-modeled environment, generated a digital replication of Watts as Ann Darrow. This was relit using a normals pass, which employs surface normals—vectors perpendicular to the surfaces of an object (in this case, the digital figure of Ann)—to analyze the light distribution in a scene. The illumination of the surface normals tells the compositor how light will be distributed across the surface of the object. Based on this information, reflection mattes and ambient occlusion mattes were used to increase the lighting on Watts's key side and lower it in her shadowed areas. The result was a convincing distribution of light throughout the scene. The digital relighting of Naomi Watts created a subliminal join of live action and computer elements. Based on the visible evidence in the lighting, Ann Darrow became an organic part of the scene's action.[16]

As this example indicates, a great deal of the work performed in compositing involves lighting and color, which traditionally has been the domain of the cinematographer on a production. Digital compositing and the use of digital intermediates have reconfigured the professional role of cinematographers. Cinematographers and directors, along with visual effects supervisors and digital compositors, now work together to create lighting (along with other camera variables, such as movement and composition), and the process spans production and post-production. Before examining this change in detail with regard to the use of digital intermediates, let's spend a bit more time looking at the nature of digital lighting in a computer-generated world.

Lighting Naomi Watts in post-production during compositing enabled a more convincing blend of the actress with the scene's matte paintings, miniature models, and digital creatures. *King Kong* (2005, Universal Pictures). Frame enlargement.

Digital Lighting

A digital lighting design can be achieved using local or global illumination methods. Using a local illumination approach, a visual effects artist works with the same categories of light as a real cinematographer. Key lights, back lights, fill and rim lights are created and positioned in virtual space, and their levels and spread must be defined in relation to the surface textures and objects in the scene. Creating local illumination is a labor-intensive process. Global illumination algorithms, in contrast, will calculate the inter-reflections of light between and across surfaces in an environment and do not require setting individual light sources. Much digital lighting in cinema is now accomplished as global illumination.

The digital realm affords many opportunities for cheating the behavior of light and shadow in ways that real-world cinematography has a harder time accommodating. Orange firelight would have made the blue-skinned Na'vi in *Avatar* (2009) look gray, an undesirable outcome, so the filmmakers decided to implement a policy they called "spectral compensation," in effect ignoring the interaction of orange and blue light in this context.[17] Digital lighting designs are found in environments that are all CGI, such as *WALL-E* (2008), *Up* (2009), and other animated films by Pixar, and in situations where CG objects are added to live-action scenes or vice versa. In most cases, the digital design strives to emulate the physical behavior of light in a perceptually convincing manner, unless a more dramatically satisfying cheat is required. As visual effects researcher Paul Debevec recognized, "This difficult task requires that the objects be lit consistently with the surfaces in their vicinity, and that the interplay of light between the objects and their surroundings be properly simulated. Specifically, the objects should cast shadows, appear in reflections, and refract, focus, and emit light just as real objects would."[18]

Accomplishing this is a challenging task because light and color interact with the environment in variegated ways. Marcel Minnaert's classic study, *Light and Color in the Outdoors*, demonstrates the physics of light under many different environmental conditions, which include reflection, refraction, diffusion, contrast phenomena, halos, coronas, curvature effects produced by the atmosphere, and the luminous properties of plants and animals. The variety of environmental lighting effects produced in nature has generated volumes of research by the computer graphics community on how to replicate this information in ways that are economical and efficient. Many of the scholarly papers presented at SIGGRAPH deal with methods of modeling light and representing reflections and shadows. Ray tracing, for example, has been an effective and widely used approach that is useful for representing specular highlights and hard-edged shadows. The method traces rays of light from the virtual camera to objects in the scene and follows the ray's path from the object to a light source, noting whether it bounces off other objects along the way. Pixar used ray tracing extensively in *Cars* (2006) to model the shiny exteriors of the cartoon automobiles and their finely detailed, reflective geometry.[19]

Ray tracing, however, is not very good at emulating soft-edged shadows, which show a gradual transition between light and dark, or at capturing the ambient light that diffuses throughout an environment. Moreover, the needs of many scenes go beyond what fixed, point-source lighting can provide. Global illumination models can emulate point-source lighting as well as diffuse and ambient effects. Global illumination deals with the reflected and transmitted light on all surfaces in a scene. Many complex CG environments—the streets of 1930s New York, for example, as rendered in Peter Jackson's *King Kong*, dense with vehicles, store signage, and pedestrians—must convincingly depict situations where there may be too many light sources to make it feasible to set up individual virtual lights or to ray-trace illumination paths. To model global illumination in such cases, environmental maps are used to calculate the global behavior of light. If the scene features live action and incorporates CG effects, a reflection ball can be photographed on location to provide a lighting reference useful in re-creating the scene's visual parameters in a CG environment. (I say more about the use of reflection balls in chapter 5 in the context of high dynamic range images.) The information on its reflective surface can be unwrapped to produce an environment map of reflected light distribution throughout the scene, and this can be used to model the computer objects that will be added to the scene. ILM refined this approach to include methods of occluding unwanted reflections and of modeling ambient light. The approach was developed for *Pearl Harbor* (2001) and quickly gained currency in the computer graphics world. ILM's "ambient environment" method included two components—creation of ambient light sources and of ambient occlusion, the soft-edged shadow effects produced from the distribution of ambient light. As an ILM artist explained, "It's . . . necessary to provide shadowing from the surrounding [live action] lighting environment. Points not fully exposed to the environment need to be attenuated properly. This process is known as 'Ambient Occlusion.'"[20] ILM's ambient environmental lighting proved to be fast and efficient. The scene in *Pearl Harbor* showing B-25 bombers on the Doolittle raid taking off from an aircraft carrier was a live action–CG blend. The CG portion used only a key light and global illumination derived from the environmental map. An ILM effects artist noted, "Not every shot goes this smoothly but it is a testament to the ease of using this simple but effective lighting setup."[21]

Other kinds of environmental maps used to calculate light distribution include texture maps wrapped around scene geometry and that are designed to capture light and shadow information. Shadow mapping, for example, is a method for calculating hard and soft shadows and point-source shadowing.[22] Occlusion Interval Maps, similarly, use texture mapping to create intervals that show when a light source is visible and when it is occluded.[23] Z-depth mapping can also provide a useful approach for calculating shadow distribution.[24]

Lighting Food in *Ratatouille*

Pixar's animated film about a gourmet rat working as a master chef in a high-class restaurant had many scenes showing delicious food being prepared in the kitchen and served to guests. Successfully visualizing the properties of good food required that the digital animation seem real, that is, it had to correspond with the finely tuned physiology of the human food response. As the film's visual effects artists noted, "We as humans have a built-in sensory system to know what looks right to our eyes and stomach, and finding that acceptable (and tasty) look was the main focus" of the film's food lighting.[25] Proper lighting and coloring provided a means for cuing a viewer's physiological food responses, and the filmmakers determined that good food appeal depended on carefully visualizing the factors of softness, reflection, and saturation. "Food needs to be colorful as this indicates ripeness or freshness. The surface should appear wet, dry, waxy or soft as appropriate. These things are visual cues of its taste, texture and feel. A fleshy or translucent appearance is essential for certain foods. It lets you know how ripe or juicy the food is."[26] Subsurface scattering provided an essential means of evoking a fleshy or translucent appearance. This technique, used in *The Lord of the Rings* movies to make Gollum's skin look naturalistic, deals with the way that light penetrates below the surface of an object, is scattered, and then exits in a different location than its point of entry. This shading technique was applied to soft and translucent foods like scallops and grapes. The latter were given a very naturalistic appearance through a careful control of scatter, diffusion, color shifting, and specular highlights. "We used tinting of scatter (with warmth), lightly patterned surface diffuse color, and allowing more translucency to dominate over the diffuse. Each grape was offset individually from the bunch by a random color shift in hue and value. We also used a very subtle diffuse blur, and a sharp reflection." All these elements enabled the lighting to create "an appealing image."²⁷ With regard to denser foods like cheeses or meats, blurring their diffuse light gave them an appropriately fleshy look, and taking the diffuse blur on cheeses to the point where details were lost contributed the right kind of waxy look.

Soft lighting made the food look appealing, even if it meant cheating the physics of the source lighting. "We always made sure that light fell on food at an angle that best revealed the broken texture of bread or the smooth sheen of sliced tomatoes, even if that meant diverging somewhat from what the rest of the set lights are doing."²⁸ In a scene, for example, where a wedge of cheese sits beside several thin slices, the key light on the cheese should create more subsurface scatter in the thin slices, but the animator might decide that the shot's aesthetic appeal demanded that more scatter appear in the large wedge relative to the slices. The Pixar artists designed a new type of light, which they called Gummi light after the fishes from *Finding Nemo* (2003). This light conveys directional transmission through an object rather than by scattering. It was used to visualize translucent objects like a glass of wine and depicted the differential absorption of varying wavelengths as light passes through the object. It complimented subsurface scattering and added color complexity and shape to areas shadowed by a key light. The ability to cheat source lighting or to invent a wholly new kind of light points to a difference between digital lighting and cinematography that is performed with real lights. A real-world cinematographer is more constrained by the physics of light. To serve an aesthetic goal, its properties can be manipulated but not altered, as can a CG lighting scheme in which shadows or light diffusion may be cheated. In a CG environment, the objectives of an aesthetic design can nudge out the physics of actual light behavior. In this respect, the Pixar artists maintained

Throughout *Ratatouille* (2007, Pixar), digital lighting establishes the physical properties of food, making it look good enough to eat. Frame enlargement.

that they were not going for photorealism in lighting and texturing the film's food because that would be distracting from the stylized world of the story. They wanted to bring viewers into that stylized world, where rats can cook and talk, a world that was not photorealistic but which needed to accommodate the recognizably real properties of appealing foods. Visual effects achieved through digital lighting served the twin goals of advancing the film's stylized fantasy and evoking the sensual properties of food in ways that were visibly true for the viewer. Photorealism is often not the goal of digital aesthetics—careful cheats in the interests of style and tone are often more important than the simulation of camera or lighting reality. We will see in the next chapter that a temperate and skeptical attitude toward photorealism by effects artists plays a major role in the aesthetics of digital performance.

The Digital Intermediate

Digital lighting effects are not confined to computer-generated environments. The ability to digitally alter light and color in movies that were shot on film using real actors and locations offered cinematographers an exciting and daunting expansion of their creative horizons. It made lighting more like painting than it had ever been. Cinematographer John Alton published a book on the art and craft of cinematography in 1949 entitled *Painting with Light*. Alton was one of Hollywood's most expressive and radical cinematographers, pushing shadows, depth of field, and single-source lighting to extremes that most of his peers didn't attempt. But expressive as his work is, his analogy of cinematography with painting was mainly a metaphor. A cinematographer creates color by working with real light; a painter does not. The painter creates color by applying pigments to a surface. Color in film is subtractive; color in painting is additive. And once shooting wrapped, a cinematographer had minimal ability to adjust and correct color in post-production. The painter can endlessly tweak and fiddle with color schemes. Cinematography as it traditionally existed was an image-creation process. The image was created and defined largely according to the decisions made during production, such as the manner in which costumes and sets were lit or the imaging characteristics of the particular stock of film on which the movie was shot. After the production phase ended, abilities to intervene and modify the existing images were highly constrained.

Scanning celluloid to a digital file has helped to alleviate these constraints. It enabled cinematographers and directors to alter colors and other image elements by working directly on the hues of pixels in what was now an additive color system in place of the subtractive system that film employed. And they now had a painter's fine control over minute image elements. What had been an image-creation process was now an image-capture process because many of the creative decisions about cinematic image definition shifted to post-production. And by expanding the capabilities of digitally manipulating photographic images, these changes made digital visual effects, broadly defined, coextensive with all of filmmaking. Digital visual effects were not the exclusive province of dinosaurs and other fantasy creatures and domains. They now could exist everywhere.

During most of the 1990s, movies originated on film and stayed there. Digital effects were created in the computer and then were scanned to film to be integrated with existing sequences. The results were printed photochemically in the lab for distribution on celluloid to theaters. Commercial advertisers and music video producers at mid-decade were digitally manipulating colors and creating other effects, but they worked in short formats. When a completed film was transferred to videotape via telecine for distribution on home video, opportunities for color control arose that did not yet exist for filmmakers during production or post-production. The telecine operator could adjust primary color channels (red, blue, green) and make adjustments to overall brightness (gain), black levels (lift), and mid-tones (gamma). Limited secondary controls enabled some adjustments of specific colors independently of others.

Outside of telecine work for video, color correction in cinema had been an analog process and had remained unchanged for generations. The director and cinematographer would view an edited work print of the film with a color timer from the lab assigned to the project and would reach agreement about where colors needed to be shifted or modified, either for dramatic purposes or to maintain consistency and continuity across shots. The lab then generated a color-timed trial print using an intermediate negative (not the camera original) and Hazeltine printing lights. The printer used a beam splitter to divide white light into the three primaries, and timing occurred by adjusting the levels of red, green, and blue light as they printed the negative. Adding blue light, for instance, would make the print look more yellow (because the negative sees in reverse, the change occurs in the complementary color). Adding more red increases the cyan level in the print. Adjustments were made on a range of 1 to 50, with an interval of eight representing one full stop of light. Thus a mid-range balanced print, ideally, would have printing values of RGB 25–25–25, though a cinematographer might wish, for instance, to have a more yellowish cast to the image, in which case the RGB values might be 25–25–30. Overall print density could be increased by raising the RGB values equally, producing a darker image. In one sense, the method was very precise. After viewing a trial print, a cinematographer who requested additional corrections might ask for two more points of red and would know exactly how this calibration would look. It would not depend on the color timer making a subjective judgment about how much red to add. The cinematographer thus retained control over color decisions, a prerogative that seemed less secure with digital timing because it lacked the Hazeltine's objective scale for calibrating color.

On the other hand, however, the method was less precise. It offered little opportunity to fine-tune individual colors. A cinematographer color-timing a film print had fewer choices than when supervising a film-to-tape telecine where, as we have seen, individual colors might be corrected without altering the overall image. Hazeltine timing could adjust the color balance but not individual hues or selective parts of the image, a major limitation on the potential for cinematography to be like painting. Moreover, prints released to theaters were always several generations away from the original camera negative (OCN). Theatrical release prints were struck from internegatives that, in turn, had been made from an interpositive that was, in turn, derived from the OCN. The generational loss of visual information was compounded by the inherent differences between the responses of negative and positive film to light. Negative film has a more gradual light curve (known as the sensitometric curve), with a longer shoulder (registering highlights) and toe (registering shadows). Positive film (printed from negative) has less latitude—a more steeply sloped curve, with less gradation in the shoulder and toe. (Video has even less latitude and a stronger tendency for shoulder and toe to reach their limit and clip or lose information.) The significance of these differences is that a print viewed in theaters could never reproduce all the visual information that was contained in the negative. Information was always, inevitably, lost. The full range of information in the negative was inaccessible. Film images remained luminous and beautiful, but the medium also claimed a quality that was astonishing to contemplate in a digital era—its images were virtual, that is, as viewed they were simulacra of a more complete but inaccessible original. An original camera negative included image information that was unrecoverable by the traditional process of photochemical printing. (Ironically, scanning that negative to a digital file enables the recovery of information that photochemical printing cannot extract.) As a Kodak image scientist expressed it, "The purpose of the negative is to capture a virtual scene, but there is no practical way to reproduce those same luminance ratios."[29] Virtuality, it turns out, is not a claim uniquely made by digital media. The photochemical heritage of cinema had always retained this characteristic.

The digital intermediate offered a new approach to color timing. By scanning film to a digital file, color timing and numerous other image corrections could be performed electronically and with greater precision and nuance than by using traditional one-light printing. As noted above, Disney was an early innovator in using a computerized scanning system to transfer animation drawings to a digital format where they could be painted and where multiplane camerawork could be created electronically. *The Rescuers Down Under* (1990) was the first animated feature to undergo this transition and to be digitally composited. In 1993 Disney used Kodak's new Cineon system to scan *Snow White and the Seven Dwarfs* (1937) at 4K resolution (4096 x 3072 pixels) so that the film could be digitally restored for a new release. In 1989 Kodak had begun researching a means of porting film into an electronic world, which it provisionally termed an Electronic Intermediate System, featuring a 2–4K scanner, a laser recorder for outputting to film, and a software file format for storing the data. In 1993 Kodak introduced the Cineon system, which Disney used on *Snow White*, and the ability to scan film at high resolution quickly moved visual effects away from optical printing and made digital compositing the new norm. As Douglas Bankston notes, Cineon "caused a radical shift in the visual-effects industry. In just a few short years, the traditional, labor-intensive optical died out."[30]

In 1999 and 2000, *Pleasantville* and *O Brother, Where Art Thou?* marked the onset of the digital intermediate in Hollywood. "Digital intermediate" (DI) referred to the electronic interval in which image adjustments were made on digital files before all corrections were exported back to film for release printing. *Pleasantville* used the technique for special effects purposes. Gary Ross's film portrays two teenagers, Jennifer and David (Reese Witherspoon and Tobey Maguire), who inexplicably find themselves trapped inside the black-and-white world of a 1950s-era television sitcom. As their presence changes the simplified moral world of the sitcom, the black-and-white world gradually transitions to color. Jennifer rebels against the constraints of the sitcom world, and her skin tones resume their normal appearance, leading to broader changes in Pleasantville. The sweater of a passing black-and-white coed glows a vibrant red. The town artist begins painting in color. An unsatisfied housewife (Joan Allen) begins to question the terms of her life, and she transitions to a color figure. The color changes symbolize social changes occurring in Pleasantville, as its denizens grapple with new gender and political issues that never before existed in its simplified television world.

Ross's symbolic use of color to shift a fantasy world closer to reality could not have been accomplished via traditional film timing. Only a digital intermediate process enabled him to work selectively on individual colors. Thus

the entire film was shot in color, and the sequences set in the TV world of
Pleasantville were scanned at 2K resolution (some 163,000 frames) so that
color could be removed except for the isolated instances in which it would
appear.[31] In contrast, *O Brother, Where Art Thou?* did not use a digital intermediate for special effects purposes. The manipulations in DI were subtler.
The use of DI on *O Brother* enabled the filmmakers to solve some very immediate and real problems. The directors, Joel and Ethan Coen, envisioned a
dry, dusty look and one that resembled slightly faded, hand-tinted postcards,
but the film was scheduled to shoot in Mississippi during the summer when
the foliage would be wet, lush, and green. Cinematographer Roger Deakins
explored traditional photochemical solutions, such as bleach-bypass, which
retains silver in the positive print and has the effect of desaturating colors
and reducing exposure latitude. While it would bring down color levels,
bleach by-pass did not provide a means for controlling selective colors, such
as the lush Mississippi greens that were going to be the main problem. No
photochemical tool seemed equipped for the job. Deakins was aware of what
had been accomplished on *Pleasantville* and, after running tests, he and the
Coens agreed that the film would be digitally graded (color corrected). "Quite
honestly," he said, "it was the only way we could see of achieving the look that
all three of us wanted."[32] He spent ten weeks digitally grading the film, and
the changes were relatively modest. "We affected [*sic*] the greens and played
with the overall saturation but little else. We only used windows, for instance,
on a couple of shots."[33] By "windows," Deakins is referring to power windows,
a selecting and masking function that enables artists to work on one part
of an image and leave the rest unchanged. Some cinematographers prefer to
avoid extensive use of power windows, while others embrace such corrective
measures. Peter Jackson, for example, used power windows to make extensive
changes throughout *The Lord of the Rings* and *King Kong*, bringing up highlights in Naomi Watts's eyes, for example, in *Kong* or changing a scene shot in
a monochromatic tone to one with more color differentiation.

　　With a digital grade, cinematographers began making changes to their
work that previously had been beyond consideration. When Jack Green shot
the rainy climax of Clint Eastwood's *The Bridges of Madison County* (1995),
he wanted an overcast day but the weather didn't cooperate. So the scene
was shot at dusk, which required constant lighting changes to balance the
actors' faces against the diminishing background light. On *Twister* (1996),
the storm scenes were shot in broad daylight, the actors brightly lit to
provide background balance, and the images were printed down during
Hazeltine timing to give them the darkness the story situations required.[34]
A digital grade can help to modify constraints imposed by weather or time

of day. On *King Kong*, Jackson routinely altered the color cast and density of scenes to suggest a particular time of day when the action was occurring. On *300* (2006), cinematographer Larry Fong shot numerous scenes under identical lighting at a mid-range color temperature and then in the digital grade warmed the color to suggest daylight or cooled it down to suggest dusk. He deliberately crushed all detail from the shadows and clipped the highlights in order to create the look of the Frank Miller graphic novel that was the film's source.

Digital grading replaced custom laboratory processes. Clint Eastwood likes very dark shadows, and on *Mystic River* (2003) and *Million Dollar Baby* (2004) he had used the photochemical process of ENR to desaturate color and intensify the blacks. ENR deepens shadows and mutes colors by adding an extra development bath during the processing of a positive print. The extra bath redevelops the silver in the emulsion, adding density to shadow areas (where most of the image-retaining silver halides are clustered). Eastwood had never done a DI prior to *Flags of Our Fathers* (2006), and when cinematographer Tom Stern ran tests comparing ENR with comparable results achieved digitally, he and Eastwood resolved to go with a DI. It gave them more creative power than working photochemically. Because ENR is applied during the creation of a positive release print, the smallest increment in which it can be used is one lab reel (about 10 minutes of film), and it cannot be varied within that unit. In contrast, working digitally Stern could not only replicate the ENR look but could vary it dynamically within a shot, changing its intensity from one corner of the frame to another. Portraying the American landings on Iwo Jima in World War II, the film has a severely monochromatic, desaturated look that is part of its ENR aesthetic, but the look wasn't achieved in the lab. Digital grading enabled Stern to modulate the film's chromatic minimalism with assertive but subtle color manipulations achieved using power windows. "There's a science to understanding where the eye will go first in a given composition. I wanted to enhance that effect by using power windows to lessen some of the contrast, or to really punch up other elements that would help control the audience's eye."[35] To avoid key details from becoming washed out by the film's black-and-white look, the digital grade retained color density in skin tones and in the blood erupting from soldiers hit by gunfire. The black of the beach sand was darkened to suggest Iwo's volcanic soil. In the American flag raised over Mount Suribachi, the reds were subtly increased.

After doing a digital grade on *Flags of Our Fathers*, Eastwood never looked back to a photochemical finish. His next films—*Letters from Iwo Jima* (2006), *Changeling* (2008), *Gran Torino* (2008), *Invictus* (2009), and *Hereafter*

(2010)—used a DI finish, and he joined numerous filmmakers and cinematographers who found in digital grading an essential tool of image control. Vilmos Zsigmond, who had pushed cinematography in historically important directions with his flashed negative for Robert Altman's *McCabe and Mrs. Miller* (1973), embraced digital grading after first trying it on Brian DePalma's *The Black Dahlia* (2006), a 1940s-era film noir. "I realize now that if we hadn't done a DI, I could not have done as good a job with the period look," he said. "The DI gives us a lot of tools that allow us to do practically anything, and I don't think I could do another movie without one."[36]

The magnitude of the changes instanced by the digital intermediate alienated some prominent cinematographers. John Bailey (*Ordinary People* [1980], *In the Line of Fire* [1993]), for example, warned that the industry's widespread adoption of digital grading threatened to erode the cinematographer's creative domain. As directors, stars, and studio executives work their way into the digital coloring suites, offering their own input into coloring, the cinematographer's prerogatives would diminish. "I fear we cinematographers may have unwittingly begun to write our own epitaph on the subject of image control."[37] Bailey asserted that a photochemical finish yielded better-looking prints than did a 2K or 4K digital finish. While industry consensus supported the view that scanning in 2K entailed a loss of film resolution, not all of Bailey's peers believed that such was the case in 4K. In a column counterpointing Bailey's criticisms, Roger Deakins wrote, "A print taken from a 4K master of a Super 35mm negative is surely superior in terms of resolution and saturation to one taken from an internegative of the same material."[38] While 2K scans were the norm in the early years of digital intermediates, at the time of this writing 4K scans have become the norm, and it is not unlikely that soon 6K will be the standard. (*Baraka* [1992] was given an 8K scan for Blu-ray release.)

Studios have embraced the DI because it economizes on the expenses incurred in post-production. When films are finished photochemically, a separate scan and color timing still have to be done for video and other ancillary markets. But a DI produces film and video masters at the same time, which is a cost savings for the studio. New Line told Bailey that he could have a photochemical finish on *He's Just Not That into You* (2009) but then changed its mind. Colorist Stefan Sonnenfeld, who worked with Bailey on the film's DI, pointed out, "There are too many ancillary deliverables these days that require digital manipulation to make a strictly photochemical finish practical. . . . The good thing about the DI is that you control the look of all deliverables from end to end."[39] A photochemical finish falls outside this evolving workflow.

Another effect of the industry's preference for the DI is an increased use of Super 35mm in production. Super 35 uses the full aperture of the 35mm negative frame, including the area normally masked for a sound track, and the image can then be formatted for release in a variety of aspect ratios. A "scope extraction," for example, is commonly performed to produce a 2.35:1 image for theatrical release in anamorphic widescreen. James Cameron's *Aliens* (1986) was shot in this manner. Before the DI, however, the scope extraction was accomplished with an optical printer, enlarging the image and anamorphically squeezing it to produce an internegative for release prints. This often resulted in increased grain, as can be seen in *Aliens*. With a DI, no optical printing is involved. The scope extraction is digitally scanned, the DI is performed, and the result is printed out to film with no generational loss of image quality. As a result, most Hollywood filmmakers working in widescreen have adopted Super 35 rather than shooting true anamorphic. Moreover, Super 35 uses spherical lenses that are faster, cheaper, and sharper than anamorphic lenses. In this regard, industry preference for the DI has helped shape the emergence of a new mode of widescreen filmmaking.

A key component of a digital grade is its subliminal character. Typically, viewers do not perceive image alterations performed in a DI as being changes to the image as photographed. It is doubtful, for example, that viewers of *The Proposition* (2005), an Australian western, thought that they were watching a visual effects film. They were, because a DI was used to stylize the color design, accentuating the beige tones of rocks, sand, and foliage in the desert landscapes and leaching most color out of the sky. Viewers of *The Duchess* (2008), starring Keira Knightley, might have thought they were viewing scenes as they had been photographed, inside sumptuous eighteenth-century historical mansions. Many of the mansions and grounds were real, but a narrative arc had been created in the lighting during the DI. As the film's colorist explained, "There's a curve to the lighting through this film—it changes as the story develops." Georgina (Knightley) moves from idealism to disillusionment as she sees the coarseness and brutality of the world. "The lighting and the tones transition from brightness and color to a faded and colder tone at the end."[40] These are invisible digital effects. Viewers do not see them as they do dinosaurs and spaceships, objects that moviegoers know are instances of movie magic. As invisible effects, image changes achieved in a DI represent a category of digital imaging that is more extensive throughout modern cinema than the effects intended to be seen as special. As such, images emerging from the DI toolbox arguably exert a more pervasive influence on contemporary film than do the more obvious kinds of effects imagery. Although the latter is

Subtle alterations in color and lighting are employed throughout *The Duchess* (2008, Paramount Vantage) to create a character curve visualizing the changing fortunes of Georgiana (Keira Knightley). The digital intermediate facilitates filmmakers' abilities to establish a narrative arc through color changes. Frame enlargement.

what media reporters, movie critics, and scholars often focus on, the digital imaging capabilities examined in this chapter—digital compositing, digital film scanning and printing, the DI—have altered production methods and professional relationships, have changed cinematography to an image capture process, have made it more like painting, and have greatly enlarged the expressive capabilities of film artists.

But the magnitude of these changes has elicited a measure of suspicion and resistance not only amongst filmmakers but scholars as well. John Bailey's declaration that he "will shoot movies on film in the anamorphic format and finish on film as long as I am able" is a matter of record.[41] Steven Spielberg, too, has said that he will shoot and edit on film as long as he can. Joe Fordham reports, "*Indy 4* VFX supervisor Pablo Helman told me that film was the first time Spielberg has agreed to use a D.I.—pretty remarkable when you realize how impressionistic some of Spielberg's films have been, working with [cinematographer] Janusz Kaminski on film negative."[42] Scholars, too, have been nostalgic and have shown some resistance toward the digital intermediate. John Belton explored the changing aesthetics of color made possible by the DI and reached a pessimistic conclusion. He points out that *Pleasantville* changed the way that color/black-and-white hybrids, such as *The Wizard of Oz* (1939), had traditionally maintained a careful separation between chromatic and achromatic domains. Dorothy's Kansas is black-and-white (sepia, actually) while Oz is color, and the two are not intermixed as they are in *Pleasantville*. He writes that this aesthetic change is both a threat and a violation. "Clearly, [digital] color manipulation poses a potential threat to our traditional understanding of chromatic and achromatic color systems and their creation of a credible narrative space." *Pleasantville*'s combination of color and black-and-white in the same frame results in "violating the integrity of the image. The image is revealed as not whole, but made up of parts. Of pixels."[43] His claims rest on a reading of André Bazin's famous essay "The Ontology of the Photographic Image," in which Bazin asserted that photographic images are uniquely credible because they have a spatial wholeness resulting from their existential connection to what was before the camera lens. Belton argues that digital images threaten "our traditional understanding of the photographic image as homogenous, as a whole constituted by the frame that groups its contents together."[44] This is because digital images involve stages of manipulation that are potentially much greater than is the case with traditional photographs and, furthermore, because it is difficult for viewers to see the extent of such manipulation. "To cast this in the language of motion-picture technology, photochemical imaging practices necessarily treat the image as a whole; digital-imaging practices necessarily treat the image differently."[45] We will encounter numerous versions of this argument as we move forward here.

It is true that digital compositing enables visual effects artists to manipulate and control many more image layers and elements than is possible when working with celluloid on an optical printer. As well, the DI facilitates global as well as selective kinds of image changes. Without question, digital tools have expanded the array of creative choices available to filmmakers. The difficulty, however, in claiming that digital undermines the photochemical integrity that cinema once possessed, and in using Bazin's discussion of photographs to make this case, is that photographs are not at issue. It is difficult to see where this photochemical integrity might be found in cinema. Moving images arranged in sequences to tell stories are not a photograph. Bazin's claims about the nature of photographic truth do not easily generalize to a medium that assembles an array of ever-changing images in order to provoke motion perception. Even if we grant Bazin the validity of his claims, he overlooks the rich tradition of composite photographs and of darkroom practices such as dodging and burning that use masks to selectively lighten or darken discrete areas of the image. These practices are not qualitatively different from anything that may be accomplished digitally. Because he neglects this tradition, Bazin at times made erroneous claims about aesthetics. As I noted earlier, some of *Citizen Kane*'s deep-focus effects were achieved using mattes and optical printing. The famous shot of Kane bursting into Susan's bedroom after she attempts suicide gives us an apparently deep-focus composition, with Kane in the doorway in the far background, Susan on the bed in midground, and a drinking glass, spoon, and medicine bottle looming in the extreme foreground. The shot was an in-camera composite that matted the foreground elements to the separately filmed midground and background. As Robert Carringer perceptively writes, "Bazin's point is valid, but his underlying premise was wrong: The shot reveals Welles not as a photographic realist but as a master illusionist."[46]

The stylistics of cinema do not favor homogenous image spaces, nor have most filmmakers treated images as whole units. Quite the contrary. Cinema is a history of techniques for creating synthetic images, for duping, matting, masking, compounding, and kaleidoscoping camera reality. In-camera mattes, traveling mattes, matte paintings, glass shots, Schufftan shots, rear projection, front projection, composite process projection, the Zoptic technique, rotoscoping, stop motion, Go-Motion, miniature models, hanging foreground miniatures, makeup, pyrotechnics, and optical printing are commonly used methods of counterfeiting what was before the camera. These pre-digital methodologies proliferated throughout the early history of cinema. In many cases, viewers did not perceive them as manipulations of physical reality. The hanging miniature set extension used for the chariot race arena in *Ben-Hur* (1925) creates a perfect illusion of unbroken space, as do the matte painting set extensions used in *Gone with the Wind* (1939). Effects images produced using these techniques are not rare instances; they are commonly found in nearly all films of the pre-digital era (especially if optical printing alone is considered). It is difficult to see how digital technology changes any of this, apart from the ways enumerated in this chapter, namely, in an expansion of creative possibilities. Cinema remains now what it always has been, a synthesis of discrete elements that collectively simulate the representational space of a depicted world. Writing in 1929, Fred Sersen, who headed the art department at the William Fox Studio, pointed out the ways that matte shots enabled filmmakers to draw closer to their artistic visions. Sersen described numerous methods for combining sets, miniatures, actors, and painted elements. He declared, "The use of a matte enables a cameraman to make the picture he visualizes. He is no longer limited by the size of the set, poor light, etc. It makes it possible for him to create and carry out the ideas he has for the enrichment of the production."[47] Little of this has changed in the digital era.

Digital Image Capture

After Thomas Vinterberg shot *The Celebration* (1998) according to Dogme aesthetics on digital video, numerous filmmakers began exploring and using digital image capture as the principal method of film production. George

Lucas filmed *Star Wars II: Attack of the Clones* (2002) using Sony's CineAlta HDW-F900, shooting 24p with a resolution of 1920 x 1080 pixels. Brad Anderson had used the CineAlta a year earlier on the low-budget horror film *Session 9* (2001). John Bailey used standard-definition cameras to shoot *The Anniversary Party* (2001), as did Zacharias Kunuk on *Atanarjuat: The Fast Runner* (2001). In a few years, Lucas had been joined by Michael Mann, David Fincher, and others attracted to the different look created by digital video relative to film and to the benefits offered by the format during production.

Two important differences offered by digital video formats relative to film were the ability of video to see into shadows and its hyper-clarity, which could make colors pop and create an almost three-dimensional look on screen. John Bailey was struck by the different way that video handled the toe of the light curve. After shooting *The Anniversary Party*, he remarked, "It's my feeling that video tends to fall off more slowly than film in the shadow end. . . . I think that the inherent greater latitude in film is at the high end [i.e., highlights], rather than in the dark areas."[48] Michael Mann was especially impressed with this characteristic and chose to shoot *Collateral* (2004) on HD for night-exterior scenes while using film mostly for interiors. The movie, about a hit man (Tom Cruise) who recruits a Los Angeles taxi driver (Jamie Foxx) to ferry him from killing to killing, was shot on location in the city, and the HD format enabled Mann and his cinematographer to view the night as if it had a kind of glowing illumination. As the cinematographer remarked, "We were able to shoot Los Angeles at night and actually see silhouettes of palm trees against the night sky, which was very exciting."[49] The movie is a modern film noir, but its vision of the city at night is starkly different from that established by classic noirs such as *The Big Combo* (1955) or *Chinatown* (1974), where blacks are rich, deep, and dark. Black areas in the night exteriors of *Collateral* are gray and semi-transparent, turning the night into a kind of milky film that hangs over the city. Darkness does not conceal and hide as it does in traditional noirs, nor establish a sense of menace or mystery. Night becomes twilight in *Collateral*, a light-toned dusk, a translucent screen rather than a cloak. The look is strikingly different and not always pleasing. Mann and cinematographer Dion Beebe frequently had to boost the gain on their Thomson Viper Filmstream cameras, which brightened the image by raising its black levels. At times this introduced considerable noise into the image. Noise is the video equivalent of film grain, an artifact of electronically processed images, and its visible presence makes some of the night exteriors in the film look coarse and harsh. They tolerated its presence in the urban backgrounds but found it too distracting in close-ups of Cruise and Foxx during scenes taking place in the taxicab. Video has less exposure latitude than film, which can comfortably handle more stops of light. Mann and Beebe found that shooting a mere 1½ stops below mid-range produced close-ups of Cruise and Foxx that were too noisy. To eliminate the noise, they overlit the actors and then, in the DI, used power windows to bring the light levels on them back down, creating the proper look of a cab interior at night.

Beebe and Mann had to contend with the noise problem when they collaborated again on *Miami Vice* (2006), shooting virtually all of that film on HD using Thomson Vipers. This time they brought the exposure levels up approximately one stop to minimize noise but found that holding the highlights—bright exteriors and skies—and keeping them from blowing out constrained many of their choices. They decided to expose for the highlights and then overlight interiors to bring them into balance. Shooting on film would have enabled up to a four-stop difference between a bright exterior and a key-lit actor indoors. HD video gave them 1–2 stops, a far narrower range, requiring the cinematographer to carefully study the exposure monitor.

This is a key change that digital video formats have introduced into cinema. Shooting on film, a cinematographer relies on a light meter to calculate exposure. This makes the cinematographer into a kind of alchemist, according to Uta Briesewitz, who has shot on film and video. Based on light meter readings in the traditional film world, the cinematographer knows how things will look; no one else does. "The director sees the set and says, '*This* is what it's going to look like?,' and the cinematographer will say, 'Wait till you see it on film.' And it's magic."[50] Cinematographers shooting on video don't use light meters; they consult a waveform monitor that displays the amplitude of the video signal and indicates where highlights and shadows are clipping or losing information. They can also view the scene displayed as a video image. As can others. Briesewitz notes, "Anyone can gather around the monitor and make an opinion known. That's a very different dynamic, for a cinematographer in particular." While this dynamic may pose issues of creative control depending on personnel, most filmmakers desire to have the ability to view their images in real time. As David Fincher said, "I will trade four or five stops of high-end shoulder exposure for the ability to have a 23″ HD monitor that allows me" to view footage without delay.[51]

In spite of efforts to control highlights, numerous exterior scenes in *Miami Vice* feature blown-out clouds and skies, lending a harsh look to landscapes that film could comfortably handle. But Mann liked the abilities of HD to see into the shadows, even though efforts to control the highlights meant that the blacks on this film would be deeper and darker than those in *Collateral*. As a result, the night scenes have a more traditional appearance than the slightly surreal look attained in the earlier film. Mann continued his usage of HD video, collaborating with cinematographer Dante Spinotti on *Public Enemies* (2009), aiming again to illuminate shadows and night exteriors and making considerable image adjustments electronically on set. This was another advantage that Mann felt HD gave him. The Thomson Viper and other top-line video cameras enable filmmakers to shoot in uncompressed RAW files. Thomson's FilmStream mode captures HD images in RAW mode, meaning that the camera applies no image-processing software, then down-converts image data to a 10-bit logarithmic format for storage. A log-encoded image looks very different from a normal RGB video image. It resembles the image on a frame of developed film negative—it looks gray and flat and has minimal contrast. Like printing a positive image from a film negative, processing a log-encoded image produces the desired levels of brightness, contrast, and color saturation. A cinematographer on set viewing footage as log images on a monitor sees scenes that look very flat and sometimes have an off-color cast. Because this can be disconcerting, Mann chose on his HD films not to work in RAW format but to use the camera's image processing software, the Viper's VideoStream mode, which compresses the image data but enables the filmmaker instantly to adjust color, contrast, and other basic image variables. This is a huge change relative to the film world, where filmmakers have lacked the ability to view final image characteristics in real time, and it can help solve problems. On *Collateral*, for example, the wide range of exterior lighting in Los Angeles created potential difficulties for a location shoot. As Beebe noted, "L.A. has a lot of mixed color at night—sodium vapors, mercury vapors, tungsten light, neon and fluorescents—and when mixed together within a frame, they often created an image that Michael thought looked too 'fruity' and detracted from the mood of the scene."[52] Using the image monitors, Mann adjusted the color levels the camera was capturing, alleviating the "fruit-bowl" problem.

The Viper—like the Panavision Genesis and the Red One—is a "data camera" because it enables filmmakers to capture images in an unprocessed, uncompressed mode, the idea being to save all image processing for post-production (though filmmakers like Mann may choose not to do this). These cameras operate like computers: they crunch huge amounts of data, require a process of rebooting after they are shut down, and get regular software and hardware updates. When Steven Soderbergh used the Red One to shoot *Che* (2008), the camera was an early-generation build; at the time of this writing it has gone through more than twenty upgrades. Using the Viper in VideoStream format, as Mann did on *Collateral* and *Miami Vice*, defeats the purpose of a data camera. Cinematographer Newton Thomas Sigel used the Genesis on *Superman Returns* (2006) and learned to mentally translate what the somewhat flat image in RAW mode would look like when fully processed in its final form. He likened the process to learning the characteristics of a new film stock.

The luminous, sumptuous imagery in *Che* (2008) and *Zodiac* (2007) show what can be accomplished with the new generation of data cameras, making these among the most beautifully rendered digital films yet produced. Soderbergh shot *Che*'s two parts (part 1 depicts the Cuban Revolution and part 2 depicts Che's subsequent, hapless campaign in Bolivia) using the Red One, which captures images in RAW format at 4K resolution (4096 x 3072 pixels, as compared with HD's 1920 x 1080). This is known as an extra- or ultra-high definition format. Although at the time the camera was still somewhat experimental, Soderbergh wanted to use it because of its portability and sensitivity to light and because he felt that working digitally would give him more control over the work. A digital workflow, from image capture to editing to color correction, enabled him to retain control over the image files. (The workflow is also convenient. David Fincher shot *The Social Network* [2010] using the Red One and remarked, "It's light and small, and I could walk away from the set at the end of the day with a wallet full of CF cards, take them to the editorial department, download them, and go back and use them again. I call it a righteous workflow.")[53] The Red One beautifully renders *Che*'s landscapes and lighting tonalities, and the film's color pops with carefully modulated intensity. While some of the night exteriors show noise, this is less excessive and more closely resembles film grain than what appears in Mann's films. *Che* has a very filmlike appearance, a product of the camera's ability to handle tones, shadows, and highlights with impressive dynamic range. Indeed, in its current build, the camera has been tested to handle thirteen stops of light and with minimal noise at the low end. Without already knowing so, a viewer would be unlikely to identify *Che*'s video origins. Disparities of resolution and exposure latitude between film and digital video have been narrowing. To a perceptive viewer, the giveaway of *Che*'s digital origin is its hyper-sharp clarity of detail and an occasional harshness in the highlights. Soderbergh indicated that even he found the clarity of super-high definition at times to be distracting and that he prefers the film's first part, which he shot with anamorphic lenses that produced a slight softening in the image relative to the second part that was shot with spherical lenses for a 1.85 aspect ratio.

Fincher and cinematographer Harris Savides shot *Zodiac* with the Viper in FilmStream mode, and Fincher, unlike Mann, was determined for the blacks to be rich and deep, a decision that helps give *Zodiac* a more filmic look than *Collateral*. *Zodiac* is a historically important film because it places digital effects in the service of banality rather than spectacle. The film is a procedural about the effort by police and newspaper reporters to learn the identity of the Zodiac killer who was terrorizing the San Francisco area in the early 1970s. As a procedural, the film's tone emphasizes naturalism, authenticity, and the mundane aspects of daily life and police work. Camera movements are uninflected, and no Steadicam is used. Lighting is natural and motivated by onscreen sources. *Zodiac* is a digital effects–intensive film, and because these effects are in service to a story told with documentary-like veracity, a viewer can watch the movie and never suspect how extensively its locations and visual designs are digitally engineered.

Fincher's respect for the tonality of darkness helps to establish the film's naturalism, in distinct contrast to the visible stylization of *Collateral* and *Miami Vice*. In researching the period look of San Francisco, Fincher watched such shot-on-location movies as *Bullitt* (1968) and *Dirty Harry* (1971) and was struck by how little one saw in the backgrounds of the night exteriors. He told Savides to accomplish something similar, feeling that CGI environments—of which the film has many—tend to look synthetic because they are often overlit. Going in the other direction helped to make the digital locations more credible. Savides shot numerous dark scenes at low F-stops with the lens wide open. This helped decrease depth of field, preventing viewers from seeing very far into the backgrounds, and also helped offset the deep-focus bias of the Viper. Depth of field reduction can be a challenge when shooting in HD because the camera image sensor is smaller than a frame of 35mm film. The Viper and Sony's CineAlta cameras use a 2/3 inch sensor, 11mm in diagonal as compared with the 27.5mm diagonal of 35mm film. This produces 2.5 times the depth of field for the same angle of view and f-stop as when shooting 35mm film. Often on *Zodiac* when the filmmakers wanted a soft background behind the performers, they established depth of field and then placed the actors at the rear border of this area. Night exteriors in *Zodiac* are dark and deep and without the excessive noise that plagues *Collateral* and *Miami Vice*. While Fincher achieved what Mann did not, he also used the Viper at times to counter the look of film and to create a subtle aesthetic tension within the visible surfaces of the movie. Like many HD cameras, the Viper produces images that are hyper-sharp. (Sharpness and resolution are not the same thing. The resolution of film is superior to that of HD, but its inherent grain produces a softer-looking image. Moreover, some HD cameras compress the image captured by the sensor to a degree that degrades resolution.) Savides thought the images looked synthetic because they captured so many details of the surface textures in scenes. "With the Viper, the audience will see more than what they normally see in a movie—literally, the pores on people's faces and every hair on the heads—so it may have an almost immersive effect."[54] This effect can be quite startling. Jake Gyllenhaal, as *San Francisco Chronicle* editorial cartoonist Robert Graysmith, stands in the background of a wide frame showing a group of editors assembled in conference with police. Gyllenhaal's face pops out of the background with a remarkable, even distracting, level of detail. Fincher uses the remarkable detailing of HD as a metaphor for the search for truth and understanding. Graysmith, fellow reporter Paul Avery (Robert Downey Jr.), and detective Dave Toschi (Mark Ruffalo) spend years delving through an avalanche of information, tips, and leads that take them down winding, often dead-end pathways. In the end there is no catharsis. A suspect emerges—Arthur Lee Allen (John Carroll Lynch)—who seems to be the guy, but there is never enough evidence to charge him. And when a witness does come forth many years later and identifies Allen as the man who attacked him, Allen dies of a heart attack before he can be questioned. The denouement is mundane and anticlimactic, yet the irresolute nature of the horrific case remains powerfully haunting. Forensics and empirical investigation provide insufficient illumination—none of the investigators can see very far into the moral darkness represented by Zodiac. Fincher explicitly equates HD's hyper-focus with the quest for truth in a scene where Toschi and two other investigators question Allen at the factory where he works. Fincher had a digital film restoration company interpolate sub-pixel information from this scene to subtly increase the resolution of the imagery beyond even what the rest of the film was showing. Savides remarked that "it makes you study the image more intently . . . it draws your eye even further into the drama."[55] But the viewer, like the investigators, will be denied the catharsis of a case successfully closed. The density and hyper-clarity of the HD imagery metaphorically contrasts with the opacity of the case and its events, and this disparity points to an epistemological paradox inhering in our desire to know and our believing that we can know and the utter resistance of the case to being known. The clarity of HD seems to promise answers, and yet none are forthcoming.

The aesthetic design of *Zodiac*, in which the heightening of image resolution visibly manifests the epistemological desire to know truth, would not be possible had Fincher shot the picture on film. And for this design to be appreciated, it must be viewed digitally. While film negative has impressive resolution capabilities, these quickly degrade through the multigenerational process needed to generate a release print that can be exhibited in theaters. In 2001, the International Telecommunication Union did a study in which a resolution test pattern presenting a maximum of 2,400 lines of information per picture height was photographed on color negative film and then printed in the usual way to generate an interpositive, an internegative, and release prints. The latter when measured were found to display a maximum of 1,000 lines of resolution that degraded further to 875 lines when projected.[56] The best way to view *Zodiac*, therefore, is digital projection. The film's HD images display best in this format, and appreciating the film's aesthetic design requires it.

New Visual Aesthetics

The shift to digital imaging has enabled moviemakers to explore new aesthetics and alternative optical domains to those established over generations using the traditional methods of celluloid-based imaging. I conclude this chapter by examining some recent striking examples in *Speed Racer* (2008), *300* (2006), *WALL-E*, and *Children of Men* (2006). This is a diverse range of movies. Not all are equally successful—and probably few critics or scholars would find *Speed Racer* particularly worthy of attention—but each film is insistently iconoclastic in its efforts to use digital methods to craft images in novel ways or to expand the boundaries of more traditional aesthetic designs.

Speed Racer is the Wachowski brothers' homage to the popular Japanese anime character, and in the film they aimed to fuse anime aesthetics with a design that subverted camera optics. They aimed to create the deep-focus look of anime graphics and make it insistent and stylized in a manner that could not be achieved through the optics of traditional cinematography. The film was shot with a Sony CineAlta camera, and the extreme deep-focus shots are the product of digital compositing. Visual effects supervisor John Gaeta noted, "When we looked closely at Japanese animation, we noticed that a lot of it is done with a large painted background and modified layers on top of

Faux-lens perspectives in *Speed Racer* (2008, Warner Bros.) include exaggerated depth of field, achieved in the compositing. Frame enlargement.

that, like traditional cel animation. It puts everything in focus."[57] To create a cinematic equivalent, the filmmakers shot separate foreground, midground, and background elements in crisp focus and then combined these as a digital composite. The resulting perspective and hyper-deep spatial articulation look very different from what would have been achieved using conventional methods. Early in the film, for example, young Speed (Nicolas Elia) drives his go-cart into his father's garage where his brother Rex (Scott Porter) is repairing an engine. The compositions place Rex in the close foreground, Speed in midground, and the house across the street as background. The spatial planes are crisply focused and layered like cel animation, and there is no attempt to evoke naturalism or photorealism, although the depth cues in the image are assertively presented in a way intended to evoke an extreme version of three-dimensional space. The depth cues are hyper-articulated. Changes in object size, for example, suggest an extreme recession of space far beyond what a suburban neighborhood street typically would engender.

The film is rife with designs that subvert camera optics. The filmmakers referred to these as "faux lensing," that is, "literally inventing optical properties that aren't physically possible."[58] Because foreground and background elements were created separately, like animation cels, their optical relationships could subvert camera reality and go beyond what camera perspective could accommodate. When young Trixie sees that Speed is going to crash his go-cart, she is presented in a shallow-focus composition, the background soft. As she grows alarmed and calls out to Speed, a rack focus occurs to bring the background into clarity, but Trixie's focal plane remains unchanged. When a real camera lens is rack-focused, the focal plane shifts so that areas that were clear become soft or vice versa. Speed Racer, instead, flaunts the paradox that rack focusing needn't alter a shot's foreground focal plane. In a subsequent scene, Speed's father (John Goodman) sits in profile in the garage in the foreground of a shallow-focus shot. When Rex walks into the background, a rack focus brings him into optical clarity without losing the focus on Speed's father. In other ways, the optical perspective within shots assumes photographically impossible forms. Many of the film's deep-focus shots incorporate paradoxical perspectives—spatial planes are mismatched, as when wide angle and telephoto perspectives are combined within the same shot. The background of a shot might be done in deep focus while the foreground is in telephoto perspective. A common artifact of lens perspective is "bokeh," the photographic term for the distinctive blurring that occurs in the out-of-focus areas of an image. Different types of lenses—spherical or anamorphic, for example—produce characteristic bokeh effects. The Wachowskis play with bokeh throughout Speed Racer, as in a scene where young Speed and Trixie realize they are in love. Each is filmed in shallow focus, and the spherical background blur assumes the shape of a cluster of Valentine's hearts.

Depth of field in *Speed Racer* is a composited effect whose aberrations point self-consciously toward its normative construction in celluloid-based cinema and the physical constraints of the optics from which camera-defined depth of field derives. The composited deep-focus shots are presented as playful subversions of camera reality, and as such they clearly depart from photorealism, as do other elements of the film. These include its intensely saturated color images and the eccentric ways that focal planes within a shot move in relation to each other. Used as a narrative tool, the focal-plane shifts enable scene transitions to occur. Background planes behind characters slide across the screen, a lateral movement perpendicular to the camera's line of sight. A new location displaces the old, signaling the scene transition, while lighting and focus on foreground characters remain unaltered. The effect is comparable to multiplane camerawork in cel animation, and it represents a 2D simulation of 3D space. Depth cues are clearly artificial and are conveyed on a 2D axis using the lateral shift of background and foreground elements. The effect flaunts the paradoxes achieved by visually disconnecting spaces that as narrative elements remain integrated in the represented action of a scene.

Critics of digital effects sometimes complain that they represent a limited aesthetic to the degree that they strive for photorealism. John Belton, for example, writes that "digital imaging technology . . . tends to simulate older, analogue, image-making conventions, not to create radically new perceptual modes."[59] Julie Turnock writes that the dominant style that ILM established is one that seeks "perfectly executed, seamless photorealism," creating a "perfect illusion" of the real.[60] These scholars are correct in pointing to photorealism as an effect that can be achieved digitally, but it is not the only goal of digital effects. Sometimes it isn't a goal at all. As we have seen, effects artists delight in revealing new optical domains. Moreover, photorealism is a slippery and somewhat misleading term. As an art-form of composited images, little about cinema is realistic if such a term is understood as corresponding with camera reality. Tromp l'oeil is deeply embedded in cinema as one of its essential characteristics.

Willful departures from photorealism are quite evident throughout *300*, a retelling of the Battle of Thermopylae that models its images on the ink and watercolor paintings produced by Frank Miller for his graphic novel, from which the film is adapted. Shot largely in a greenscreen studio with minimal sets, the locales are computer-generated, and the filmmakers never seek to persuade viewers that they are seeing landscapes that could be photographed.

The digital skies are monochromatic and toned like a watercolor wash, rocks and mountains are minimally textured, and oceans, storms, and the Persian foes are depicted in a surreal fashion. Distant vistas are digital matte paintings presented as 2D constructions. The film's landscapes do not include realistic depictions of atmospheric perspective, namely, visual haze and a color shift toward blue. *300* was shot on film, which creates the soft tones necessary for the watercolor style, but in the DI the blacks were crushed (detail in shadow areas was eliminated) and the highlights were clipped. The resulting effect looks very different—more velvety, less harsh and hard—than what HD video would have achieved. But none of the film's stylistic attributes seeks to persuade viewers that they are real. Stepping into the film, viewers imaginatively enter a digitally painted domain, in which the small spaces on set are opened up as digital set extensions but with minimal effort to provide credible 3D depth cues. The painted and two-dimensional qualities of the matte backdrops are unconcealed.

When depth cues are vividly rendered, they count among the film's most extreme departures from photorealism. One of the film's especially flamboyant effects employs digital zooms to create the appearance of an extended moving camera shot; the zooms actually conceal a series of cuts. The zooms create depth of field effects and hide the cuts in a way that maintains the viewer's phenomenal impression of seeing a stream of action unbroken by editing and contained within a single shot. The effect is displayed most strikingly during the first battle scene between the Spartans and their Persian foes. King Leonides (Gerard Butler) charges into the fray hurling a spear and using his sword to lop off the limbs of his enemies. A moving

300 (2006, Warner Bros.) avoids a photographic look even though it was shot on film. Instead, it emulates the distinctive painterly style of the Frank Miller artwork on which it is based. Frame enlargement.

camera follows him as he defiantly rushes across the battlefield, slaying his antagonists. At key moments—as he hurls a spear or slashes at foes—the shot abruptly and rapidly zooms in to provide a close view of the action, then quickly zooms back out, and these optical changes are accompanied by speed changes (known as "speed ramps") during which the action slows down to a few frames per second in order to highlight details, such as a blood spray or flying limb. The abrupt zooms and speed ramps give the shot a hyper-kinetic quality, a herky-jerky, spasmodic energy, a degree of artifice so pronounced that the viewer is forced to take notice.

The "shot" actually contains twenty-seven cuts and incorporates footage assembled from two takes. It was created using a special three-camera mount that filmed the action simultaneously from three lens perspectives—wide, medium, and long—each aligned on the same axis of view.[61] The zooms are digital creations used to cover the cuts from one lens perspective to another, and morphs blend the views imperceptibly. Thus a zoom-in to highlight a detail such as a sword thrust by Leonides is actually a cut between a wide-angle shot and a telephoto shot, with digital frame interpolations used to simulate the zoom effect and provide the lead-in and lead-out of the join between the shots. The speed ramps were created during compositing, and they are more dynamic than what might have been achieved using celluloid methods. When shooting film, a modest speed change can be achieved within a shot by altering the camera's speed (or, after filming, by using the optical printer), but the ramps in *300* are more extreme. A technique called optical flow, a form of motion analysis, enables the computer to analyze the motion vectors occurring across the frames in a sequence and from these to generate new frames that can be used to shorten or expand the action. This method creates perfect image blends and models the alterations of motion blur that correspond with the speed changes. Acceleration produces greater blur, deceleration less. The other tool necessary for the sequence to work was matchmoving, a method of analyzing a live-action camera move and live-action elements such as actors and using this data to create corresponding moves in a CGI environment. Gerard Butler charged into action on a greenscreen set; in the finished shot the CG backgrounds have been carefully matchmoved so that the camera's simulated optical perspective on them matches what happens in the live action.

What emerged from these manipulations was a digitally realized long take. The action appears to be covered in a single camera move, and this appearance conceals the actual basis of the sequence that lies in montage. The wholeness of space here is a digital palimpsest, but one that advertises its constructed origins through the insistent artifice of the speed ramps. Imperceptible simulations of a long-take aesthetic can be found throughout

Children of Men (2007), a futuristic tale about a time when the human race
has become sterile. Director Alfonso Cuarón wanted to compose the film in
a series of extended moving camera shots, a long-take style that he felt would
lend the story the immediacy and credibility of a pseudo-documentary such
as *The Battle of Algiers* (1966).[62] Unlike the extended camera moves in *300*
that present themselves as part of a visual effects sequence, the long takes in
Children of Men unfold in a more naturalistic manner and are perceptually
indistinguishable from true long takes. I make this distinction because, while
Cuarón did shoot the film with extended takes, he lengthened these by digitally conjoining several takes to create scenes that seem to unfold in a single,
unbroken camera perspective. The joins between the shots cannot be seen
even if a viewer knows where they are. The digital stitching is that perfect.

A striking example occurs in the film's first scene. The hero, Theo (Clive
Owen), is in a coffee bar listening to a newscast about the death of the world's
youngest citizen. He leaves the bar, followed by the camera in a Steadicam
shot. He walks out the door and down the street, through a throng of pedes-
trian traffic, as the camera follows close behind. He pauses by a newspaper box
to pour some liquor into his coffee. As he does so, the camera circles around
to show him in the foreground; in the background is the street he has just
walked down and its coffee bar. At that moment, a bomb blows out the front
of the building and Theo ducks to the ground. The camera rushes past him
toward the ruined building as a woman staggers out clutching her severed arm.

Subtle compositing of multiple takes creates a sustained optical flow that connects
Theo (Clive Owen) with the exploding coffee bar that he has just left. The digital
long take enhances the abrupt and shocking effect of the scene's action. *Children
of Men* (2006, Universal Pictures). Frame enlargement.

The shot is composed as a continuous camera move, and its emotional effect—the bomb destroying the building from which Theo has just emerged—depends on a viewer's subliminal sense that the shot has unfolded in real time and within a space that is whole and contiguous as presented in the long take. The continuous optical flow that has connected Theo and the coffee bar makes the sudden explosion more shocking than if the scene had cut from Theo in the street to the building blowing up. But while the shot's design works well in this regard, the basis on which it is achieved is deceiving. The long take is constructed from two shots, and the scene was filmed over two days. The reason was entirely pragmatic. The bar had to be fitted with an effects explosive, its extras recostumed as wounded patrons, and this was easier to accomplish if the shot cut at the point where Theo leaves the bar, enabling the set changes to be made for the next day's shooting. The "cut" is imperceptible. It occurs as Theo steps through the doorway into the street. The camera briefly pans away from him toward the door as a double-decker bus passes by in the street outside. The two takes were joined at that moment, with matchmoving used to align the backgrounds of the door in each take. The passing bus enabled the compositor to apply a traveling matte as a digital wipe. As the bus passes, its bulk blocks the camera's view of the street, and the rear edge of the bus effectively becomes the blade of an optical wipe, enabling the compositor to insert the street background from the second day's filming. This background is revealed as the rear edge of the bus crosses the screen. The solution enabled the views of London's Fleet Street, with different traffic patterns over the two-day shoot, to blend perfectly.

Numerous other scenes in the movie create long takes as digital conjunctions of separately filmed material. A bravura six-minute moving camera shot depicts action in which Theo and his ex-wife Julian (Julianne Moore) reconcile while driving in a Fiat van; they are then attacked by thugs who chase their van; Julian is shot and killed; Theo flees in the car; he is then stopped by police; and he must flee again when an accomplice kills the officers. The shot was not done as greenscreen. It was filmed over eight days, in three separate, real locations, and was broken apart as six small sequences for filming. Numerous digital transitions blend background plates of different locations into what appears to be a single passing landscape, and digital blends were used inside the car to hide sections of the action that were discontinuous because they were shot at different times. The Fiat had no roof so that the camera could descend into the car and film the actors, and the camera crew sat atop the open-roofed vehicle. To hide the crew, a CG car roof was used, and digital lighting effects simulated the look of an enclosed vehicle.

During the attack, a Molotov cocktail hurled by a thug and the fiery explosion are digital effects, as is the bullet strike through the windshield. Julian's head when she is shot is a digital model tracked onto Julianne Moore's shoulders. When Theo hits a pair of pursuing motorcyclists with the Fiat, the stuntmen fall into the underbrush, but the flipping cycles and victims are digital creations, as is the splintering, crumbling windshield. When police stop the Fiat and Theo gets out, a digital matchmove centering on the open door enables the camera to look back (in another take) at a real Fiat without a camera crew on top of it.

Like the digital blend that joins the two views of Fleet Street in the earlier scene, none of these manipulations are apparent. Viewers experience instead an unbroken extension of time and space, dramatic action unfolding within a continuous optical perspective. The long take aesthetic is a digital achievement, and as such we should ask whether its visual effects sleight-of-hand is consistent with the kind of realism that Bazin famously claimed for long takes. Bazin argued that a long-take aesthetic was counterposed to montage aesthetics. The latter, he wrote, is anti-cinematic because it does not respect the unity of space. It creates meanings derived from image juxtaposition rather than from the content of an image itself. He wrote that montage is "an abstract creator of meaning," one that "preserves the state of unreality" demanded by spectacle.[63] It would be far too easy to claim something similar for digital effects, that their use in *Children of Men* preserves a spectacle-based state of unreality. Quite the opposite, in fact, is the case.

In contrast to montage, Bazin emphasized the ways that deep focus and extended takes preserve a unity of space that he believed was an essential constituent of realism in cinema. He held that the continuity of dramatic space, achieved via these techniques, was a cinematic analogue for the spectator's experience of the real world. To the extent that cinema could model that experience, it drew closer to reality. He praised, for example, Renoir's use of camera movement to extend shot duration, regarding this as an important alternative to montage. "It is based on a respect for the continuity of dramatic space and, of course, of its duration."[64]

If a filmmaker can model the continuity of dramatic space and its duration in a fictional screen world, does it matter how this is accomplished? Does it make any difference if the long takes are existentially real or are digitally simulated? Much depends on the context of a scene, of course, but if spatial continuity is what counts, then surely there are many routes to its attainment. Cuarón filmed *Children of Men* in long takes; they simply aren't as long as what is represented on screen. These long takes indeed exist in the film as a stylistic alternative to montage, even if their construction involves a process of montage as the various digital elements are assembled. A viewer watching the digital long take has a phenomenological experience of duration and not montage. Cuarón uses visual effects in order to respect the integrity of space. That space is often simulated, but the stitching between shots or other visual effects elements does not show. The unity of space is perceptibly whole, and it is sustained across complexly choreographed dramatic action. The film is utterly Bazinian in its preference for creating scenes as large blocks of action sustained without a fragmentation of the represented dramatic space. What is cinema in *Children of Men*? It is a medium of digital realism or, to be more precise, a medium in which the Bazinian ideals of realism are sought and digitally attained. The aesthetic design is consistent with that found in the work of all Bazin's heroes—Welles, Renoir, Rossellini, Flaherty—while representing as well an approach to spatial unity that was technologically beyond Bazin's horizon of filmic experience. *Children of Men* demonstrates that long takes can be virtual and remain consistent with the aesthetic of realism to which they historically have been attached.

Criticism of digital imaging on the basis that it strives for photorealism overlooks a prime motivation on the part of effects artists when they do seek a photo-real appearance. Such an appearance minimizes the artificiality of computer-generated imagery, and it creates continuity with the historical traditions of cinematic imaging that are photographic. Pixar's *WALL-E* (2008) exemplifies this quest to create an all-digital world on screen that is fanciful and fantastical yet evokes the conventions of cinematic perspective familiar to moviegoers. These serve to soften the tendency for computer images to look overly calculated and excessively designed, cold, and hard. The film's director, Andrew Stanton, said, "Life is nothing but imperfection and the computer likes perfection, so we spent probably 90% of our time putting in all of the imperfections." Jeremy Lasky, the director of photography, emphasized the strategic value of designing imperfections into the film. "The little inconsistencies that you can put in CG . . . make it feel like [objects] were really filmed and not studied pixel for pixel, month after month, which is what we do."[65]

The imperfections mostly involved the proper replication of anamorphic lens perspective and the flaws that distinguish it from spherical lens perspective. Many of these involved depth-of-field simulations to emulate the focusing characteristics of anamorphic lenses. (As with lighting a CG environment, the difficulties of representing depth of field in CG have elicited numerous algorithms and methods of simulation.)[66] Stanton wanted the movie to look reminiscent of 1970s-era anamorphic widescreen science fiction films. Pixar's virtual camera package, as used on films such as *Ratatouille*, calculated camera variables, such as f-stops, depth of field, focal lengths, and created optical perspectives consistent across these variables, but these lens perspectives had always been spherical. The package was not equipped to emulate the look of an anamorphic film, even though many Pixar movies were in a 2.35:1 aspect ratio. The films had always had a spherical look as if they had been a Super 35mm scope extraction. Cinematographer Roger Deakins worked on the film as a consultant, showing Pixar's artists the subtle distinctions between spherical and 'scope perspective and also demonstrating how a cinematographer might light some of the film's scenes and locations. Successfully replicating the appearance of anamorphic cinematography required redesigning the studio's virtual camera software so that the optical distortions found in anamorphic movies would be on display in *WALL-E*. These include elliptical-shaped bokeh and lens flares, barrel distortion, astigmatism, field curvature, and optical breathing artifacts.[67]

When filmed with a spherical lens, point-light sources that are out of focus appear round, whereas blurred light sources filmed anamorphically appear as horizontal or vertical ellipses. This effect is especially evident in the close-ups of EVE, the sleek robot with whom our hero, WALL-E, a discarded waste removal robot, falls in love. In the close-ups showing her from WALL-E's perspective inside his trailer, the background Christmas lights assume the characteristic elliptical form that would be found in an anamorphic movie. Anamorphic lens flares tend to spike horizontally, and this effect is simulated in the glare of the rocket engines when WALL-E hitches a ride on the spaceship carrying the surviving Earthlings. Barrel distortion is visible as the outward curvature of straight lines, especially when filmed at wider focal lengths. The film's evocation of barrel distortion is especially subtle and can be seen at the edges of the high-rise buildings in many wide shots. Astigmatism is one of the most serious problems found in anamorphic lenses and makes it difficult to achieve fine focus across the field of view. The outermost quadrants of the frame tend to go soft, and *WALL-E* is especially attentive to the peculiarities and defects of anamorphic focus, particularly evident in shots involving close-focus distances. An extreme close-up of WALL-E gazing at his companion cockroach, for example, does not resolve cleanly across the width of his face. The limited focus points to the constraints on anamorphic depth of field and the lens' relatively small "sweet spot," the area capable of delivering fine-focus imaging.

Simulating anamorphic field curvature—the warping of lines and objects as they move across the curvature of the lens—required Pixar to construct a different type of virtual camera because the studio hitherto had relied on one that was nodal. A nodal camera is specially mounted so that it will pan around the optical center of its lens, creating a shifting view but no change in perspective. It is often used in visual effects work employing foreground miniatures because it permits limited pans. These do not create the perspective shifts that would reveal the presence of the miniature model. Most tripods are not nodal. Cameras mounted on them do record changes in perspective during a panning shot. These perspective changes were a new level of visual information created for *WALL-E*. Throughout the film, panning shots cause objects in the scene to warp as they move across the frame. A related type of object displacement, visible as a focusing artifact, is the phenomenon of optical breathing. Large focal changes, as when racking focus from a very distant object to a very near object, produce changes in field position. In the film's last act, when WALL-E is hiding in the spaceship captain's cabin, a large rack focus shifts from EVE in the far background of the shot to WALL-E in the near foreground. As EVE is defocused, her position in the frame changes as a result of anamorphic lens breathing.

All these effects in the film are fairly subliminal and are probably felt by audiences more than seen. Lasky believed that they would be noticed subconsciously by viewers and would help audiences to "feel like there's a camera in the CG space."[68] The realism induced by these artifacts is not a first-order level of realism in the way that ambient occlusion establishes the impression of 3D space by representing the soft shadows cast by environmental light. It is a more derivative form of realism, tied to the peculiarities of anamorphic optics as these were instantiated in cinema by generations of films, most especially during the high period of anamorphic widescreen that lasted until the 1980s. By emulating the eccentricities of this optical system, *WALL-E* locates itself in this distinct period. It is a paradoxical gesture. This is a futuristic film in a double sense—its story world is a science fiction set in the future, and it is

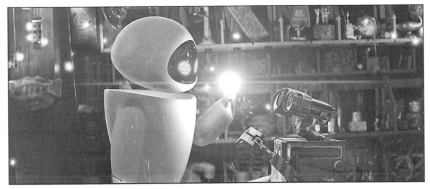

The animation in *WALL-E* (2008, Pixar) emulates the characteristic look of anamorphic cinematography, which includes features such as this horizontally spiking lens flare. Frame enlargement.

an all-CGI film in which nothing was photographed—yet its aesthetic design looks toward the past and the way that films were once composed. With this backward glance, the film distinguishes itself from the spherical cinematography that is commonly found in modern cinema and that digital imaging tools have helped to make more prevalent, and it aligns itself with a format that emerged in the 1950s as a means for cinema to compete with television. It is photorealism in a very restricted sense. The objective is not to convince audiences that what they are watching is real, but rather to suggest that WALL-E could have been filmed by a cinematographer working in anamorphic widescreen. Audiences know that the film is all-CG, but this visual conceit serves to introduce a historically grounded aesthetic perspective into the film, ironically, by connecting it with the mechanical imperfections that once were rife in cinema and that lens manufacturing has worked very hard to overcome.

Berys Gaut has written that the long dominance of photographically derived images in cinema has led scholars to identify the characteristics of photography with those of cinema. But the advent of digital imaging tools has moved cinema away from its near-exclusive reliance on photography. He writes that the task now is "to disentangle systematically which aspects of photographic films depend on their photographic nature, and which on their being moving images."[69] As moving images, *Forrest Gump*, *Zodiac*, *Ratatouille*, *Speed Racer*, *300*, *WALL-E*, and the other films examined in this chapter incorporate a photographic aesthetic but also go considerably beyond this. Digital imaging tools enable filmmakers to extend the visual properties of cinema in ways that are consistent with photographic images and also in ways that subvert, alter, or otherwise depart from what the optical system of camera machinery dictates. This flexibility opens up new creative freedoms without destroying the old ones. Martin Scorsese's *Shutter Island* (2010), for example, contains nearly 650 visual effects shots that simulate the island location using bluescreen mattes, digital painting, and 3D computer effects. But the final shot of the film employs a hanging miniature, one of the oldest and most traditional of visual effects techniques. Digital imaging coexists with cinema's traditional aesthetics, but it is not confined or constrained by them. Using its tools, filmmakers have taken audiences to new visual domains foreclosed by the optics of real, nonvirtual cameras. Cinematography has been transformed in the process, and light—a filmmaker's most basic tool—has retained the physics of its behavior while becoming a virtual energy, one that is infinitely malleable.

CHAPTER 3

Actors and Algorithms

A decade into Hollywood's digital revolution, Andrew Niccol wrote and directed *S1mone* (2002), a speculative fantasy in which film director Victor Taransky (Al Pacino) replaces a temperamental star (Winona Ryder) with a digital actor. His move saves the production. The film becomes a huge success and so does Simone, its digital star. She commands constant media attention and a huge and devoted fan base. Taransky now has a new problem—keeping Simone's true identity secret. The public believes she is flesh and blood, and Taransky struggles to prevent the fraud that he's perpetrated from being known.

Niccol's film is whimsical, but it expresses real anxiety and some bitterness. The movie conjures a world in which digital simulations of human beings are unperceivable as such and in which actors are replaced by computerized surrogates. The film envisions a time when filmmakers no longer need flesh-and-blood actors because digital replacements are cheaper and can be designed to have star quality. Simone represents the death of the actor and even of reality. Sitting at his computer, manipulating Simone, Taransky playfully mutters, "I am the death of real." Simone tells an interviewer, "I relate better to people when they're not there."

Fittingly, Simone is the invention of a mad scientist, Hank Alano (Elias Koteas), a whacko who has developed an eye tumor from staring at his computer screen too long. He bequeaths his invention to Taransky. Using the figure of Alano, the movie casts the genesis of digital images in the terms of a Frankenstein myth. Simone is the product of a lone inventor rather than decades of research pursued by many institutions, the process that actually gave us CGI. Taransky can interact with her in real time, make her speak, and move by pushing a few keys at his computer, an ease that still eludes digital animators.

Feeling remorseful about his deceitful behavior, Taransky tells his ex-wife, "There's no Simone. She's pixels, computer code molded by me from a mathematical equation I inherited from a madman." But Simone represents the new reality, according to Niccol. Taransky can't walk away from her or the success she's brought him. The film ends as he and Simone tell the media that they have decided to go into politics. The illusion and sleight-of-hand they have been practicing will be very much at home there.

"The creation of realistic digital humans [is] the high watermark in computer animation."[1] So wrote Remington Scott, who supervised the motion-capture work on *The Lord of the Rings: The Two Towers* (2002). This is an oft-repeated idea (especially by advocates of motion capture), that lifelike digital humans are the Holy Grail of computer animation. Its corollary—why use actors anymore?—elicits the anxieties that *Simone* addresses. Indeed, Pamela Wojcik writes that we now face "a crisis in the conception of acting, a crisis that is seemingly historically and technologically determined: the issue of acting in the digital age."[2] The notion that digital imaging poses crises for our understanding of cinema, however, seems to exaggerate the nature of the changes that have occurred.

In his book on film acting, James Naremore writes that there is "no such thing as an uncontrived face in the movies."[3] Humphrey Bogart wore a full wig throughout *Treasure of the Sierra Madre* (1948)because his hair was thinning. John Wayne wore a toupee and was rarely photographed without it. Orson Welles regularly appeared onscreen in false noses. Nicole Kidman did likewise when playing Virginia Woolf in *The Hours* (2002). Charlize Theron dimmed her natural beauty to play a serial killer in *Monster* (2003), and many stars today require that digital intermediates be used for cosmetic purposes such as erasing skin blemishes and wrinkles. Just as faces are contrived for the camera, so, too, are bodies. Alan Ladd famously stood on boxes to be photographed with his taller co-stars. Al Pacino and Dustin Hoffman are carefully framed in movies to hide their short stature from viewers.

Actors provide the human element in cinema, a medium that otherwise is heavily dependent upon machinery for creating light and color and capturing images and sounds. And yet the actor's presence is paradoxical. A viewer's impression of wholeness—the actor as a unified being in front of the camera—and of psychological and emotional continuity—the actor-as-character unfolding in narrative time and space—is a manufactured impression that often fails to correlate with what was. The discrepancy between the actor as a real being and the sleight of hand performed with makeup, editing, and camera angles can raise questions about what, precisely, the actor contributes to cinema. (In point of fact, an actor's ownership of a character's through-line is only possible in live performance, not in cinema.)[4] Where are the boundaries between what an actor creates and what filmmakers have crafted? In their study of screen performance, Cynthia Baron and Sharon Marie Carnicke acknowledge this problem, which they call "the still uncertain status of screen performances. Are they instances of authentic acting? Or are they the result of filmmakers' sleight of hand?"[5] The problem endures. Has cinema's digital revolution complicated it?

Because films are shot out of continuity, performance and character often must be constructed in the editing. As actor Michael Caine observed, "If the last scene in a picture takes place outside, you can count on the fact that it will get shot first and then you will move to the studio to shoot all the scenes leading up to it. You might shoot the master in the morning, then rush out in the afternoon to shoot another scene because suddenly the sun came out. Then you have to come back some other time and continue with the morning scene, then perhaps do the medium shot and close-up a week later."[6] Professional courtesy mandates that actors who are off-camera in a dialogue scene remain on set to feed lines and reactions to their co-stars. When this fails to occur, the footage will be edited to suggest the missing actor's presence. Rod Steiger complained that Marlon Brando didn't stick around when Steiger filmed his close-ups in *On the Waterfront*'s (1954) famous taxicab scene. "I did the take with him, when the camera was on him, but when it came for the camera to be on me—he went home! I had to speak my lines to an assistant director."[7] According to Steiger, he played the scene with an actor who wasn't there, but a viewer watching the film cannot tell. The screen reality created by the framing and editing, and by Steiger and Brando's performing, alters the conditions that Steiger said prevailed during filming. Is this situation different in kind or degree from one in which an actor plays to a missing digital character that will be composited into the scene at a later time?

Mark J. P. Wolf correctly observes that "performance in film has almost always been more than the straightforward recording of actors."[8] Actors perform on set but their work is reconstructed during post-production as picture and sound are edited and as effects shots are composited. Performance in cinema always has been a construction synthesized from discrete elements removed from their original contexts, rearranged, reordered, reshaped. As Wojcik emphasizes, "Discussion of film acting must find a way to account for the role of technology in performance." She points out that film acting "is always already mediated" by technology.[9] This is true in analog as well as digital cinema. Digital tools, though, have given filmmakers new powers to manipulate light and color and to composite images; they have augmented the existing practices of completing or creating performances in post-production.

As Wolf writes, "Today with digital effects, we are seeing an unprecedented degree of technological advances that allow the breaking up, recombining, and reconfiguring of actors' abilities as multiple forms of input."[10]

This chapter examines the forms and methods by which digital performances are commonly created and the creative possibilities and challenges that result. At the outset, it will be very useful to distinguish between "acting" and "performance" along the lines suggested by David Fincher, whose *The Curious Case of Benjamin Button* (2008) pursued a novel approach to virtual performing and is examined later in the chapter. Fincher said that "acting and performance are two different things. Acting is what you do; the performance is the thing that you make from the acting."[11] On stage, performance and acting often are interchangeable. In cinema, acting is a subset of performance. For our purposes, then, *acting* is the ostensive behavior that occurs on set to portray characters and story action. *Performance* is understood as the subsequent manipulation of that behavior by filmmakers or by actors and filmmakers. This distinction will enable us to recognize the ways that cinema employs technology to mediate the actor's contribution, via such things as editing, music scoring, lighting, makeup, and compositing. The distinction also enables us to incorporate the tradition of animation that has been so important throughout the history of cinema and that is typically omitted from discussion of film acting. Stop-motion animation, for example, has created very persuasive cinematic performances, from the expressive bugs and foxes in Ladislaw Starewicz's *The Dragonfly and the Ant* (1911) and *The Tale of the Fox* (1930) to Willis O'Brien's *King Kong* (1933), Ray Harryhausen's *Jason and the Argonauts* (1963), Henry Selick's *Coraline* (2009), and Wes Anderson's *The Fantastic Mr. Fox* (2009). The animators at Pixar have crafted some of the most affecting performances in modern cinema, in *The Incredibles* (2004), *WALL-E* (2008), *Up* (2009), and other films. Performances by digital creatures, fanged, furred, or scaled thespians, are key elements in the success or failure of their respective films. We need, then, to work with an expansive concept of performance in cinema, one that encompasses all these traditions. As Lisa Bode writes, "Rather than 'splitting' acting from digital animation or technology, we might instead imagine a screen performance continuum encompassing all the modes of technological mediation and augmentation of performance."[12]

Acting and Animation

Of particular importance is the tradition of animation. Indeed, all digital performances are to some degree the work of animation. Some characters—WALL-E or the family of superheroes in *The Incredibles*—are completely realized through animation, whereas others—Gollum, Benjamin Button—incorporate the contributions of a live actor whose movements or facial expressions are photographically captured and then used as the basis for constructing an animated character. Scholarly and popular discussion of performance in cinema tends to limit it to the contribution of a human actor working on set before the cameras during production. Acting in these other contexts is rarely considered, and performance traditions that extend away from the live actor or that build digital bridges from live acting to animation are often regarded suspiciously. A larger bias is at work—a general disregard for animation, which film theory and aesthetics have virtually excluded from consideration. Tom Gunning has rightly identified this marginalization of animation as "one of the great scandals of film theory."[13] To the extent that an aesthetic bias exists against digital performance, it may be connected with the marginal status that animation itself occupies in film theory and aesthetics.

This bias precludes us from seeing the manifold ways that acting exists in the digital domain, albeit not as traditionally configured with a live actor emoting before cameras that capture a performance subject to modification afterward. Actors exist in the digital world in three ways. They may be present as the live action component of composited shots (for example, Naomi Watts acting with King Kong). They may give a performance that is motion-captured for use in animating a digital character (for example, Andy Serkis as Gollum). The third condition is the most significant and influential and the one that is perhaps the least obvious—the animator is an actor and works with the objectivity that an actor in live theater does not have. (As Patricia Raun notes, "The challenge in live theatre is that the actor is both the artist and the medium and s/he cannot see the effect of the work s/he is creating. S/he has no objective eye.")[14] The animator who creates a digital character onscreen must give a performance, expressed through the character as it is created, shaped, and given movement in the expression of feeling and attitude. Ray Harryhausen, who brought many classic monsters to life as stop-motion puppets, remarked, "I always tried to give my characters little habits that made them seem more believable. It doesn't take much, just small habits such as taking a quick look at the ground before they step forward."[15] Hanging from the roof of a tall building, mortally wounded by gunfire, the alien monster in *20 Million Miles to Earth* (1957) glances downward in fear and panic, knowing it cannot sustain its grip and that death from its impending fall awaits. The creature is a miniature puppet brought to life through the illusion of stop-motion photography, and yet its demise is very affecting. Harryhausen's animation often made the fates of his fantasy creatures more deeply moving than the lives of the pallid human characters that populated the films.

Brad Bird, director of *The Iron Giant* (1999) and *The Incredibles*, points out that animation typically is regarded as more technique than art, "its practitioners little more than technicians with pencils (or clay or pixels or puppets)." When a character is successful, the voice actor often gets the credit. "What is typically lost in discussions about animation is the fact that when you watch an animated film, the performance you're seeing is the one *the animator* is giving to you."[16] To accomplish this, the animator has to stay "in the moment" for weeks, comparable in a fashion to the work of an actor in live theater where weeks of rehearsal precede and contribute to the creation of the right moments on stage. Ed Hooks, who has taught acting to animators at Disney and other studios, emphasizes that acting by animators is sustained, analytic work: "A good animator must go through a similar process of motivating his characters on a moment-to-moment basis, but he then must keep re-creating the same moment over and over and over again, sometimes for weeks on end, while he captures it on the cell or computer screen."[17]

In this regard, digital animation continues the traditional practices of hand-drawn and stop-motion animation. Disney animator Mark Davis, who designed the villainous Cruella de Vil in *101 Dalmations* (1961), said, "To be an animator, you have to have a sense of the dramatic, a feeling for acting; you have to be a storyteller." He noted, "Drawing is giving a performance; an artist is an actor who is not limited by his body, only by his ability and, perhaps, experience."[18] Disney animators Frank Thomas and Ollie Johnston wrote about this connection: "The actor and the animator share many interests; they both use symbols to build a character in the spectator's mind. By using the right combination [of gestures and expressions] the actor builds a bond with the people in the audience." The audience comes to care about the actor and the character and to understand the character's thoughts and feelings. "These are the animator's tools as well, but while the actor can rely on his inner feelings to build his portrayal, the animator must be objectively analytical if he is to reach out and touch the audience."[19]

In numerous contexts, animators work as actors. Phil Tippett won an Emmy for his puppet animation in the CBS documentary *Dinosaur!* (1985). With his knowledge of animal behavior, he conducted acting classes for the digital animators working on *Jurassic Park* (1993). "I would physically pantomime some of the animal behavior to demonstrate it to them. Sometimes you just have to show people."[20] The animatronic velociraptors in *The Lost World: Jurassic Park* (1997) were animated by puppeteers using a telemetric device to send commands to a computer that, in turn, relayed them to the character. The puppeteers were professional actors. Stan Winston said, "The operators who animated the dinosaurs were members of the Screen Actors Guild, because the performances entailed real acting. The gestures of the raptors were powerful, quick, natural. In a word, these dinosaurs became the best actors!"[21] Or, one might say, these actors made the best dinosaurs.

Professional courses and guidebooks enable digital animators to train as actors and understand the craft. A SIGGRAPH course, "Acting and Drawing for Animation," teaches animators physical exercises and moves, methods of emotional projection and sensory recall, and techniques of emotional staging and drawing. The Disney principles are incorporated throughout, as in a series of "squash and stretch" warm-up exercises. "As a physical warm-up this exercise helps to loosen up the hands, face, and whole body. . . . Imagine balling your face into a fist. Scrunch it down as tight as it will go. Think about trying to tuck your forehead into your bottom lip. Release!"[22] Ed Hooks writes that the quickest way to provoke a room full of animators is to take away their mirrors. "Animators love mirrors! They like to make facial expressions in them, and act out scenes in front of them. Little mirrors, big mirrors, hand mirrors, full-length mirrors, animators will usually have one close at hand." As the authors of a textbook on acting lessons for animators write, "Your instrument is not the same as an actor who uses his own body, voice, and emotions to create the character. Your instrument is the hardware and software available to you. Nevertheless, your character still has a body, voice, and emotions as with the actor's character, so understanding and employing the techniques of an actor can only aid in your artistry."[23]

Disney artists honed their craft by taking acting classes and used this knowledge in the practice of character animation: animation that expressed the personalities, thoughts, and emotions of characters through line and form and movement. Convinced that "we cannot do the fantastic things based on the real, unless we first know the real," Disney began requiring his animators to attend action analysis classes.[24] Starting in 1936, they studied live-action motion pictures and analyzed the ways that people, animals, and inanimate objects moved and from this empirical work they evolved the famous twelve principles of character animation. These included "squash and stretch" methods of deforming objects to suggest weight, mass, and personality. The latter is also conveyed through proper "timing" of actions. Disney's animators discovered that natural movements are not linear but occur through "arcs" and also realized that "exaggeration" of action and form could get them quickly to the essence of a story idea or emotion. The ultimate principle was "appeal," creating characters that an audience enjoyed experiencing. This included villains—Cruella de Vil and the witch in *Snow White* (1937) are very appealing characters. Indeed, here is an important distinction between the live actor on film and the animated character. "Spectators enjoy watching something that is appealing to them, whether an expression, a character, a movement, or a whole story situation. While the live actor has charisma, the animated drawing has appeal."[25]

In 1986, Pixar demonstrated the relevance of the Disney principles for 3D computer animation. Pixar's first production, after Edwin Catmull and John Lasseter formed the company upon leaving Lucasfilm, was *Luxo, Jr.* (1986), a short written and directed by Lasseter. The charming two-and-a-half-minute film shows a comic situation enacted by two Anglepoise (extension) desk lamps, one large and one small. The animation endows these with personalities and the roles of father and child. A ball rolls onscreen. Dad bats it away with his lamp hood, and Junior chases it enthusiastically, hopping across the screen. Squash-and-stretch, timing, and exaggeration delineate the characters and their emotions. Dad moves slowly, with gravitas, Junior with quicker, chippier actions. Both characters hit the ball with their heads, but, as Lasseter wrote, "Dad, who is larger and older, leans over the ball and uses only his shade to bat it. Jr., however, who is smaller, younger, and full of excited energy, whacks the ball with his shade, putting his whole body into it."[26] Movements were based on physics and the structural characteristics of Luxo lamps but were exaggerated to convey emotion and thought. "In designing the characters, the feeling of a baby lamp and a grown-up lamp was very important. The effect was achieved using exaggeration in proportion, in the same way a puppy is proportioned very differently than an adult dog, or a human baby is different from an adult."[27] The bulbs in each lamp are the same size, but Junior's shade is much smaller than Dad's. The springs and support rods have the same diameter, but Junior's are shorter. Dad moves only from neck, head, and shoulders; Junior moves with his entire body. Dad's electric cord lies on the floor without moving. Junior's wags and undulates behind him, signaling emotion like a dog's tail.

Lasseter intended for *Luxo, Jr.* to shake up the world of animation by showing what computers could do. It was also intended to show the application of Disney principles in a 3D digital world. Bad computer animation, Lasseter argued, "will be due to unfamiliarity with the fundamental principles that have been used for hand drawn character animation for over 50 years. Understanding these principles of traditional animation is essential to producing good computer animation."[28] Disney's principle of exaggeration, for example, enables an animator to precisely capture and visualize emotion, attitude, and thought as these are enacted in movement and facial expression. The Luxo lamps have heads, formed by the light bulb and surrounding shade, and the hinged support rods connecting the bulbs to the base suggest shoulders, arms, and legs. When moving, the lamps lead with their heads, signaling to viewers the presence of intentionality, purpose, attitude, and emotion. Creating a performance from inanimate objects requires creatively segmenting their structure, in particular devising a head area. "When you imagine a character, you not only have to address its personality, its design, and its 3-D articulation, but also manage to create the illusion that its movements reflect its thoughts, its emotions," Lasseter said. "You immediately define where the head's going to be. No matter if the object doesn't have two eyes and a nose. You choose the part of the 'body' that will follow the action, like the head, which will be 'looking,' will be dictating all the other positions."[29] In *Luxo, Jr.* this practice endows the lamps with what Disney animators referred to as the illusion of life.

Much character animation takes advantage of the human perceptual system's fine-tuned propensity to scan objects and environments for signs of intention and to read these signs often on the basis of scant and incomplete evidence. Disney's animators discovered, for example, that the simplest shapes could express attitude and emotion. Exploring the squash-and-stretch principle, they created a series of line drawings showing a half-filled flour sack stretched and bent so that the sack became, alternately, dejected, joyful, curious, cocky, amused, belligerent, sad, and happy. The sack displays the reactions of a biological being, and the emotions come through vividly in the drawings, despite their graphical simplicity. The sentient automobiles in Pixar's *Cars* (2006) and the mechanical robots in *WALL-E* and *Transformers* (2007) exemplify this ability of animation to endow inanimate objects with personality and performance. Animation can do this because the perception of biological motion is hard-wired into observers (and animators as well), who extract from it a wealth of information even when cues are minimal. Numerous empirical studies, for example, have demonstrated that viewers can perceive emotions and even gender identity in abstract point-light motion displays. These are motion-capture experiments in which movements by one or more actors are recorded as a series of point-light sources from markers placed on the actors' joints and extremities. All a viewer sees in the display is a two-dimensional cluster of small, moving lights. When point-light sources are used to capture a dance performance expressing the emotions of surprise, fear, anger, disgust, grief, and joy, viewers watching only the abstracted pattern of captured lights were able to understand the expressed emotions.[30] Viewers have been shown to recognize facial expression from point-light displays[31] and emotions expressed in the point-light display of an isolated arm in motion.[32]

The biological basis of emotion perception is overdetermined, and animators rely on this attribute routinely in order to create performances in cinema. WALL-E has no speaking voice, and his body is completely mechanical—a trash compactor for a torso, tank-like cogwheels and treads for feet, short metal arms ending in a pair of retractable grippers, a hinged extension rod for a neck, and a camera-like sensor for a head. His face is a pair of binoculars. His eyes—the glass lenses at the large end of the binoculars—are highly emotive and give the character appeal. The binoculars operate more like camera lenses. The diaphragm inside the lens barrel opens and closes like the pupil in an eye and gives WALL-E's gaze varying degrees of keenness and intensity. The focal ring on the lenses is motorized and spins clockwise and counter-clockwise, signaling that WALL-E is struggling to understand a strange sight in the environment like the sudden arrival of the sleek robot EVE, with whom he will fall in love. EVE's reflection on the outer glass of his lens-eyes expresses this infatuation. WALL-E's eyes have brows—little mechanical levers—that raise in alarm when he sees an onrushing dust storm; and when he is frightened—the rocket bringing EVE to the barren planet threatens to land on top of him—his neck contracts and his head drops onto his shoulders in a turtle-like gesture. Lasseter said the filmmakers were surprised at how much expression could be conveyed. "The animators actually added little levers that come up that gave a little bit of an eyebrow expression, but they found that they didn't need it all that much. Just by taking it and bending these binocular eyes up and down, they gave it a tremendous amount of expression."[33]

If he lacks the charisma that a live actor might supply, WALL-E gives a performance of great appeal. Likewise Remy the rat in *Ratatouille* (2007). Pixar's animators had to figure out how rats can win empathy since rodents typically elicit disgust from audiences. By carefully exaggerating key body features, the animators made Remy and his cohorts into pleasing and appealing personalities. The rat body was modeled in a teardrop shape, giving it a soft contour and a low center of gravity that enabled the animators to switch between upright bipedal poses and quadruped ones. The rat shape was kept simple and often posed in silhouette for a cleaner and smaller appearance. (Playing action in a silhouette or side view was another Disney principle.) Deforming the muzzle and cheek conveyed emotion to the face. Deformation changes the shape of an object, and in the digital world it can be accomplished by the manipulation of motion dynamics or by the use of point clusters, splines, patches, and paths to bend or twist the surface of an object. To create Remy's appealing face, "squishy cheek mass is manipulated by the corner of the mouth and creates the most appealing smile. We extend the effect of cheek deformation in a wide region to link eyes and mouth connectivity. Setting the direction of the deformer to lead into the eyes creates a connection between the mouth and eyes. This is especially helpful when characters are delivering long lines or when the mouth disappears from certain angles under the muzzle."[34] When this happened, responses in the cheeks signaled the mouth's movement and drew the viewer's attention to Remy's eyes, thus directing the eyes by way of cheek and mouth movements. "Allowing the deformation to flow from one feature to another creates the illusion of connectivity and the ability to read the whole body as emotion."

Deformers also were used to simulate contact within and between the film's human and rodent characters. When Linguini captures Remy inside a large glass jar, Remy fearfully squishes against the glass and Linguini's fingers flatten menacingly against the outside. The Pixar artists believed that 3D digital animation had avoided simulating contact behaviors because these were difficult to model. Animators were making acting decisions that minimized believable character contact, and thus *Ratatouille* would implement approaches that would "allow animators to easily setup collision relationships, make acting decisions with contact response interactively, and alter the resultant shapes."[35] While Disney animators hand-drew squash-and-stretch responses, the digital animators had to create software to emulate the desired deformations of surface and volume, the right "cartoon contact look." All the film's human and animal characters were built with collision detectors that simulated flattening and bulging reactions appropriate for particular body areas—a belly, for example, should deform more than a hand. The fleshy surfaces of foods also needed to deform as when being sliced, chopped, or chewed.

Crafting the film's performances, then, entailed building the algorithms to simulate these properties of real-world physical behavior, albeit

Remy the rat, the appealing hero of *Ratatouille* (2007, Pixar). Frame enlargement.

exaggerated appropriately to achieve a cartoon look. Virtual performance, in this context, entails more than directing or animating the actor or character. It is an art of cosmo-genesis, of total world design, the programming of an array of movement extending from facial expression to the texturing of hard and soft surfaces and the visualizing of collision behaviors among them. Virtual performing requires continuing, sustained analysis by the animator, to achieve believable characters performing in accord with known physical laws (which themselves have to be programmed and created inside the fictional world) and in accord with the stylistic demands of the particular film. These can vary tremendously. Where the style is extremely photorealistic, the characters in Robert Zemeckis's *Beowulf* (2007) sported finely detailed body hair and beard stubble. By contrast, textures in *The Incredibles* were stylized and simplified. Instead of rendering individual hair follicles, a light wash of color indicated beards. Joe Fordham found this approach highly pleasing. "I always thought characters in *The Incredibles* looked like beautifully sculpted stop-motion puppets, which were visually very satisfying to watch emoting."

Character Rigging

With the shift from 2D to 3D digital methods, the animator has remained an actor but is now required to be more analytic and precise in delineating the creative choices that make a character successful and appealing. This is because the range of choice is now so much bigger. Digital methods enable the actor's instrument—face, voice, and body—to be infinitely varied, infinitely malleable, and the abundance of choice can take artists down cul-de-sacs. The instrument—face, voice, body—must be constructed, and the animator-as-actor literally builds the performance through a process called "character rigging." The character is built first as a wireframe model and is assigned joints as the first step in constructing a functioning skeletal structure. The joints are positioned inside the wireframe model and are programmed to rotate and twist in an anatomically correct manner. This is critical for achieving credibility with digital human and animal creatures whose behavior an audience knows from experience. Fantasy creatures may present novel problems of skeletal articulation. Nobody knows how dinosaurs moved, and in the *Jurassic Park* movies skeletons had to be designed according to speculative rules of locomotion, which the filmmakers derived from studying the gait of lizards, ostriches, and other animals and then extrapolating these to accommodate the scale of the oversized reptiles. The Na'vi horses in *Avatar* (2009) have six legs, and the animators had to figure out how such an animal might run.

The monsters in the *Alien* movies have tri-segmented legs, like dogs, and yet walk upright as a biped does on two-jointed legs. Rigging the character as a first-ever digital being in *Alien Resurrection* (1997), the effects artists had to solve this problem because the earlier films had not shown extensive alien locomotion. Fordham points out that on *Alien*, "Ridley Scott specifically directed the suit performer to move very slowly, like a dancer, to avoid the look of a man in a suit running about; he constantly disguised the creature's orientation."[36] Portraying the alien through digital means expanded the performance capabilities of the character, which was already an iconic horror figure, enduringly popular with viewers and uniquely creepy. Digital tools enabled the familiar icon to be burnished with new motion capabilities and personality characteristics. To figure out how an alien might walk, the effects artists tried putting an actor into an alien suit and having him move about, but they found the results looked awkward and unconvincing, too humanoid. Their digital solution was to develop a novel form of locomotion for the creature, one that served the performance by conveying an attitude—that of a canny and crafty predator that moves in a way that disguises its power and lethality. "Our solution sounds contradictory, but the alien moves like a sort of vulnerable predator. He reduces his size and looks very protective, but he really has no fear. It's just a way for a giant creature to minimize his space. He walks at a diagonal, which I think is predatorially efficient."[37]

Once joints are in place, bones are placed to connect the joints and these are programmed to work according to a hierarchy of action involving parent and child objects. "Forward kinematics" flow from parent to child—shoulder to upper arm to forearm to hand, for example. "Inverse kinematics" work by stipulating all that follows from the child object. The animator moves the character's hand, and the upper-body skeletal structure responds appropriately. When the bones are in place, connective tissue is added. Muscle and tendon are programmed to have the right amount of elasticity, with muscles flexing and bulging and sliding over the bones. Soft-tissue character rigging developed considerably after the first *Jurassic Park* movie. Apart from joint rotation, the dinosaurs in that film show very little activity beneath their highly textured skin surface. In subsequent films, muscle and tendon articulation becomes more pronounced and defined. Once muscles and tendons are articulated, character rigging proceeds by adding skin, and it, too, gives a performance, varying in tightness and elasticity, and in relation to underlying fat, depending on where in the body it is. Skin will behave differently when located over a kneecap than when covering the wattles beneath a portly man's jaw. The animator has to consider these differences and build them into the performance.

As Disney's animators realized long ago, movement conveys attitude and personality, and creating digital monsters in *Alien Resurrection* enabled the animators to design a more expressive creature than the man-in-a-suit version that appeared in the earlier movies. While the film suffers from script and story problems that make it one of the weaker entries in the series, the digital actors—the slimy, goo-covered xenomorphs—give first-rate performances. Like the digital dinosaurs in *Jurassic Park*, the aliens move more fluidly, quickly, and more expressively than did the animatronic models or suited performers in earlier films. In fact, the animators designed one of the film's shots as an open homage to the digital monsters in *Jurassic Park*. After a colony of aliens breaks loose on board a huge space station, one climbs over the body of a human victim and over the camera positioned at floor level near the body. As the monster moves down the corridor, its tail swishes into the camera's face with frisky aggression. The shot emphasizes the Z-axis staging that Spielberg brought to *Jurassic Park* and the anatomical details of the alien's physiology. Speaking of the character rigging in the shot, the effects supervisor noted, "As the foot lands on the floor in close-up, the toes spread, the mass settles out, and the calf muscle tightens."[38] Animating the character to achieve the requisite physiological realism for the shot required several weeks, but the monster's performance is sinuous, and it conveys an evil sensuousness that is not as vividly realized in the earlier films. The tail swish is just like a cat's as it studies the half-dead prey it intends to continue torturing.

The alien's digital performance had to be physically credible and also had to convey, as all actors do, the essence and personality of the character. Designing the character as a digital being enabled it to do new things, such as swimming. Pursuing Ripley (Sigourney Weaver) and other space station workers, the alien swims through a flooded kitchen, and the animators had to decide how it would move in the water. They decided it would propel itself with its tail, and they modeled its performance on the movements of sea iguanas, which tuck their legs close to their bodies and use their tails as a propeller, thrusting themselves through the water. When the alien submerges and gives chase through the flooded kitchen, the movements are startling in their anatomical detail, convincing and menacing, and they take the character to a new and previously unsuspected level of physical skill and prowess. The rules governing alien locomotion convey attitude and make the creature a being with intention, desire, and, above all, an intensely visualized malice. The film's director, Jean-Pierre Jeunet, wanted the monster to move with the calmness and deliberation of a western gunslinger. "It's like John Wayne or Clint Eastwood—very purposeful. We could accomplish those slow movements because our CG model was so detailed. The tail has a nice, whippy motion and a dagger-like feel, but the head moves very slowly. The alien's motions are really graceful, very purposeful and fearless."[39] A baby alien gives the film's most affecting performance when it realizes that Ripley is its mother. Ripley's DNA has been used to clone an alien queen capable of live birthing, and the baby bonds emotionally with Ripley. As Ripley kills it, the baby fixes a dying gaze upon her mother that is infinitely sorrowful and supplicating.

The remake of *The Mummy* (1999) replaced the actor-in-bandages of the Boris Karloff original with a digital mummy that, over the course of the film, regenerates from a bony husk to a flesh-and-blood being played by actor Arnold Vosloo. Character rigging for the digital version of the mummy included a skeletal build from a wireframe model and the provision of an elaborate musculature. All muscles in the legs and upper torso—shoulder, arms, neck—were built, connected to joints and then wrapped around bones so as to replicate an accurate physiology of human movement. The muscles had to stretch and flex convincingly because they were often visible under the mummy's decayed skin. Procedural animation specifies a set of rules that will govern the movement of a character or object. With procedural rules, movements need not be keyframed (animation of key positions in the movement cycle). The animator sets the rules and then runs simulations to refine them. The method provides an economical way of moving the rigged character. Accordingly, a walk-cycle was set as well as rules for the behavior of muscles and skin. Skin was applied according to a volume analysis of the geometry of the creature's body. As a result, skin animation convincingly responded to the movement of muscles underneath. Rigging according to forward kinematics enabled the animators to move the skeleton and produce the corresponding changes in the movement of muscles and skin. Throughout, the goal was to produce the visible impression of a real physical being. The mummy's performance was achieved by this cluster of procedures—rigging the character, defining the rules by which it would move, and mapping skin and muscle to bone in ways that elicited the audience's horror. A hole in the face opened onto functioning muscles and even bone beneath. Viscera showed through the chest cavity. The character's progressive physical regeneration established its narrative arc. When Imhotep is resuscitated in the flesh, his powers will be undimmed: he will become immortal and unleash an apocalypse. The movie's heroes (Brendan Fraser, Rachel Weisz) need to stop him before this happens. The character rig and the visual effects create the performance by taking Imhotep from a decayed husk to a monster ever more arrogant and confident of success.

Motion capture and tracking placed Arnold Vosloo's performance inside the digital character in *The Mummy* (1999, Universal Pictures). Frame enlargement.

While many scenes featured the mummy as a digital character, others depicted actor Vosloo wearing prosthetic makeup as well as matchmoved digital effects. When he is partly regenerated, for example, and is half-mummy, half-human, portions of his face are missing. Gaping holes reveal teeth and jawbones surrounded by sinew and skin. The shots blended prosthetic appliances and digital animation. The prosthetics were fitted over Vosloo's face while digital effects portrayed the holes and the interior surfaces. Elaborate matchmoving was required to ensure that the digital effects were anchored to Vosloo's face and followed it as the actor moved about and also to ensure that they blended seamlessly with the prosthetic makeup. Throughout the film the mummy is based on Vosloo's performance. Even the all-digital version seen when it first appears as a skeleton incorporated the actor's movements. These had been motion-captured to provide a baseline for character definition. The character's performance, then, is recombinant. It synthesizes the contributions of a live actor, a prosthetic makeup artist, and digital animators and compositors.

Performance as a Composited Element

Benicio Del Toro's lycanthropic transformations in *The Wolfman* (2010) are a blend of similar components. When Larry Talbot (Del Toro) first changes into a werewolf, he's alone in a moonlit mausoleum, and the first signs of the coming change are signaled with 2D painting effects that increase the reflectivity in his eyes and accentuate the veins in his forehead. Talbot looks at his hand and sees his fingers elongating and growing hair. The hand was a 3D digital element joined to Del Toro's arm. Both 2D painting and 3D prosthetics deformed his face, making it progressively more lupine, and digital replacements of his foot, his leg, and his lower back were selectively applied to alter the contours of Del Toro's body and to visualize the werewolf's emergence as the actor moved about the set. Throughout, Del Toro remained on camera, and the final performance incorporates the live actor and the digital alterations. When the change was complete, Del Toro stood at the top of the mausoleum stairs wearing elaborate prosthetic makeup designed by Rick Baker (who had also done the werewolf transformations in *An American Werewolf in London* [1981]). Del Toro's head was covered with a prosthetic nose, ears, muzzle, fangs, and hair, a nondigital makeup effect that Baker designed to evoke the appearance of Lon Chaney Jr. in the original *Wolf Man* (1941). (A subsequent transformation scene in the film, when Larry is strapped in a chair at an insane asylum, is all-digital, executed without prosthetic makeup.)

The werewolf transformations in the original Chaney Jr. version were static and lacked the dynamic energy of those in the remake. (*Werewolf of London* [1935], Universal's initial werewolf movie, used traveling mattes and colored filters on the camera to stage transformations that were more dynamic than the Chaney Jr. version.) As Vivian Sobchack writes, the viewer is "aware that the metamorphosis represented before us is visibly marked by temporal gaps—during which, exempt from our sight and enduring hours of make-up and stop-and-go filming, the physical body of the actor Lon Chaney Jr. was being made more or less lupine and hirsute."[40] Makeup artist Jack Pierce applied a prosthetic nose to Chaney Jr., along with fangs and yak hair. Each layered element was filmed a shot at a time with lap dissolves connecting the stages of transformation. The camera was locked down, and Chaney had to lie absolutely still so that the positioning of his head would match from shot to shot across the dissolves. The scenes are charming, but the staging makes Chaney's character seem like he's sleeping through the transformation. When it's complete, he wakes up, snarls, and stalks off to do mischief. By contrast, using digital tools to extend the performance of a live actor enables the Del Toro sequence to be composed in continuous motion, with Larry *acting out* his confusion, fear, and pain. The viewer sees these expressed in the behavior of the character who is tortured and anguished, not static and comatose. The performance in the transformation scene is better—more emotional, more dramatic, more expressive—in the remake than in the original. While Del Toro is a finer actor than was Chaney Jr., the performance differences are also a function of different filmmaking tools. The locked-down camera and the lap dissolves of the original worked against drama and performance. Match-moving digital effects to an actor playing a scene that is covered with a mobile camera produces a more immersive dramatic experience for the viewer.

Digital tools helped to make the lycanthropic transformations in *The Wolfman* (2010, Universal Pictures) much livelier than in the Lon Chaney Jr. original. Frame enlargement.

Del Toro and Vosloo participate as live actors in the scenes where they are portraying their fantasy characters, and their bodies and faces are extended digitally through alteration and modification. Thus in contrast to conventional, analog cinema performances, the viewer sees actor and digital character as a kind of layered composite image. The actor is there but must be discerned through the digital makeup, at the interior of the effects rather than their exterior. At other times the actor is a trace, a presence implied by the design of the effects. Although Larry Talbot's transformation in the asylum is all-digital, Del Toro enacted it as motion capture and then was replaced with digital animation modeled from the capture data. A multipass render transformed Del Toro's data into the digital werewolf replete with fangs and fur. Del Toro remains a part of the digital character even though the actor is not truly on camera throughout the scene. Virtual performance does not end with the contours of an actor's body. The body itself is malleable and susceptible to alteration and extension, and the performer on camera may be a recombinant product formed of flesh and computer algorithms. This does not negate the contributions of the actor, but it does sharpen the ambiguities that always have defined acting in cinema, where actors play to nonexistent locations in a process shot or to other characters not present in a close-up. As Mark Wolf points out, "Film performance itself was really a Gestalt rather than an isolated element."[41] Digital tools elicit the viewer's customary gestalt but using new methods and procedures and with the potential of realizing new kinds of characters.

Caricature and Photorealism

The most significant of these new characters have been achieved using motion capture (mocap) to model digital characters based on the dynamics of a live performance. As used in such films as *The Lord of the Rings*, *Final Fantasy* (2001), *The Polar Express* (2004), *Beowulf*, *A Christmas Carol* (2009), *The Curious Case of Benjamin Button*, and *Avatar*, digital characters created from mocap data exemplify two broad stylistic objectives—caricature and photorealism. Caricature includes styles of representation that aim for exaggerated, cartoonlike, or nonhuman kinds of portraiture. Photorealism aims to create perceptually convincing digital representations of human beings. The monster Grendel in *Beowulf*, the Na'vi in *Avatar*, and Gollum in *Lord of the Rings* are stylized or exaggerated characters whose design does not aim to replicate the exact appearance of a human being. In contrast, Benjamin Button and the characters portrayed by Tom Hanks in *The Polar Express* or by Anthony Hopkins and Angelina Jolie in *Beowulf* are intended to look as photorealistic as the digital animators can make them.

Photorealism poses special challenges that caricature avoids. Exaggeration, as the Disney animators knew, provides a pathway not just for emotional expression but for establishing the credibility of a cartoon character. Teacups, automobiles, candles, broomsticks—Disney animators brought these to life with defined personalities and often did not provide faces. The flour sack exercise demonstrated how simply drawn objects could be invested with emotion. As Disney animators Frank Thomas and Ollie Johnston wrote, "If the shapes in the face and body can be caricatured just a little, the characters will be easier to animate and more convincing to the audience."[42] It's the seven dwarfs in *Snow White* who come to life most vividly, not Snow White or her prince, who are composed more realistically and who were drawn from photostats of live actors who played the roles. The caricatures expressed in the dwarfs—Grumpy's scowl and bulbous nose, Dopey's big ears—and their squash-and-stretch moves give them the illusion of life. Snow White, by contrast, moves according to realistic canons of behavior, and the natural contours of her face are less expressive than those of the dwarfs. She can't squash-and-stretch running down a staircase, as do the dwarfs, legs akimbo, noses bumping and thumping the steps.

In the popular mind, the ultimate goal of digital animation is the replication of photorealistic human beings. The anxieties in *Simone* focus on the looming threat posed by digital animation to the live actor in cinema. Pixar Studios is producing some of today's finest digital animation and consciously incorporates the twelve Disney principles into its work. John

Lasseter has said, "Ever since I've worked in this branch of film, it's always been said that the Holy Grail in terms of synthesized images is to succeed in creating perfectly realistic human beings." But, he continued, "that's not of great interest. What interests us is the fantastic."[43] Pixar's films have embraced caricature, not photorealism. Brad Bird's *The Incredibles*, for example, depicts with humor and pathos a world of retired superheroes who have been litigated out of their storied careers saving those in distress. The filmmakers aimed for a stylized simplification of texture and line. The characters were rigged for 3D with skeleton and musculature, and their skin was lit with subsurface scattering, but only to provide a minimal means for locating them in an approximation of physical reality. The emphatic goal was to depart from the kind of minute texturing of hair and skin pores that movies like *Beowulf* have pursued. Bird and his team believed that caricature provided a surer route to the interior of the characters' personalities. Bill Wise, the character team's technical lead, summed up the paradox. "You want a stylized design for human characters, but they need to have a believable complexity."[44] Teddy Newton, one of the film's character designers, said, "We all wanted the cast of characters to look like cartoon people instead of photo-realistic people. In animation, it really takes a bit of exaggeration to make something look convincing. The great caricaturist Al Hirschfeld most typified this. He could perfectly capture a person's identity by simply sketching curlicues for hair and pinholes for eyes. The faces and attitudes he drew were often more recognizable in the abstract than if they had been rendered out realistically."[45] Ralph Eggleston, an artistic coordinator on *The Incredibles*, said, "It's always been a fallacy, the notion that human characters have to look photo-realistic in CG. You can do so much more with stylized human characters. Audiences innately know how humans move and gravity works, so if a human character doesn't feel right, they'll feel something's wrong."[46] *The Incredibles* renders its characters as digital 3D beings, with a believable musculature and subsurface scatter (a first for Pixar), but it embraces exaggeration as the pathway for evoking a truthful performance.

Digital tools, however, have proven very good at emulating the surfaces of the visible world, and as render costs have declined and computing power has increased, the challenge of doing a human digital character in photorealistic terms has proven irresistible. Robert Zemeckis has pursued digital filmmaking in aggressive and often keenly intelligent ways. In *Who Framed Roger Rabbit?* (1988), he said goodbye to the world of analog compositing, traditional cel animation, and optical printing. *Forrest Gump* (1993) explored the new digital tools then becoming available to filmmakers and crafted a tale that portrayed the existential dilemmas that had bothered Dostoevsky, namely, is life orderly and purposeful or simply a random (and therefore valueless) collision of particles? Zemeckis then went after digital photorealist animation with a vengeance, pursuing this elusive goal in *The Polar Express, Beowulf,* and *A Christmas Carol.* The results were mixed, as I explain shortly. Before turning to Zemeckis's films and Fincher's *Benjamin Button,* the storied saga of the travails in crafting convincingly real-looking synthetic characters begins with a film that in its time was much anticipated and heralded and is now widely reviled, *Final Fantasy: The Spirits Within* (2001).

It started as a wildly successful computer game designed in 1987 by Hironobu Sakaguchi, who harbored dreams of doing a feature-length digitally animated film. After the game became a bestseller, Sakaguchi pursued his filmmaking aspiration. He formed a production company, Square Pictures, and attracted $70 million in investment monies from Columbia TriStar for the venture. Setting up shop in Hawaii to attract animation talent from the United States and Japan, Sakaguchi aimed to create animated characters that would look photographically real. The realism of the characters would be achieved by emulating in microscopic detail the texturing of skin, hair, and clothing. "The transparency of the skin, the small defects in pigmentation, the degree of brightness and different shades of color of the teeth, the watery appearance of the eyes. In short, everything you perceive without paying attention to it when you look at a real human being."[47]

Achieving this goal required extraordinary computational powers within the period's resources. The film contains some 1,300 shots, and its 142,000 frames each required a render time lasting from fifteen minutes to seven hours.[48] Just opening a file to begin work sometimes took over an hour. The story depicts the efforts of scientist Aki Ross and military Captain Gray Edwards to defeat a legion of alien monsters roaming the earth and decimating its population. The landscapes and environments were digitally created, as were Ross, Edwards, and the rest of the characters. The filmmakers relied on mocap data to stage the broad outlines of character movement. They hired a group of actors to portray the action that had been visualized in storyboards, but the faces and overall visual design of the main characters had already been modeled in the computer before any mocap sessions occurred. The sessions supplied the broadest coordinates of character movement, but the subtleties of facial expression and personality quirks had to be animated by keyframe.

In a mocap session using optical or infrared sensors, actors wear special markers that reflect or emit light to a series of cameras arranged around the performance stage (which typically is bare except for wireframe props). Markers are positioned on performers' joints and extremities (such as hands and feet) and occasionally on their faces. The markers establish a series of vertices in three-dimensional space, and the cameras capture only this vertex data. The actor in effect becomes a cloud of illuminated moving points, digital data that is easily translated into the wireframe models used to build CG characters. Mocap sessions are filmed with multiple cameras arranged in a 360-degree configuration. Each camera captures a 2D display of point-light information, but by triangulating the views of several cameras a 3D spatial view can be assembled. When facial markers are used, mocap sessions are called "performance capture." In such cases, mocap data is mapped to a digital facial model and used as a partial source for the animation. Facial data was captured from Tom Hanks in *The Polar Express*, Anthony Hopkins and Angelina Jolie in *Beowulf*, and Brad Pitt in *Benjamin Button*. In contrast, mocap facial data was not used to animate Gollum in *Lord of the Rings*, nor was any used in *Final Fantasy*. On *Avatar*, the actors' bodies were mocapped but not their faces. A live video feed from mini-cams mounted to helmets worn by the actors transmitted low-resolution images of their facial performances during mocap sessions.

The *Final Fantasy* animators had been keenly focused on trying to achieve expressive, photorealistic faces. Roy Sato, the lead animator for Aki Ross, refined a library of fifty basic expressions with controls that subtly altered and manipulated them. "I could do very detailed things like control the size of her pupils or make her nostrils flare a bit. . . . The eyes communicate so much, so they were very important."[49] The animators used mirrors to model their own expressions for the characters, which, as a result, took on qualities of the animators' performances. Animation supervisor Andy Jones said of Aki, "You see a lot of Roy [Sato] in that character. The timing of Aki's blinks [is] the same as the timing of his blinks. The way she talks is similar to the way he talks."[50] And yet, despite this attention to detail, character faces remained less expressive than a real human face. As Jones candidly admitted, "There are so many little things that happen in a facial expression. When the jaw opens, for example, the skin doesn't just stretch down. It actually rolls over the jawbone. Temple muscles move when you chew. . . . We know, instinctively, what a face looks like when it moves. So we did a lot of that subtle movement in the facial expressions—but even so, it is missing certain components, and that makes the character look less real."

The daunting complexity of digitally modeling a perceptually convincing human face was exacerbated by cost constraints on the production that limited the information that could be rendered. Scaling detail appropriately for close-up and longer views of characters was a particular problem. The animators lacked the resources to modulate facial data in accord with changing camera views and so aimed for a median solution, balancing detail at the same level of resolution for both close and far views. The median solution was not ideal for either perspective. A bigger problem lay in the depiction of characters' skin. It was not animated as a 3D organ system. Instead, it was a 2D paint effect, textured with wrinkles, moles, and other surface features and then wrapped around the wireframe model. Skin was a painted surface on the digital characters, and it exhibited little translucency because methods of subsurface scatter were not yet widely available and in use. (Weta Digital implemented subsurface scatter for Gollum in *Lord of the Rings*, and Pixar used it for the first time on *The Incredibles*.) The results fell short of the ambition. As visual effects animator Peter Plantec wrote, Aki Ross comes across as "a cartoon character masquerading as a human. As she moves, our minds pick up on the incorrectness. And as we focus on her eyes, mouth, skin and hair, they destroy the illusion of reality."[51]

The Uncanny Valley

Today, the perceived failure of *Final Fantasy* is widely regarded as a demonstration of the paradox known as "the uncanny valley." Roboticist Masahiro Mori used this term in an influential essay published in 1970. He described what happens when a robot or other artificially designed humanoid form draws closer to fully replicating human features. At first, the increasing resemblance elicits a growth in empathy and a feeling of familiarity from

Photorealism instead of caricature: Aki Ross, the hero of *Final Fantasy* (2001, Columbia Pictures), fell into the uncanny valley. Frame enlargement.

the viewer. But then, "as robots appear more humanlike, our sense of their familiarity increases until we come to a valley. I call this relation the 'uncanny valley.'"[52] A threshold is crossed where the imitation becomes so close and exacting that its remaining incompleteness points to its status as a surrogate, as something not real, and this results in a loss of empathy from viewers, a pulling back, as what had seemed so familiar becomes defamiliarized. Mori pointed out a converse principle, namely, that perceptions of high familiarity can be induced by nonhuman or by semi-humanlike designs. His example was Japan's bunraku puppet theater: "I don't think a bunraku puppet is similar to human beings on close observation." But audiences sit some distance from the puppets that move in humanlike ways. "So although the puppet's body is not humanlike, we can feel that they are humanlike owing to their movement. And from this evidence I think their familiarity is very high." Mori's insight is consistent with the realization by Disney and Pixar animators that caricature provides an effective mode for expressing emotion and for eliciting audience participation in the narrative and the lives of the characters. Caricature conveys emotion in concentrated form. Viewers intuitively understand what the exaggeration conveys, and no sense of the uncanny is evoked. Digital characters whose stylization avoids photorealism are very effective at reaching audiences and have never fallen into the uncanny valley. The human and animal characters in *Shrek* (2001), for example, or squid-faced Davy Jones in *Pirates of the Caribbean* (2003) do not trip viewers' warning sensors. The stop-motion puppets in *Coraline* (2009) have extraordinarily expressive faces, in part because the expressions are stylized. Because the faces aren't meant to look real; they appear very lifelike. The stop motion reproduces natural eye mechanisms—saccades, blinks, changes in size produced by widening or contracting the eyelids. These changes convey Coraline's feelings as she grapples with parents who have no time for her and as she enters a secret passageway into a nightmare world that is the inversion of her own. The Coraline puppet does not closely resemble a human being, but her movements are humanlike, with special attention from the animators toward realistic eye behavior. As a result, her level of familiarity is very high, and she does not fall into the uncanny valley.

Why, then, have faces proven to be so problematic for digital photorealism? Partly the problem is a function of its complexity. The face contains fifty-three muscles that move in complex, subtle ways to generate a multitude of expressions, and these movements cannot be captured as vertex data. As anatomist Elizabeth Rega and biologist Stuart Sumida point out, "Unlike every other body area, the movements in the face are not principally the movements of skeletal elements around joints. Rather, most facial movements are the result of highly variable thin sheets of muscle which attach—not to bone—but from skin to skin. This results in movement that does not proceed along a vector from a clear anchor point, but rather a surface deformation approximating various skin attachment points."[53] Mocap supplies vertex data. The moving, illuminated dots on the actor's bodies visualize vectors connecting feet to knees, hands to elbows, heads to neck, and the rotational properties of these vectors. Faces are quite different because the data involves subtle and intricate surface deformations. Optical mocap systems do not grab these, except by gross implication. Tom Hanks's face was outfitted with 152 markers for the mocap sessions employed on *The Polar Express*, and while the markers furnished some information about the flexing and stretching of his face, it was incomplete information. With respect to faces, mocap aims to sample an information-rich analog process using relatively few data points. These do not provide enough information to work backward from the sampled points to a reconstruction of the surface deformation. Moreover, on *The Polar Express* and *Beowulf* the actors' eyes were not mocapped, and the animators had to infer the behavior of eyes and the precise direction of the actors' gazes from markers placed around the eyes. This resulted in one of the films' most widely criticized qualities—the vacant and lifeless appearance of characters' eyes.

Peter Plantec observed some of the *Beowulf* mocap sessions and felt that things were being lost. Anthony Hopkins's subtle expressions weren't being captured. (Hopkins plays the debauched King Hrothgar.) "He had a subtle, nasty little smile that held so much meaning and some of it is missing in the final print. That tiny bit of smile apparently held a lot of emotional information, because I could feel the difference."[54] One of the film's software engineers said that the amount of labor from digital animators necessary to provide all the subtle expressions of character that a live actor might contribute would be far too expensive to create. Thus calculations of cost efficiency contribute to the phenomenon of the uncanny valley.

It has been a formidable phenomenon because it is biologically coded at a deep perceptual level. As Rega and Sumida note, "The average human (or even chimpanzee) audience is the end result of selection from ancestors whose very evolutionary success was dependent on successful decoding of facial signals. Unlike other body areas, the face will be subject to an intense unconscious scrutiny deeply embedded in our biology."[55] This scrutiny attends to fine details, which include facial asymmetry and nonsymmetrical expressions that are normative for many people. The *Final Fantasy* faces look too symmetrical, too balanced, and therefore unsatisfying as real replicas of human beings. Ontogeny creates challenges when an animator seeks to scale performance data by an actor to a character of a different age. Skull and facial

Detailed texturing of skin and hair failed to solve the uncanny valley problem in *Beowulf* (2007, Paramount Pictures). Frame enlargement.

bones and the muscles layered atop them differ proportionally between children and adults, affecting the way that muscles are involved in facial expressions. Using mocap data from Tom Hanks to play the young boy who is the main character in *The Polar Express* produces a child that doesn't look like a child. Instead, the depiction of "hero boy" resembles the Renaissance practice of painting young children as if they were miniature adults. The scaling of actor to character is incorrect, which undermines the resulting performance.

Rega and Sumida emphasize that the failure of mocap data to supply accurate eye information—particularly blinks and saccades—is responsible for the zombie-like quality of many photorealist digital characters. Blinks are produced by relaxing, not by tightening, eye muscles, and few mocapped films have captured this distinction well, nor the association of blinking with situations in which a character is lying or being evasive or is embarrassed. Saccades vary as a marker of focal distance, being faster, more frequent, and of larger amplitude when one looks at near objects. Once again, few digital characters originating from mocap data have exhibited proper saccadic behavior in response to focal distance and emotional intensity. Ironically, animation outside the tradition of photorealism often features these cues. The stop-motion puppets in *Coraline* exhibit lively saccadic responses because the animators realized that replicating these would be a key means for increasing the puppets' level of humanlike familiarity.

Thus, the zone in the uncanny valley between familiarity and defamiliarization is affected by many variables. In *Beowulf* Zemeckis and his animators rendered clothing, hair, and skin surfaces with unprecedented levels of detail. Getting at the emotional truths conveyed in the actors' performances became a quest for depicting the exact textures of clothing, skin, and hair. The film's visual effects supervisor felt that by adding more detail, the actor's performances would become more engaging. "We got to the level that we said he should have hair coming out of his ears, he should have hair out of his nostrils. In fact he should have peach fuzz all over his face. . . . That was the level that we thought was interesting."[56] They also aimed to portray saccadic responses in the eyes of the characters, and while these are not especially robust, they do make the eyes look more lifelike than in *The Polar Express*. But while surface texturing is rendered in microscopic detail, getting the full repertoire of expressive behaviors was another matter, and the performances by Anthony Hopkins, Ray Winstone, Robin Wright Penn, and John Malkovich come off as remote, lacking presence despite the abundant surface texturing of their bodies. The film's software engineer noted, "We're making good progress, but the amount of hand tweaking that would have been required to enunciate all subtle expressions on every character in a movie [of] this scale would have been expensive."[57] Anthony Hopkins's nasty smile is lost, along with other paralinguistic information. To date, none of Zemeckis's mocap films have been wholly satisfactory emotional experiences. Their odd, unidentifiable nature—some strange admixture of cinematography and animation—sends up contradictory and irresolvable cues to the viewer. The screen world is stranded somewhere between a dream and a real physical landscape. It is stylized but not enough in relation to the photographic texturing of hair, clothes, and other surfaces.

Zemeckis regards his mocap movies as experiments, as novel hybrids, a strange blend of animation and live action. This is perhaps why their photorealism seems so strange and disconcerting. It inhabits a stylistic zone that simultaneously asks viewers to suspend disbelief and to embrace realms of fantasy while the image design erases distinctions between live action and the painted look of animation. The films create a modal ambiguity—a confusion of representational modes—that is neither addressed nor resolved in their cinematic design. To put this differently, the films exhibit an insufficient level of exaggeration and caricature. In this respect, it is notable that the most emotionally affecting character in *Beowulf* is also the most exaggerated. Grendel (played by Crispin Glover) is an anguished creature whose body is twisted in exquisite agony, and rather than speaking he makes wrenching animal cries of distress. Grendel's visual design portrays—via the special condensation of meaning that caricature enables—a condition of unendurable misery. The animation design was intended to "make him look like a giant mutant child suffering from every known skin disease."[58] Grendel is frightening, but his suffering makes him less than a monster. His childlike nature comes through very clearly, as does his distress, and this complicates the viewer's response in ways that benefit the film, enriching its moral perspective. As the slayer of Grendel, Beowulf comes off as both hero and brutal charlatan. This moral complexity emerges because Grendel is a differently conceived and designed character. He is not born of the quest for photorealism but from the use of bold strokes that define an emotional truth. The startling success of Grendel as a digital character—the merging of Glover's outstanding performance with animation that visualizes the creature's suffering—points to the limitations of the textural route to photorealism.

An important point remains. Zemeckis's working methods have elicited great praise from his actors who report that mocap sessions enable them to work in a manner conducive to good acting and unlike the conditions that typically prevail on a film production, where the actor spends much of a day waiting to go on camera and then delivers short pieces of business enacted shot by shot. Mocap proved to be more like theater, with the actors performing in very long takes covered by multiple cameras. John Malkovich and others have said they experienced a new kind of freedom in these methods. Colin Firth, who appears in A Christmas Carol as Scrooge's nephew, said that it was exhilarating to play a whole scene without stopping. "In some ways you had to rise to the occasion of having all that freedom. There is no proscenium. There's no camera to play to. . . . It's even more authentic than doing theater because there is no imaginary fourth wall."[59] Bob Hoskins, who plays Fezziwig in Christmas Carol, said, "What was extraordinary was the fact that once you're covered in all this stuff [mocap markers] you got nothing else to do but to concentrate on your performance. They've taken all responsibility from you. It's extraordinary."[60] Zemeckis likened the process of filming mocap performances to an elaborate tech rehearsal in theater, where an entire scene is run through from beginning to end with the freedom to change blocking and allow actors to try out alternatives to what is scripted. While these methods of working proved to be exhilarating for many cast members, the downside was that much facial information from their performances could not be rendered into the final screen characters.

Composited Characters, Recombinant Performances

If mocap landed Zemeckis in a cul-de-sac on his quest for photorealism, does that mean that no filmmaker has crossed the uncanny valley? We turn now to three examples of emotionally expressive digital performance elicited from mocap data and that achieve credible perceptual realism, although the problem of the uncanny valley is relevant only to one. These are Gollum in Lord of the Rings, the titular character in The Curious Case of Benjamin

Button, and the Na'vi in *Avatar*. The character of Gollum has been called "perhaps the first truly emotionally expressive CG character ever created for a film."[61] He is also, in the words of Weta Workshop head Richard Taylor, "one of the most iconic and loved folklore images of the twentieth century. To be tasked with the job of designing the definitive, quintessential fantasy character from our literary past was tough."[62] The book's legions of readers had strong mental images of Gollum—doing the character in visual terms on the screen was risky. That Gollum would be CG was a decision made early in production. The creature was too far removed from human form and had to perform impossible stunts for an actor to complete. As Jackson said, "Gollum was so emaciated and twisted, walking on all fours, scrambling up and down cliff faces—it just wasn't conceivable that we could have done that with a human."[63] But the digital creature originated from live acting. Gollum is based on a physical performance provided by Andy Serkis during production of the second and third films, *The Two Towers* (2002) and *The Return of the King* (2003). Gollum originally appears during the prologue in the first film, *The Fellowship of the Ring* (2001), as an all-digital character who had been visualized and designed before Serkis was hired (initially as a voice actor, tasked with supplying the character's vocal track). Gollum looks different in the prologue—he is more frog-like, with large eyes, a pug nose. After Serkis joined the production, the character was remapped to resemble the actor's facial features. Serkis found that he needed to physically act the character in order to produce Gollum's extraordinary voice, and his anchoring of the voice to a physical performance convinced director Peter Jackson that Gollum's CG animation ought to be revised and based on Serkis's live-action performing. He believed this would make the digital creature more credible and human.

Serkis performed the character in several contexts. In the first, he played as an actor on set with Elijah Wood and Sean Astin (as the hobbits Frodo and Sam) so that they could hone their performances in relation to a Gollum who was physically there, with the aim of achieving greater emotional authenticity in the acting. For these shots, Serkis wore a skin-tight, flesh-colored unitard to provide the animators with a lighting reference for Gollum. The unitard defined Serkis's silhouette, which made it easier to rotoscope him out of selected shots. These reference passes enabled animators to view the scene's action with Serkis performing on camera as the character. This was especially important for animating moments when Gollum physically interacts with the hobbits, as when he scuffles with Frodo and Sam for possession of the Ring at the beginning of *The Two Towers*. The reference passes provided a basis for matchmoving the digital animation. Serkis was rotoscoped, then digitally painted out, and Gollum was inserted. Serkis, though, is a large-framed man, and Gollum is thin and wasted, so their forms couldn't be interchanged easily. The animators had to cheat by compositing in views of the landscape (extracted from a clean plate filmed without any actors) to bridge the difference in size between Serkis and Gollum or by covering these areas with painted dust and debris effects. At moments where Serkis's bulk obscured Sean Astin's face and the digital Gollum did not, Astin's face from a clean take was matchmoved into the scene. (Fordham points out that the filmmakers "sometimes had to scavenge alternate takes because the clean plates weren't usable, and I'm not sure it was always possible to shoot clean plates."[64] Filmmaking does not always proceed in a methodical fashion.)

After reference passes with Serkis in the unitard were completed, scenes were filmed again with Serkis now off-camera, feeding Gollum's lines to Wood and Astin, creating a clean plate to be used for compositing digital action. The other performance contexts for Serkis were the ADR and mocap sessions. In the former, Serkis voiced the character for sound recordists, actors, and editors. In the latter, he physically reperformed all of Gollum's scenes, this time in a body suit with optical markers on his joints, hands, and feet, and on a relatively bare stage (which included basic props for him to manipulate) covered by a range of sixteen to twenty-four cameras, depending on the session. The mocap data were mapped to a 3D skeletal model that was deformed to change Serkis's big-boned, fleshy frame to the wizened proportions of Gollum. The digital Gollum was character-rigged with a complete human skeletal system that drove more than 700 muscles attached to it, along with simulated respiration and heart activity. Skin was animated to the muscle system to respond with sliding, stretching, folding, and compressing actions. Lighting the skin realistically—avoiding the solid, painted look so prevalent in *Final Fantasy*—provided a particular challenge, but a 2001 SIGGRAPH paper on subsurface scattering suggested methods of achieving light dispersal through skin surface.[65] Rather than do the complex and costly rendering outlined in the paper, the animators achieved similar results by applying painted digital layers that emulated scatter effects.

Gollum facial animation was entirely a digital creation. Serkis's performances in the reference passes were used as models for the animators, and Serkis occasionally came to their desks and modeled expressions for them. Three video cameras did record Serkis's facial performance in the mocap sessions, and the animators consulted this footage. But, apart from these references, Gollum's face is an all-digital creation by a team of twenty animators using a process of blend-shape animation (a technique that had been used to create Yoda's expressions in *Star Wars* Episodes II and III). Blend-shape animation creates a performance by using a series of sculpted expressions as templates and then animating from one to another. Bay Raitt, who was the lead facial animator for Gollum, sculpted a digital facial puppet that contained hundreds of expressions that could be interchanged to produce the anchor points of a performance. Each one of these basically provides a keyframe for Gollum's animation, representing how he looks when he is angry, frightened, sullen, scheming, and so forth. Gollum's facial performance was animated using these basic sculpts from which intermediate blends were created, establishing the character's transitions from one emotional state or thought process to another. Animators refined the basic facial poses using a set of sixty-four controls targeting micro-movements of lips, brow, nose, and other facial features. Expressions could be visually blended, edited, and saved for later use. "'Terror,' for example, could be programmed, its settings saved for instant recall."[66]

If this sounds like a kind of Muzak programming for acting and emotional performance, it's not. The filmmakers aimed for perceptual transparency. Viewers would relate to Gollum as if he were one of the flesh-and-blood characters performed by actors without extensive digital mediation. About Gollum, Peter Jackson said, "We wanted to recreate what is compelling about a human performance." Animation supervisor Randall Cook said, "I always thought that animated characters in live-action movies . . . were often achieved by the use of animation solutions rather than acting solutions."[67] Gollum first appears in *The Two Towers* when he attacks Frodo and Sam at Emyn Muil. In thrall to his obsession with possessing the Ring, he creeps down a rock cliff toward their encampment below. These movements were keyframed without a performance by Serkis because they are beyond human capability. He moves like a spider down the rocky cliff. The animation aggressively stages action on the Z-axis, in the manner that Spielberg had defined for CG imagery in *Jurassic Park*. Wide-angle framings accentuate Gollum's lanky arms and legs as they extend toward the virtual camera in the extreme foreground. By contrast, the animation based on mocap data does not feature such extreme Z-axis staging. Snarling his hatred for them as unworthy possessors of the Ring, Gollum attacks the hobbits, and the fight features a 2D Gollum painted overtop Serkis's live-action struggle with Astin and Wood (with Serkis rotoscoped out). Because the action is so fast, the deceit works well.

Fordham covered the film for *Cinefex* and calls this "a brilliant scene, still today. I watched it recently, and it still holds up because the performances are so compelling and the characters are so strong. My theory is Gollum was so effective and such a breakthrough because they were inspired by Tolkien's story. Randy [Cook] is also one of the world's finest animators and he really carried the torch and inspired his animation team, many of whom were quite young and from all corners of the world. At least, that's how it appeared to me, sitting in on their sessions toward the end of *Two Towers*."[68]

The digital character's physical interaction with Astin and Wood is convincingly portrayed, but the scene's real performance challenge was not the physical struggle among the characters but the emotional one. To make Gollum a convincing character, his emotional arc had to be acted through in the scene's visualization. Searching for a way to understand Gollum's personality and determine a manner of playing him, Serkis decided that the character was in the throes of a physical addiction, like a drug addict or an alcoholic. His overweening desire to possess the Ring had crippled and deformed him physically, filled him with hatred for others and a self-loathing, and had corroded his mind to a state of psychosis. The schizophrenic dialogues throughout the film between Gollum and Smeagol, his former self, express this psychic violence and duality, contests of personalities poised between pure lust and unbearable shame. The striking voice Serkis created for the character expresses the tortured, debased, and lustful qualities of his self-immolating desire for the Ring. Gollum sounds like an anguished animal, feral, savage, and suffering psychological pain. His cunning and aggression are frightening and make him a formidable adversary, and yet his suffering complicates the viewer's response, evoking empathy in spite of his grotesque appearance and mannerisms. Gollum is rent by an internal conflict unique in the film trilogy. No other character suffers such torments or exhibits such turmoil. Gollum is the most psychologically driven character, the one performed and animated with the most depth of emotion. He is, of course, a digital being, and his ability to elicit sympathy, antipathy, and fascination provides a benchmark of virtual performing. Live acting and animation work synergistically to create a character that could not be rendered in such terms in either domain alone.

Serkis's brilliant performance preserves the character's humanity and anchors the animation with an emotional center, as Jackson had wanted. But the animators, too, performed the character and created his emotional arc across the films. They did this by being attentive to eye movements and facial expressions, as well as bodily inflections. When Gollum attacks Sam and Frodo at Emyn Muil, he lurches for the ring bound around Frodo's neck, and an extended close-up shows his face twisted with rapacious desire, his eyes distended with the anticipated bliss of touching the Ring. As he clutches Frodo, Gollum's digital eyes behave as would those of live actors. They show retinal convergence in focusing on Frodo. They are moist and contain surface reflections of Frodo and the landscape. And they are surrounded by textured skin that reflects and absorbs light in a realistic manner.

The emotional turn in the scene comes when Frodo struggles free and brings his sword to Gollum's throat, thwarting the creature's aggression. Serkis thought carefully about how he would play the change that sees Gollum turning from aggression to submission, as he swears to serve Frodo as the master who holds the Ring. "I was interested in finding a way to play the transition from the aggressive Gollum to the moment he gives in." Serkis determined that it would be right to play Gollum "as a manipulative child throwing a tantrum to get his own way and then playing the sympathy-inducing passive-aggressive child" as he swears allegiance to Frodo and agrees to guide Frodo and Sam on their quest.[69] When Frodo puts the sword to Gollum's throat, he commands the creature to release Sam, whom Gollum is choking with his forearm. The editing cuts between close-ups of Wood's face and Gollum's, their eyes equally prominent and *equally lifelike.* Wood's eyes shine with anger and reflect pinpoints of light from the environment, as do Gollum's. But more critically, Gollum's emotional transformation—from aggression to the passive-manipulative child—is played mainly in his eyes and in Serkis's vocal performance, a fusion of live acting and digital animation that is seamless. When Frodo tells Gollum to release Sam or have his throat cut, Gollum responds with saccadic eye movements registering his calculation of a new stratagem. This response, conveying the character's inner life in recognizably human terms, is wholly a matter of digital animation. His eyes skitter back and forth and then downward, not focusing on anything nor tracking movement but registering the thoughts ricocheting through his psychotic mind. The saccadic jumps are augmented by changes in pupillary reaction. Gollum's pupils swell as he determines what his best response will be. This is a stylized physiological response that provides an index of emotion and thought. Pupillary responses of this sort follow changes in the levels of light in the environment and none have occurred here. The dilations, therefore, mark an internal change that is occurring in the character and function as an emotional and psychological symbol. These and the saccadic responses resonate in three ways—they are autonomic and therefore reflect real, inner transformations rather than a prevarication on Gollum's part. They express the despair accompanying Gollum's shift in strategy, and they manifest his thoughtfulness and calculation. This triple resonance makes the emotional turn taken by Gollum—from attacking the hobbits to serving them—very persuasive. In concert with the way that Gollum's eyes provide a window onto his being, Serkis vocalizes a cry of anguish and resignation that seals the character's surrender not just to the hobbits but to a continuing and chronic state of abjection. The performance is in the voice and it is in the keyframed eye movements and the matchmoving of Serkis's physical actions. Gollum is a composite being—stranded by the Ring's power between human and inhuman and as a screen character in the synthesis of live action and animation, the composite layers seamlessly joined.

Subsequent scenes capture comparable levels of behavioral complexity, with eye animation providing a key means for tracking Gollum's shifting allegiances. His schizophrenia shows itself in a series of soliloquies as the two sides of his personality vie for control—the monstrous Gollum who will commit any act in order to possess the Ring, and Smeagol, the former self who descended from a hobbit family. Smeagol murdered his cousin to get the Ring, and the addiction progressively turned him into the psychotic and emaciated Gollum. The first of these soliloquies occurs as Frodo and Sam continue their journey to Mordor after Gollum has sworn to follow and serve Frodo. As the hobbits sleep, Gollum's shattered mind produces the startling dialogue between the two selves. Gollum spews his hatred for the hobbits, and Smeagol defends them, saying Frodo is his friend. Gollum attacks Smeagol and tells him he is friendless and a thief. The switches in personality are very fast; Jackson films some within a single take, while covering others by cutting between the dueling personalities as if they were two separate beings. As Gollum heaps invective on Smeagol, Jackson uses shot-reverse-shot cutting to separate them, and the alternating compositions serve to emphasize the difference in eye and facial animation. While Gollum's face contorts with hatred, Smeagol crouches submissively, his eyes narrowed and hooded with shame and guilt. The camera tracks in slowly on Gollum's face as he delivers the coup de grace, calling Smeagol a murderer, drawing out the word at sadistic length. Gollum's eyes are wide with anger and have a bright sheen. In the reverse-angle cut,

Gollum, an emotionally expressive CG character and a breakthrough for digital performing, represented a perfect synthesis of live action and animation. *The Lord of the Rings: The Two Towers* (2002, New Line). Frame enlargement.

Smeagol's eyes are heavy, dull, and filmy. Then the emotional contest between them turns: Smeagol says Frodo will take care of them, and he tells Gollum to leave now and never come back, repeating the command several times with increasing authority. With each iteration, his eyes shine more brightly, as a reflected key light comes up to accentuate them visually. When he realizes his command has worked and Gollum is gone, Smeagol reacts with a flurry of confusion, fear, and disbelief. His saccadic responses increase their amplitude and speed, and he looks about incredulously, not daring to believe his good fortune. Smeagol's complex emotional reactions flicker across his features as they would on the face of a live actor. Because most of the soliloquy is filmed in extreme close-up, it is wholly dependent on the quality and conviction of the digital performance.

In a later sequence, Smeagol dives into the Forbidden Pool after a fish, and Faramir and his Rangers, hidden nearby, prepare to execute him, but Frodo intercedes and persuades Smeagol to come with him. "You must trust Master," he tells Smeagol, who does not know the Rangers are waiting to seize him. Smeagol's hesitation, his suspicion that something is wrong, and his inner conflict over whether to trust Frodo register clearly on his face and in his eyes, as does the awful realization when he is seized that Frodo has betrayed him. Gollum/Smeagol is the most psychologically rendered character in the film trilogy. No other figure has the kind of sublime scene that ends *The Two Towers*, a final battle between the personae of Gollum and Smeagol that is filmed in a single moving camera shot that lasts nearly two minutes. Frodo's betrayal of Smeagol has reawakened the spiteful Gollum personality, and it persuades Smeagol to plot the hobbits' destruction. Smeagol battles for his better self but loses the psychic struggle, surrenders to his addiction, and embraces Gollum's venomous outlook. Covering this action in a single shot enables the performance to unfold in real time, understood, of course, as real *screen* time since the character was created from multipass rendering and from several performance passes by Serkis. Nevertheless, by presenting the performance as a real-time construction, the filmmakers draw on an acting solution rather than an animation solution to the question of how best to stage this climactic soliloquy. The staging of the reference pass in a long take played to an actor's best instincts—Serkis could play the difficult scene as an organic whole, without interruption. About the sustained takes used to film the soliloquies, Serkis remarked, "It was like being back on stage performing a monologue."[70] Randall Cook and his team of animators also drove the performance. Serkis keenly summarized the novel nature of the collaboration. He wrote that they had taken a great character from literature and proceeded to "filter that character through great screenwriters, then take the emotion, physicality, and voice of an actor's performance, which had grown organically from acting with other actors on set, and synthesize them with a range of animation techniques and motion capture."[71] Roger Ebert paid their work a left-handed but significant compliment when he remarked that the trilogy as a whole lacked psychological depth, that the films "exist mostly as surface, gesture, archetype and spectacle," but that Gollum's death nevertheless made him feel true human emotions because he had come to know who this character was.[72]

Gollum is the trilogy's most memorable creation, the one that arguably affects audiences most deeply. Visual effects artists, as well, were impressed. Rick Baker said, "The stuff in *Jurassic Park* was great. But those were still dinosaurs stomping around. Gollum was a real *character*. That's what excited me." For Richard Edlund, "Gollum was the most exciting visual effect to happen in the last decade—a totally believable CG character."[73] Since then, other believable CG characters have appeared in high-profile films, such as the Na'vi in *Avatar*. These six-foot-tall, blue catlike creatures living on the planet Pandora originated in motion-capture sessions facilitated by director James Cameron's ability to direct live actors alongside digital characters in real time. Innovative camera and computer systems—dubbed Simulcam—created composited footage of CGI and live action as Cameron directed the actors. In an early scene, for example, wherein Jake (Sam Worthington) awakens in the hospital lab as his Na'vi avatar, Cameron shot mocap footage of Worthington performing the scene on a stripped down, minimalist set. This footage subsequently was streamed through the Simulcam system, which mapped Worthington's performance onto a primitive visualization of his Na'vi avatar. Cameron could then direct this digital character in the fully dressed lab set with live actors and follow the action with a hand-held camera. In other instances, he filmed actors on greenscreen sets while viewing them on a monitor in the digital environment they would inhabit in the final, fully rendered scene. He could also do virtual camera moves through the digital sets in real time.

A goal throughout was to take mocap from being a post-production tool to one that was integrated with the filming and directing of live actors. In the past, mocap sessions followed principal cinematography. Brad Pitt's motion-capture sessions in *Benjamin Button* came after David Fincher had shot his movie. As a visual effects supervisor at Weta Digital remarked, "For Gollum, we had shot all the plates, and *then* we captured Gollum's performance with Andy Serkis."[74] Cameron's use of Simulcam enabled the actors to be filmed as their digital characters during production, which incorporated four sets of cameras: mocap cameras, the real-time virtual camera, HD witness cameras to provide visual references of actors' performances for the animators, and face cams mounted to a headpiece worn by the actor and capturing a low-resolution record of facial performances in the mocap sessions.

To animate the digital faces, the filmmakers turned to Paul Ekman's Facial Action Coding System, a classification scheme that maps the face in terms of zones and micro-expressions and the muscles involved in producing them. Using FACS, the animators numerically encoded every facial muscle and created a character rig with this data that could produce minute responses such as an eyelid twitch or an upper-brow raise. Close attention was paid to eye animation and to subsurface light scatter and transmission in the Na'vi skin. Na'vi characters were created with the familiar facial features of the actors who voiced them or who also appeared in the film as human characters, such as Jake and Grace (Sigourney Weaver). In Weaver's case, her features were imported to those of her avatar even though some, such as her patrician nose, were inappropriate for Na'vi faces. In this way, digital animation preserved the live actor's presence in the CG character.

Mocap and digital compositing enabled facial and bodily performances to be reconfigured and even uncoupled. In some scenes, Na'vi characters, such as the princess Neytiri (Zoe Saldana), appear with athletic bodies animated from mocap data supplied by stunt performers while the heads derive from facial animation based on the star performer. Facial Performance Replacement sessions enabled the actors to come back after scenes were shot and redo elements of their performances, akin to what is routinely accomplished with sound during an ADR session. Cameron said, "We were uncoupling the facial performance from the physical performance, but in a way that the actors embraced. It actually freed them up to perfect their performance without having to worry about how they were jumping or rolling around."[75]

Across the Valley

About the film's innovative streaming of live action and digital performances, producer Jon Landau said, "We wanted performance capture to be the 21st century version of prosthetics, something that would allow actors to play fantastic characters that they could not otherwise play."[76] The synthesis of mocap and keyframe animation enabled actors to inhabit fantasy characters at high levels of perceptual realism, characters that traditional methods of screen performance could not achieve. The uncanny valley, however, does not afflict these characters. They are humanoid but not human. Their features are exaggerated—the Na'vi are blue and have tails, Gollum has fish-gray skin and creeps about on all fours. As such, they do not invite viewers to regard them as photorealistic renditions of human beings. They provide vivid levels of perceptual realism—Gollum's facial animation, the texturing of his skin, the lighting of his eyes give him the spark of life. But Gollum and the Na'vi are stylized beings, which enables them to avoid the uncanny valley problem. The concept is not relevant for understanding how they interact with an audience. *Final Fantasy, The Polar Express, Beowulf*—these are the films that aimed to cross the uncanny valley and could not climb the other side.

David Fincher, who had used digital effects to such innovative ends in *Zodiac* (2007), made the first film to solve the uncanny valley problem. *The Curious Case of Benjamin Button* offers a parable about the corrosive effects of time, presented via the life story of the titular character whose life runs backward. During childhood, Benjamin has the outward appearance of a man in his eighties, and as he grows up he becomes visibly younger until, in his advanced years, he takes on the appearance of a child. Dying, he looks like an infant. With his life running backward, Benjamin cannot forge emotional connections with other people, except fleetingly. He loses everyone he loves, as do we all, but in his case the reversal of time accentuates this existential dilemma by making him come unstuck from the lives of the people around him. It is a film about people missing each other in time, a melancholy and soulful work.

It is also a film that could be made successfully only in the digital era. Its performance requirements were too challenging to be handled by the traditional solutions. A conventional approach to showing a character aging across a span of story time is to have the character played by different actors. But no matter how skillfully executed the performances may be or how closely the actors resemble one another, viewers feel the deception and know they are seeing different actors. In *The Notebook* (2004), for example, Ryan Gosling and Rachel McAdams play young lovers who marry, spend their lives together, and then in their later years turn none too convincingly into James Garner and Gena Rowlands as the characters. Another traditional approach portrays extreme changes in a character's age by using prosthetics and makeup, as Dick Smith did when aging Dustin Hoffman to a centenarian in *Little Big Man* (1970) or F. Murray Abraham from a youthful to an aged and decrepit Salieri in *Amadeus* (1984). No matter how brilliant the makeup— and these instances are supremely accomplished—viewers feel quite rightly that the actors are wearing things on their faces. Visual effects supervisor Eric Barba clarified why this approach doesn't work well: "The problem with old-age makeup is that it is additive whereas the aging process is reductive. You have *thinner* skin, *less* musculature, everything is receding. There is no way to do that 100 percent convincingly by adding prosthetics."[77]

Brad Pitt as a digital head replacement, anchored in the scene with exacting attention to lighting detail. *The Curious Case of Benjamin Button* (2008, Warner Bros.). Frame enlargement.

Brad Pitt, who plays Benjamin, wanted to do the film only if he could play the lifespan of the character rather than doing one or two age intervals and then handing the character off to other actors. The trick was to age Benjamin backward from his eighties all the way to an infant's appearance while still retaining the viewer's conviction that the character's many forms remain Brad Pitt, that the character's transformations are anchored by a single actor's performance. Digital solutions brought Pitt's performance to this wholly new level, and for this reason *The Curious Case of Benjamin Button* is a film of historical importance, as is *Zodiac*. In both instances, innovative visual effects serve the naturalism of the respective stories, immersing viewers in screen worlds that could not be photographed as real environments or populated with actors giving performances that were photographically captured in the traditional ways. During the film's first hour, Pitt appears as a digital head replacement on the bodies of three different actors who are performing Benjamin's physical movements in the scenes where he is aging from his eighties to his late sixties. These actors had the right body types to convincingly portray Benjamin as he would be at these ages. Then, beginning with sequences showing Benjamin working as a crew member on a tugboat, Pitt physically appears as a full-body actor and no longer as a head replacement. To play Benjamin in his sixties, Pitt wore prosthetic age makeup that was digitally enhanced, and as he aged backward into his teen years, Pitt was progressively "youthened." Digital facial alterations made him look as he did in *Thelma and Louise* (1991) and then even younger. These included changing the geometry of his eyes, altering the eye sockets, and reversing the effects of ptosis, a condition in which aging eyelids protrude down over the eyes.

Fincher shot all the scenes featuring the three stand-in actors as the old Benjamin, and then he edited this material to identify the exact takes that would require head replacements. Only then did Pitt come in to perform Benjamin's facial responses and voice the scenes. Pitt, in other words, acted the role after these scenes had been shot and edited. The key creative challenge was placing Pitt's facial performance convincingly inside the aged Benjamin. To accomplish this, the filmmakers captured Pitt's facial data in several ways. Three-dimensional sculpted plaster models were built from a lifescan of Pitt's face. These depicted Benjamin in his sixties, seventies, and eighties by remapping Pitt's features to imagine how he might appear at these ages. The sculptures then were scanned to create digital models for animating. (Creating a sculpture or maquette as the basis for a subsequent digital model is a common procedure. Complex organic forms are easier to design this way than trying to start from scratch in the computer.) CG animation of the digital model utilized a large reference library of Pitt's facial expressions. This had been created using non-marker-based motion capture, a facial contour system developed by Mova that employed phosphorescent makeup worn by the performer and triangulated in 3D space by the array of mocap cameras. The makeup provided more data points than a marker-based system. In the reflective makeup, Pitt modeled a series of micro-expressions that were broken down according to the units specified by researcher Paul Ekman in his Facial Action Coding System (FACS).

During the performance sessions when Pitt was enacting Benjamin's facial responses in the scenes that had already been filmed, four high-definition Viper cameras recorded his performance, covering him from different angles. After each take, Fincher and Pitt assessed the goodness of fit between the body movements of the actor who had been filmed in production and the facial and head movements provided by Pitt. The body language and the facial performance had to seem in synch. Image analysis software helped transfer Pitt's live-action facial performance to the digital model built to resemble the aged Benjamin. Keyframe animation drew upon the reference library of Pitt expressions to shape and modulate the character's responses moment to moment. But to bring off the illusion required perfect rendering of Benjamin's skin and eyes, the lighting on his face to match the environments that had been lit on set, and flawless motion tracking of the head replacement to the character's body as supplied by the three actor stand-ins. Bumps, pores, blemishes, age spots, and tissue thinning were rendered using displacement maps (a form of texture mapping that alters the shape of the model), ray-tracing, and subsurface scattering.

Because eyes had always been a big problem in previous efforts to render photorealistic human beings, a special animator was tasked solely with visualizing Benjamin's eyes. Barba said, "We knew if we didn't get the eyes right, it wouldn't matter how good the rest of it looked. Without the eyes, it wouldn't be Brad Pitt, and it wouldn't be Benjamin Button."[78] Multipass rendering isolated essential characteristics of lifelike but aging eyes. "Every element— the amount of water in the eyes, the different layers of the skin, the red in the conjunctiva of the eye—was rendered out separately for control, and then the compositors layered those things together again, shot by shot."[79]

Executing the film's 329 digital head replacement shots required precise motion tracking to ensure that the head replacements aligned properly with the character's spine and also required matching the light effects to those created on set during filming. When Benjamin walks through a dimly lit corridor in a New Orleans brothel, for example, the movement and the lighting of head and body had to look identical. The filmmakers accomplished this by surveying every light source on set and every bounce card and then replicated this information in a CG environment in order to light Benjamin's digital face interactively with his environment.

The results seamlessly suggest that the actor portraying Benjamin inhabits a unified space onscreen. The "actor," of course, is a composite presence, deriving from the on-set performer enacting Benjamin's body movements, Brad Pitt's performance as Benjamin's face, and the team of animators who meshed the body and head through facial animation and lighting cues. Hard light sources on set visibly reflect off the digital head replacement, and characters moving off-camera cast shadows over Benjamin's features. The matching of specular highlights, ambient occlusive shadows, global illumination characteristics, and color tone between on-set lighting and digital animation create the perceptually convincing bridges between Benjamin's head and body and the acting performances that unite them. It is easy to overlook the contributions of the body actors, but they provided the physical performances that gave the character solidity and personality as he moved through the spaces of the narrative. The eighty-year-old Benjamin hobbling on crutches after a departing streetcar provides a striking image of his vulnerability and spirited nature.

Pitt's presence in the character across the story arc gives Benjamin the continuity of personality that makes the character conception work. Benjamin is a reflective personality, quiet and meditative, not aggressive and verbal. His affliction—being born old—cuts him off from other people who are aging in the opposite direction from his own and forces him continually to confront what everyone faces during intervals of crisis, the loss of friends and loved ones. As a result, Benjamin develops a patient, restrained, passive demeanor. The mysteries of life and time puzzle him, as they must, but he accepts these and seeks no answers in any of the traditional ways, from religion to debauchery. He is not loquacious, and this characteristic both facilitates and challenges the facial animation necessary to bring the character to life. It facilitates facial animation because Benjamin doesn't say much and, therefore, dialogic inter-actions with other characters are minimal and often need not be portrayed. Benjamin listens to what the old people say at his mother's boarding house where he lives, and he forms attachments to them, but these relationships are dramatized in visual terms rather than verbal ones. Speech, therefore, is not a major requirement of Benjamin's facial animation. But getting the way that he reflects upon and reacts to what others say and do was a difficult chal-lenge. Benjamin's digital face is quite expressive, convincingly so because the emotions are implied, subtle, and indirect rather than being telegraphed in the broad manner of caricature. The transformation of Pitt's motion-capture performance to digital terms is subliminal—Benjamin's face does not seem like an animated creation, as the faces did in *The Polar Express*, *Beowulf*, and *Final Fantasy*. Brad Pitt enacts the character through a set of carefully controlled and focused reactions and responses, and his thoughts are presented mainly in voiceover narration, which Pitt handles in a quiescent manner that suits the character. Benjamin lives onscreen in the ways that he reacts and responds to events around him. As he gazes out the window of the front door of the boarding house for the first time, curiosity is mingled with passivity. Framed by a bedside lamp, he listens patiently as a close friend says goodbye. He gazes reverently at the deceased form of an old woman who taught him to play piano. He endures the scolding of Daisy's grandmother, who finds Benjamin and the young girl in close quarters and believes Benjamin is molesting her.

In portraying Benjamin's range of responses, Fincher did not aim for total photorealism. He gave viewers a clue to the character's invented and synthetic nature by insisting that the head replacement shots incorpo-rate a head that is slightly too large for the character's frame. This subtle disproportion points to Benjamin's ontologically deviant nature, to his backward-running biological clock, and it enables viewers to enjoy a modest but important amount of perceptual and critical distance. Seeing Benjamin as a visibly odd character, as someone whose head is too large for his body, induces a critical framing process whereby the character can be understood as a fabulous one, as a fictional construct through whom the lesson of the film's narrative can be developed, a parable about how we are meant to lose all the people whom we love.

The success attained in the character's conception and execution—that Brad Pitt is Benjamin and that Pitt as actor inhabits the character across all

Digital tools enable an actor to move forward or backward in time. Brad Pitt was "youthened" for scenes in which Benjamin grows old chronologically (but not physically). *The Curious Case of Benjamin Button* (2008, Warner Bros.). Frame enlargement.

his mutations in time—becomes especially apparent when it breaks down. We last see Pitt as Benjamin when he visits a now aging Daisy at her dance studio. Pitt has been youthened to look even younger than he did in *Thelma and Louise*, via virtual skin grafts and subtle remodeling of his head. Thereafter, when Benjamin next appears, he is twelve years old and is now played, for the first time in the film, by another actor whose face is visible on camera. Child actors were recruited to portray Benjamin's advancing years (which produce an infantilizing of his body and face), and this switch is jolting and undermines what had hitherto been achieved with the character. Heretofore, Pitt's features defined the character's continuity of being. Benjamin always looked like Brad Pitt, no matter how aged he was. Now, seeing the child actor who is demonstrably not Brad Pitt, the viewer wants to shout at the screen, "That's not Benjamin!" Fincher said, "We decided we would have to go with child actors to play Benjamin when he looks 12 and younger; but by then, we felt we would have made the case that this was the same guy, and people would roll with it."[80] Fincher is a very astute filmmaker, and he perhaps underestimated how well the digital head replacements would work. Abandoning this strategy in the last act of the narrative produces a jolt that breaks the audience's illusion that it is seeing a single character enacted by a single performer, an illusion developed seamlessly to this point. The film now falls into the dilemma of every other movie that employs different actors to play the same character—viewers feel an emotional disruption that creates a breach in the story and screen world.

Despite this fumble in the final act, *Benjamin Button* demonstrates the creative and expressive power of digital tools in forming credible characters and providing an actor with new methods of performing. The filmmakers wanted viewers to relate to Benjamin as a real character and not a visual effect. As Eric Barba said, "We didn't want anyone to be taken out of the story by some kind of obvious effects technique."[81] The technical modes by which Benjamin is realized as a character reimagined what a live actor contributes to cinema. A gallery of performers enacted Benjamin onscreen, some as body-only performers, while Brad Pitt is a digital head and face in some scenes and a whole body performer in others. In the head replacement shots, Pitt is not a photographic element. He is there as an image-analysis transformation, moving from HD video capture to a low-resolution 3D digital head model that was animated to be emotionally expressive and then rendered with detailed texturing and lighting effects. But it would be a mistake to conclude from this that Pitt had been replaced by digital technology, that he was merely a ghost in the machine. Pitt's perceptible presence is essential to selling the character's reality, and this is why it is so startling when the movie offers in its last act another screen performer as the face of Benjamin.

Benjamin Button is an actor's film, just as Gollum in *Lord of the Rings* is an actor's character. That they are also digital-intensive creations does not diminish the importance of the actor in helping to realize them. Rather than being displaced by technology, the actors remain visible onscreen, glimpsed inside and through their digital characters. Zoe Saldana's performance as Neytiri is very apparent in the screen character, as is Pitt's in *Benjamin Button*. These films point to the compatibility of screen acting and digital effects. Moreover, the novel production methods furnished performers with substantial creative pleasure. As numerous actors have stated, mocap can be a very liberating method of working, enabling performance in real time unlike the fragmented mode of performing that is traditional in live-action film production. Directors, too, report a satisfying creative experience. Steven Spielberg said, "Motion capture brings the director back to a kind of intimacy that actors and directors only know when they're working in live theater."[82]

Gollum and Benjamin Button are not characters that could be created successfully in traditional performance modes, where an actor wears a costume and elaborate facial makeup. Costuming, makeup, and masks continue as essential components of acting in cinema. Spike Jonze's *Where the Wild Things Are* (2009) derives splendid returns from putting actors in large animal costumes and having them deliver dialogue. The masks were digitally animated in small ways only to achieve lip-synch as well as other minimally expressive movements. The film embraces the artifice of being in costume and mask. Few observers would deny that an actor performs a character when wearing a costume or a mask or elaborate prosthetic makeup. No one says that the mask replaced the actor. Digital extensions of these traditional tools do not undermine the actor's craft, although they can make the boundaries between live performance and animation harder to discern and therefore more elusive. This is the chief reason that controversy has surrounded efforts to credit actors with awards for performing digital characters. James Cameron, for example, publicly expressed disappointment that Zoe Saldana was not nominated for an acting Oscar for her performance as Neytiri. "There's a learning curve for the acting community, and they're not up to speed yet," he said.[83] Writing in *Entertainment Weekly*, Mark Harris vehemently disagreed that Neytiri was Oscar-worthy.[84] He maintained that Neytiri was a special effect, not a character informed by an actor's creativity.

The notion that digital characters might earn acting awards seemed scary to some in Hollywood. Jeff Bridges, who won an Oscar for his performance in *Crazy Heart* (2010), complained, "Actors will kind of be a thing of the past. We'll be turned into combinations. A director will be able to say, 'I want 60% Clooney; give me 10% Bridges; and throw some Charles Bronson in there.' They'll come up with a new guy who will look like nobody who has ever lived and that person or thing will be huge."[85] As Kristin Thompson discussed, the *Avatar* animators altered Zoe Saldana's facial features and added details that enhanced the emotional content of expressions and shots: "Despite actors' and directors' claims to the contrary, the movements and expressions caught by performance capture are changed in many obvious and not so obvious ways."[86] And she asked where the boundaries are between acting and special effects. I have avoided using the term special effects in this book because digital tools have created so many new imaging possibilities that visual effects are no longer "special" as they were in earlier generations, when a filmmaker shot the footage and matte painters, model builders, and optical printer operators came in at discrete points to do a few shots. Visual effects no longer are segregated in production in a manner that justifies calling them "special." Thus in films like *Benjamin Button* and *Avatar* there is no clear boundary between domains that we might call acting and those we would term visual effects. Actors become effects and effects derive from actors. They are synergistic and mutually informing, each permeating the other. Steven Spielberg has provided a good working description of what new tools such as Simulcam and digital animation-from-mocap bring to performance. He sees it as digital makeup, a new form of prosthetics so thin that one can see the actor's every move.[87]

Few of cinema's traditional expressive formats have been undermined by digital tools, and the live performer remains as important as ever. But myths about replacing actors with digital effects are commonplace in popular and academic criticism. Kirsten Moana Thompson, for example, concludes a very fine essay on the camerawork in *Lord of the Rings* with this familiar lament: "The traditional photography of real actors and props is fast becoming replaced by the digital manufacture of the mise-en-scene, and, like the mocap technology used in the creation of Gollum, by the replacement, in whole or in part, of the live actor as a filmmaking staple."[88]

All involved with *Lord of the Rings* agree that Andy Serkis's performance was essential to realizing Gollum as a believable and vivid digital character. Animation supervisor Rob Coleman, whose credits include numerous *Star Wars* films and *Men in Black* (1997), dismisses complaints that 3D animation will replace the need for actors. "No, no and NO! Even with CG characters, you will have people like Andy Serkis in front of the camera, and people like me and my team behind the scenes. You have on-set actors for the live actors to relate to, you have voice talent. It isn't HAL 9000 sitting in the back churning out all this footage!"[89] And, of course, CG characters are not cinema's exclusive future. Live-actor-centered dramas will continue to proliferate, partly because they are less expensive to make and because, if you want Al Pacino or Meryl Streep for characters that don't need digital extensions, you hire them. You don't hire a team of animators to create elaborate facsimiles of them. Actors remain a centerpiece of cinema, whether in its analog or its digital forms. Digital offers new stages on which an actor might perform characters and new ways of visualizing performance. Actors like Andy Serkis find this irresistible because it can get at truth. Animation doesn't substitute for acting. "You can't enhance a bad performance with animation. You can't dial it up, lift the lip or the eyebrow. It has to be right at the core moment."[90] He has said that not recognizing the acting in animated characters derived from performance capture is a Luddite outlook. Writing about his mocap experiences, Serkis asserted that mocap allows acting to "retain its purity." The absence of costume, set, and makeup on the mocap stage requires "pure, truthful acting" and offers in return an infinite range of characters that can be mapped onto an actor's performance. It is acting for the twenty-first century, he maintains, and yet it "feels strangely close to the older acting arenas of theater, puppetry and plain old sitting around a campfire telling stories."[91] Digital tools look backward as well as forward; they embrace tradition while configuring new possibilities. They emphasize a medium characteristic that is easily overlooked—the performer as a recombinant element of cinema, transacting relationships with elements of style across scenic action and composited image layers. Rather than foreclosing on the contributions that live actors make to cinema, digital effects provide arenas in which actors may continue to furnish the human presence so vital to the medium.

CHAPTER 4

Digital Environment Creation

Aerial flyovers—moving camera shots taken from a helicopter or an airplane—are a traditional way of introducing important story locations. In a helicopter shot in *Bad Boys II* (2003), the camera flies toward a Cuban beach and circles a mansion surrounded by trees and smaller houses. The location is a composite. The mansion was shot in Miami. The surrounding houses were shot in Puerto Rico and appear in the film as textures projected onto a 3D wireframe model of the Cuban location, and the distant mountains in the background are a 2D matte painting. The midground showing a river and additional houses is composed of 2½D matte paintings, so-called because they are arranged on a series of 2D planes in the 3D computer environment to provide a minimal but necessary amount of motion parallax. A flyover shot in *The Ring* (2002) shows an island lighthouse surrounded by trees and a road. The lighthouse is a wireframe model on 3D terrain, textured with motion picture footage and still photographs taken by helicopter of Oregon's coast and of farmland in California. Ten matte paintings projected on underlying computer models furnished the camera's changing perspective in the flyover. The environments that viewers see in these flyovers are amalgamations composed of digital modeling and painting and with textures supplied by photographic and motion picture images.[1]

In *Pirates of the Caribbean: At World's End* (2007), pirate captain Barbossa (Geoffrey Rush) and crew, searching for Jack Sparrow (Johnny Depp), sail their junk, the *Hai Peng*, into a strange, arctic domain known as the Farthest Gate. Huge icebergs surround the ship whose hull cuts a visible wake through the partly frozen waters. The *Hai Peng* is an eight-foot miniature model composited into a location composed, depending on the shots, of a Greenland sea and a real wake cut by a camera boat or, alternatively, a CG sea and CG icebergs textured with footage of ice formations filmed in Greenland. The

CG icebergs are also 3D matte paintings, and the geometry of Greenland's ice floes was changed to make things look more dramatic. A visual effects supervisor at Digital Domain, one of the effects houses working on the film, explained, "We took cues from the [Greenland] plates—the quality of the ice, scale of detail and size relationships of the huge ice cliffs relative to the boat—and we extrapolated from there, changing the geography into tall, looming spires that converged above the ship."[2] Later, when the *Hai Peng* drifts dangerously close to a huge waterfall at the edge of the world, fluid simulations based on research conducted at Stanford University establish the surface detailing of the water along with its energy, dispersed in motion, and its internal dynamics, bubbles, and froth. But the CG waterfall also incorporated photographic references based on footage filmed at Niagara Falls using camera angles that approximated those employed in the sequence's computer design. "That footage became a library of information for the water's scale and its behavior as it went over the edge. It was such a wild concept, we wanted to ground the fluid dynamics in reality, in terms of acceleration and drag from the air as the water particles atomized."[3] The viewer sees a virtual environment that is modeled on reference data supplied by physics and photography.

In *Batman Begins* (2005), Bruce Wayne (Christian Bale) journeys to a Himalayan monastery where he learns ancient forms of martial arts. The monastery is a 1/48-scale miniature composited into a digital landscape created using a scan of footage of a mountain and glacier location in Iceland. Digital painting blended the real location with the miniature model. As Joe Fordham points out, "They went with a miniature here because they had to blow it up, and [director Christopher] Nolan wanted to ground that in reality."[4] In the film's climax, villains on Narrows Island dump toxins into the water supply of Gotham City. Narrows is a 40-foot-by-80-foot miniature model detailed with working lights, and Gotham's cityscape beyond it is CG. The CG buildings were created from photographs of Chicago buildings and textured with their architectural details. HDRi (high dynamic range images, explained below) furnished data that enabled full 3D views inside the windows of the CG buildings, complete with reflections of the urban environment on the surface of the glass.

A major location in *Iron Man 2* (2010) is Stark Expo, Tony Stark's (Robert Downey Jr.) exposition promoting Stark Industries' latest research and manufacturing. The locale is a blend of CG environments and photographic references from real places, such as New York's 1964 World's Fair with its distinctive Unisphere globe and Tent of Tomorrow. These objects were built into the film's CG scenery, and virtual camera moves could be digitally matchmoved to blend with the plate photography taken by helicopter. About the real landscapes in the plate photography, effects artist Ben Snow said, "That was useful to us in several ways. . . . There were real freeways that we could use in our shots. The photography also included the Unisphere—a giant metal globe of the world—and the skeleton of the 'Tent of Tomorrow,' which we were going to use as the Stark Pavilion in our film. There were these core pieces of environment that [we] could shoot and work out camera moves on."[5] A subsequent sequence in which Stark races in the Monte Carlo Grand Prix uses an establishing shot of the Monte Carlo site with digital augmentations. The race itself features CG cars, but these are composited with location plate photography of the actual track. Costuming, too, is a blend of practical and CG elements. Rather than wearing a full-body Iron Man suit as he had done in the first film, Downey wore a chest-piece on his torso and the outline of a helmet on his head, leaving his arms and legs free. The full-body suit was tracked as a CG element into the shots using a proprietary motion-capture system developed at ILM that enabled actors to work on real sets as well as the greenscreen environment traditionally used for motion capture. In the film, depending on the scene, Iron Man can be an all-CG character or may be created from mocap data supplied by a stunt man or may be Robert Downey in a costume blending practical and CG elements.

Digital visual effects blend such disparate image sources as live action and animation, still and moving photographic images, paintings in 2D and 3D, and objects modeled in computer space and textured with photographic or painted details. Digital toolsets conjoin these various image categories, deriving from real locales and synthesizing new ones. So what, then, is real? A scholar investigating digital imaging might conclude that such practices undermine the photographic basis of cinematic realism, that they offer simulacra that mimic the real, and by doing so create an epistemic doubt as to the status of all images that look photographic.

But how adequate is a photographic conception of realism in cinema and how useful is photography for understanding the nature of narrative cinema? How much has really changed in the way that narrative cinema portrays environments and locations? Before turning to our topic in this chapter—onscreen environments achieved through digital production design—it will be helpful to explore the limitations of the photographic model for our understanding of digital visual effects. Environment creation in cinema cannot be understood fully in terms of this model. I have raised the issue in earlier chapters, and an expanded discussion is warranted here. I want to demonstrate continuities in the representation of locations by cinema in the analog and the digital eras in ways that go beyond the photographic model. To do so, I spend some time in the first part of this chapter discussing analog visual effects as they bear on scenic design and the representation of story locale.

Limitations of the Photographic Model of Cinema

Few essays have been more influential about the nature of cinematic realism than those by André Bazin, most particularly "The Ontology of the Photographic Image" and "The Evolution of the Language of Cinema," in which he claims that the realistic elements in cinema derive from the objective nature of photography. The development of photography, he argued, freed painters from the obligation to depict the world as it appears and enabled them to pursue instead poetic and subjective imagery. For Bazin, in this respect, photography's objectivity made it radically dissimilar from painting. The mechanical formation of an image by the camera provided the basis of this objectivity. Bazin famously wrote, "For the first time, between the originating object and its reproduction there intervenes only the instrumentality of a nonliving agent. For the first time an image of the world is formed automatically, without the creative intervention of man."[6] Its automatic nature made photography more credible than all other traditions of picture-making: "We are forced to accept as real the existence of the object reproduced."

A corollary of this view is the idea that photographs are best understood as indexes. Bazin wrote that photographs model the reality of what they depict. Photographs transfer reality "from the thing to its reproduction."[7] Roland Barthes wrote that photographs demonstrate the existence of their referents, which, for Barthes, are necessarily real: "Every photograph is a certificate of presence."[8] Rudolf Arnheim emphasized photography's objective nature, that is, "the fundamental peculiarity of the photographic medium: the physical objects print their image by means of the optical and chemical action of light."[9] Photographs take viewers "on vacation from artifice."[10] Photographs are said to make documentary claims about the nature of reality that are dissimilar from the appeals of painting. Barbara Savedoff writes that viewers "irresistibly see the photograph as faithfully recording for us the appearances of the world."[11] Even Sergei Eisenstein adhered to this traditional view. Montage was necessary, he wrote, in order to shape the recalcitrant content of a single shot, which was "more resistant than granite. This resistance is specific to it. The shot's tendency toward complete factual immutability is rooted in its nature."[12] For Eisenstein, as a photographic image the shot was a fragment of nature.

Viewed in these terms, photography's change from a chemical medium to a digital one seemed to change its ontological status and its relation to viewers. As Philip Rosen points out, "Accounts of the digital gravitate toward a postulate of radical change in arenas of representation, discourse, culture, and sometimes even society as a whole."[13] An oft-repeated idea is that because digital images are more easily manipulated, photography loses its privileged claims to truth, its credibility as a visible document of the world. Savedoff writes, "It is the digital image's enhanced alterability that precludes it from ever having the credibility attributed to photographs."[14] For Steven Shaviro, "Digital photography is no longer mimetic."[15] He claims that, in an era of digital image manipulation, "photographic images themselves are no longer objective in Bazin's sense. They can no longer carry their own self-evidence." If cinema is regarded as a photographic medium, then what is seen as true for digital photography also holds for digital cinema. The authenticity of its images cannot be trusted in the way that those of its analog forebear could. Keith Griffiths states, "What gave cinema part of its value—a confident, assured and unchallenged recording of reality and one that was extremely difficult to modify and manipulate—has now been fundamentally changed by the new digital technology."[16] He fears that live-action images will become increasingly displaced by digitally engineered spaces, places, and people. Berys Gaut writes that informed viewers must necessarily suspend judgment about the "evidential authority of the digital image" and that in this respect digital cinema's pursuit of realism is self-defeating. "Digital cinema has greater powers to achieve realistic-looking images than does traditional film, but when viewers come to know of these powers, they have every reason to be suspicious about whether what they seem to have evidence for happening really did happen."[17]

The key ingredient of such claims is the idea that in a digital era, where images can be imperceptibly altered, digital photographs can no longer function as indexes. Rosen notes that "it is common for theorists to treat indexicality as the defining difference for the digital, so that the photographic image often becomes the most exemplary 'other' of the digital image."[18] As Braxton Soderman points out, "Contemporary discussions of the digital image often focus on the annihilation of the indexical status of mechanically produced images such as photographs."[19] Manovich, for example, observes that cinema "is no longer an indexical media technology."[20] Shaviro claims that "the indexical character of the photographic image has disappeared" and "there is no longer any ontological distinction between a 'true' image and a 'false' one."[21] Tom Gunning, on the other hand, has argued that the concept of indexicality has reached "the limits of its usefulness in the theory of photography, film and new media" and that it may not be the best way of thinking about cinematic realism.[22] He points out that the sheer perception of motion in cinema provides a strong reality effect, regardless of whether movement occurs in a photographic image or in an animated or an abstract image, and he speculates that the impression of reality that cinema conveys may have more to do with its simulation of motion than with indexical referencing. As a consequence, he suggests, as I have been arguing in this book, that realism is a descriptive category that can be applied to categories of cinematic image that traditionally have not been considered as realistic.[23]

Soderman and Mark Wolf point out that digital images can retain indexical properties. For Soderman, digital indexicality refers to the algorithms of the program that executes the operations necessary for creating the image. Digital images function "as indexical signs of an algorithm."[24] For Wolf, digital images carry two types of indexicality: "a perceptual indexicality, which is similar to that of the analog image and deals with visual appearance, and a kind of conceptual indexicality as is present in the data sets represented in the digital imagery of computer simulations."[25] Rosen's view of digital indexicality is more broadly considered and closer to my own view. As he points out, "Digital information and images can have indexical origins, the digital often appropriates or conveys indexical images, and it is common for the digital image to retain compositional forms associated with indexicality."[26]

As I suggested in chapter 1, the dinosaurs in *Jurassic Park* are perceptually realistic even if, as nonexistent beings, they cannot be indexes as this category is conventionally understood. Nevertheless, the persuasiveness of the effects makes indexical claims. The detailed texturing of the animals' skin, the spatial complexity of their movements, and the suggestions of sentience and personality conveyed in their behavior—all make strong perceptual claims upon us that these beings exist within the film's fictional world. The dinosaurs are perceptually realistic. The cinematic images point to the existence of the dinosaurs—they indicate their existence in terms that would be indexical but for our conceptual knowledge that such creatures do not exist to be photographed. While the reader might object that this is a spurious indexicality, consider the example of Brad Pitt when he appears as a digital head replacement in *The Curious Case of Benjamin Button*. He is an animated computer model, not a photographic image, but this model was derived from a Lidar scan of Pitt's face. The model was constructed based on that data, and altering it selectively enabled the filmmakers to change the character's age. So although Brad Pitt does not physically appear as an actor in these sequences or as a photographically derived image, the computer-based image that we see is indexical. It persuades us that it is an age-altered version of Pitt because it carries his trace. And if one accepts the translation of physical space into binary data, then one must accept that the Pitt head replacement is physically connected to the actor as an index. There is little difference between this example, whereby Pitt's face is quantified and then regenerated as an image and a conventional, analog photograph in which light furnishes the medium of translation from the object to the image. In this regard, Bazin's claim that the object impresses itself directly upon the photographic image is incorrect. Cameras record light, not objects. (Three-dimensional scanners record three-dimensional geometry, and motion sensors used in mocap sessions record movement.) Photography in both analog and digital contexts remains a medium of translation. In the analog world, a photograph is the output of the translation of luminous information by camera optics and then by the development bath and fixer. In the digital world, the translators are algorithms, and these need not be false or falsified.

What we know of 9/11 and the Iraq War, we know largely by virtue of the photographic record supplied by digital cameras in the hands of witnesses to the events. Digital images of 9/11 have achieved iconic status in contemporary culture, and few doubt this visual record, apart from conspiracy theorists. But even conspiracy theorists search the record of digital images for empirical evidence to bolster their claims that the event was an attack by the government on its own citizens. The abuse at Abu Ghraib prison in Iraq elicited worldwide revulsion when digital images taken by prison guards were made public. Charles Graner, one of the instigators of the Abu Ghraib abuse, is now in prison because of the images captured on cheap, consumer-grade cameras. The army prosecutor in that case used the image time stamps to sequence the photographs taken from multiple cameras into a progression showing what acts were done and when. And Sabrina Harman, one of those involved in the abuse, took her own digital photos of Manadel al-Jamadi, an Iraqi captured by U.S. forces and killed during interrogation. Her superiors at the prison ruled the death accidental, and, suspecting a cover-up, she wanted images that would document signs on the corpse of physical abuse. In these contexts, digital images clearly established indexical and evidentiary connections with what they depicted.[27]

Digital imaging technologies have gained widespread acceptance throughout the field of medicine. These include imaging systems such as magnetic resonance imaging, computer tomography, and nuclear scanners, and they provide capabilities for surgical telepresence, virtual operations, and surgery simulation. Indeed, as Markus Gross writes, "From the early days of computer graphics, the medical field has been one of the most important application areas."[28] If these imaging capabilities lacked indexical value, they would be not merely useless but harmful. As Scott Curtis points out, the images are manipulated to enhance their informational value, but this does not mean the images cannot be indexes or that the manipulations result in falsification. "While it is true that the images created by the CT or MRI scanner are not 'pictures' of the body in same way that X-ray films are, this does not mean they are not indexical. Even though the information gathered by the machines travels to the computer in the form of binary oppositions, ones and zeros, that information is nonetheless 'indexical' in the sense that there is a necessary physical connection—even if only at the molecular level—between the object and its representation. It must be so; otherwise, the images would have no informational value."[29]

There is nothing inherent to the nature of digital images that rules out indexicality. The context in which images are created and used is the determining factor that affects whether an image may also be an index. In this respect, the digital revolution does not represent a break with the past. Curtis argues that there is an "essential continuity between the way physicians *understand* analog and digital medical images."[30] I believe this point is generalizable beyond the field of medicine. Writing about digital images broadly considered, Timothy Binkley correctly emphasizes the importance of aesthetic continuity. "Despite its novelty, the digital revolution builds upon long-standing, if sometimes misunderstood, traditions in the arts." He notes, "Digital media augment rather than undermine their analog forbears."[31] Fordham concurs and states, "Ask any great visual effects designer what is important for young up-and-coming VFX artists to learn, and most often they will emphasize the need for a good foundation in art and art history (as well as film history, acting, physics, photography, anatomy, you name it). Many young kids cut their teeth on digital tools without being able to draw or sculpt, and they will eventually hit a wall that they cannot break through if they don't master the principles of perspective [and other analog tools]."[32]

The photographic and the indexical are conjoined in Bazin's account. Measuring the nature of cinema as Bazin and his descendants have done according to concepts and functions like "recording reality," "evidential authority," and "live action imagery" produces a necessary but incomplete model of the medium and one that interferes with our ability to see the continuities of style that connect digital imaging to the production practices of earlier eras. The camera's recording function played a key role in the development of cinema, and without it modes such as the documentary could not exist. Even within the realm of fiction, motion picture cameras often document the appearance of a world on screen. Watching Chaplin's *Modern Times* (1936), we see what sections of Los Angeles looked like in the mid-1930s. As noted earlier, the impact of John Ford's westerns depends in part on a viewer's knowledge that the Monument Valley vistas onscreen are real.

But as the examples of 9/11 imagery and productions such as *Winter's Bone* (2010) demonstrate, digital cameras also can perform this recording function. Technology is inflected by aesthetic use and social context. When these value reportage, documentation, and indexical presence, it matters little whether a camera's image is captured on film or a memory card.

It is important, as well, to remember that the evidential authority of a camera's image is ambiguous. Documentary filmmakers know this very well; the framing of a shot is a necessarily rhetorical act, as is editing. Philip Gourevitch and Errol Morris have written about how the cropping performed on several Abu Ghraib abuse photos alters the meanings they proffer.[33] Photographic images are not formed in a manner that is free from creative intervention. The limitations of cameras require that users make a continuing series of calculations and tradeoffs. Photographic film responds to a narrower range of light than does the eye, and f-stop and shutter speed impose severe demands on a photographer who must determine where the shoulder and toe of a film stock's light curve ideally ought to located for a given shot. The optics of lenses impose their own characteristics upon photographic space, upon what and how much can be captured. The creative decisions continue into the darkroom. Slightly overexposing an image in camera will create a denser, thicker negative that then can be printed down to achieve rich contrast. To take a photograph, a photographer must already see the picture in his or her mind's-eye, must a priori have processed physical space as a pictorial composition and made a decision to capture that perception. As Joel Snyder points out, photography is an intentional act of picture-making and therefore lies within the aesthetic conventions of representation. Photography does not do an "end run" around representation. "There are no end runs that get us out of language or depiction to the really real."[34] He notes that the idea that a photograph might be objective in the sense of showing us what we would have seen if we had been there "has to be qualified to the point of absurdity. A photograph shows us 'what we would have seen' at a certain moment in time, *from* a certain vantage point *if* we kept our head immobile *and* closed one eye *and if* we saw things in Agfacolor or in Tri-X developed in D-76 and printed on Kodabromide #3 paper."[35]

Explaining cinema in terms of a photographic model produces a limited account of the medium. This claim seems counter-intuitive. Aren't movies photographic? A cinematographer works with lights and lenses, f-stops and T-stops just as a photographer may do. Many movies give us photographic images of real people, even if they are actors, and of places that are real locations or sets designed to look as real as possible. Doesn't this make cinema a photographic medium? As Joel Snyder notes, Bazin and other theorists of

The actors are real, the sea and sky are a digital matte painting, and the lighthouse is a miniature model. Setting in cinema often is an amalgamation of image types and tools. *Shutter Island* (2010, Paramount Pictures). Frame enlargement.

photographic realism try to explain photography's special status in terms of its origins. Photography is thought to originate from an authentic, non-artificial, visibly accurate, and mechanically achieved capturing of the physical reality before the camera, giving photography a different status from that of painting. For Bazin, since cinema is photographic, it shares this originating impulse. And, according to views that connect the aesthetics of cinema with photography, the endlessly redactable nature of digital images threatens to undermine the medium's authenticity and take it back into the domain of painting, erasing a distinction, pointed out by Bazin and others, between subjective and objective images that the invention of photography had made possible. For Bazin, the objectivity of photography freed painters to pursue subjective styles and visions. Lev Manovich has stressed the point. As I noted previously, he claims that digital images have returned cinema to its prehistory, to "the practices of the nineteenth century when images were hand-painted and hand-animated."

Painting and animation, however, have been core features of cinema throughout its history and not simply at its inception. Cinema is photographic, yes, but it is also, among other things, a medium of painting, and I mean that literally. Movies are not photographs, nor can they be explained as moving photographs. The normative practice of filmmakers in cutting from shot to shot takes the medium closer to the principles of collage than to photographic composition. Bazin's emphasis on long takes privileged an atypical element of film style and minimized the larger edited structures within which a long take might be found. The long takes in *Citizen Kane* (1941), for example, are surrounded by numerous rapidly edited sequences.

Amalgamation and Synthesis

The key point to be made here is that cinema synthesizes different traditions of picture-making—in regard to visual effects, these are, chiefly, painting, animation, and photography. Cinema is a combination of image types that have differing derivations. In this sense, it is not a photographic medium. As Noel Carroll has emphasized, "Film is not one medium, but many media."[36] He points out that films have been composed from blank leader, words, numerals, still images, abstract and nonfigurative shapes and forms as well as the more normatively considered photographic images. He refers to cinema, therefore, as a medium of moving *images* rather than moving *pictures* because the latter tend to be representational and cinema need not be representational. "Photographic representation," he concludes, "cannot be regarded as the essence of cinema."[37]

Because our theoretical and historical accounts of cinema have tended to neglect the role played by visual effects, the importance of this process of amalgamation and synthesis has been underappreciated. If we have a bias in our thinking about cinema that emphasizes live action, this is consistent with the way that the industry itself operated for many decades. Studio chiefs and filmmakers during the Hollywood period regarded visual effects as a form of trick photography, as something that had to be hidden from the awareness of viewers. Norman O. Dawn, who pioneered the use of glass paintings and matte shots, worked at Universal for five years beginning in 1916, and he recalled that studio heads "didn't believe in telling anybody about effects. . . . They considered anything that was a drawing or a glass shot a fake. So they didn't want to let the exhibitors know that this was a cheap picture full of fakes. They kept all that quiet . . . no matter if it was nothing more than an ordinary double exposure."[38] This tradition of concealment continued over succeeding decades. Matte painters during the studio era worked behind locked doors, in conditions of secrecy. More than any other single event, the release of *Star Wars* in 1977 altered these attitudes and the subterfuge they had inspired. George Lucas's enthusiastic embrace of visual effects, and the popular response to the film, ushered in a new era of publicity surrounding visual effects and a supportive fan base devoted to them, as well as journals like *Cinefex* that chronicle the history, technology, and aesthetics of visual effects. Since then, visual effects have held tremendous interest for audiences, and industry practices are no longer bashful.

Visual effects point to the medium's disparity from photography, that is, from capturing or recording live action placed in front of the camera. Many of the locations that we see onscreen, for example, were radically incomplete at the point of filming and are compendiums of nonadjacent and dissimilar types of environments and image types. Many iconic movie locations— Xanadu, Skull Island, Metropolis, Gotham City—have no photographic reality. They don't exist as places that could be put in front of a camera. This much is obvious, but perhaps less obvious is the fact that most of the time our sense of place in cinema is a manufactured perception, achieved by conjoining different categories of images and environments. One of Warner Bros.' great swashbucklers, *The Sea Hawk* (1940), stars Errol Flynn as Captain Geoffrey Thorpe, a sixteenth-century English raider targeting Spanish ships. Thorpe leads his men on a guerrilla raid into Panama to seize Spanish treasure. The Panamanian jungle, of course, is no such thing. It was created with fog machines and tropical plants dressed on a studio backlot. Thorpe and his men escape from the jungle to the shore and row out to their ship to head for England. They walk onscreen from the jungle backlot into beach shots filmed at Point Mungu, west of Los Angeles, and from there to the mockup of a rowboat placed in a studio rear projection set, and thence to shots in which they clamber aboard a full-scale model of a 135-foot man-of-war in a specially constructed studio maritime soundstage surrounded by a muslin cyclorama painted with a skyscape.[39] Their transit from jungle to ship is built from the layering of these different environments, in which the sea and sky are, alternatively, real, a photographic projection, and a painted backdrop.

This process of amalgamating environments is a routine condition in cinema, and it was practiced in especially thorough ways during the studio era. As Hollywood art director Robert Boyle, a frequent collaborator with Hitchcock, noted, "If we were shooting in New York on a street, we would shoot somebody driving up to a building in a cab and the next shot you're in the studio. The front door was built to match the location and be a part of the studio-built interior. What you saw out the windows of the interior were painted or photographic backings."[40] Hitchcock was especially fond of visual effects, and on *Saboteur* (1942) Boyle simulated on an indoor studio set the image of a lengthy circus caravan traveling a dusty desert road. The film's hero, Barry (Robert Cummings), is running from police and takes refuge in the caravan. Several point-of-view shots show the line of trucks halted as police with flashlights search them. The caravan and the cops seem to stretch from the foreground way into the distance, but this was an illusion created with forced perspective. The road was painted on the concrete studio floor and outlined with dirt and was ramped up on the rear of the set to simulate recession in space. Real trucks in the foreground were succeeded by painted toy trucks in the background, and cops played by actors in the foreground became tiny cut-out figures with lights in the distance. Speaking about the methods of forced perspective used in the shots, Boyle said, "You're achieving a large space in a limited space. You bring the background up, and you force everything smaller."[41]

Spaces depicted on screen tend to be fragments of the larger spaces referenced by story situations. Production design is the art of making a part stand for the whole. An art director only builds or dresses that part of a set or location that will be seen on camera, and often it is necessary to extend a viewer's impression of the space that can be placed before the camera. Glass shots, matte paintings, miniature models, rear and front projection—all these furnished filmmakers with enduring methods for extending the boundaries of the represented action. The Shufftan process, for example, places a mirror at a 45-degree angle to the camera to combine live action with the reflected image of a miniature model. The live-action elements are filmed through portions of the mirror that have been scraped away to leave transparent glass. Hitchcock used the process in *Blackmail* (1929) to combine actors with miniatures of the London Museum. The Shufftan process famously was used throughout *Metropolis* (1926) to place live action inside miniature sets of the futuristic city, and the technique furnished a short-cut means for building a shot in *Aliens* (1986) that required a larger set than could be constructed on budget. "We needed a shot of two characters entering a bar in the boom town, but we had no time or money to build a whole set. We built a full-size door area that actors could interact with and a matching miniature of the building and surrounding areas." The two were combined using a mirror, and clouds of dust obscured the join between set and miniature. "Even in the digital age, these techniques still work perfectly, and you can get your shot done in one take without any additional processes."[42]

Cinema as Painting

The environments seen on screen frequently are painted ones. Painting is fundamental to cinema. Filmmakers have always used paintings to enlarge their sets or to create landscapes and environments that cannot be photographed. The painter's art is different from a photographer's. While a cinematographer works with real light, the matte painter works more impressionistically, creating texture and atmosphere with paint and brush (or pixels and mouse). Matte paintings lack detail when seen up close. They are designed to be filmed with the camera at a distance. They didn't need crisp details in the analog era because film resolution couldn't retain the detail, and it would be lost anyway in the optical printing. Some of this has now changed with digital compositing and high-definition video—paintings need to be crisper now and with more detail. The matte painter's artistry achieves different objectives than photography. As Sean Joyce, a matte painter for ILM, remarked, "I wanted to be a matte painter because I loved the paintings and the impact of the images. A matte painter can create amazing angles you could never get with a camera, dress a scene with fantastic props and lighting. . . . Matte painting appealed to that part of me that wanted to have control over the consciousness of an audience. It was also the artistry that made it work."[43]

Matte paintings illustrate the limitations of the photographic model of cinema. The medium owes nearly as much to painting as it does to photography, measured in terms of the extent to which paintings have established locale and landscape throughout its history and the unobtrusive ways they have been blended with live-action cinematography. As soon as cinema was invented, it drew upon painting, and painting has remained an essential tool for visualizing images that cannot be photographed. The earliest films often had painted backdrops, and filmmakers quickly grasped methods of enhancing the painted illusion. While working as a photographer in 1905, Norman Dawn learned the common technique of placing a painting on glass in front of the camera to change undesirable elements in a scene that was to be photographed. In this case, a painting of trees obscured unsightly telephone poles from the property of a house he needed to photograph. Dawn brought the technique to cinema and augmented it in 1911 by pioneering the matte–counter-matte process used to marry a painting with a live-action film element. This process, known as original negative matte painting, provided a convenient alternative to the often cumbersome and awkward procedure of painting onto glass on location. A painting could be created in the comfort of a studio by projecting a frame of film from a live-action scene. The scene would have been filmed with a matte to obscure the area that would be filled in by the painting. Tracing the image onto glass or onto another surface, the artist could produce the painting with a precise fit to the matte line and then photograph the painting onto the original negative by using a counter-matte to prevent further exposure to the original live-action area. Working on the original negative preserved image quality, unlike the duping of a negative that optical printing frequently required.

Matte paintings as glass shots done on location or as Dawn's matte–counter-matte process proliferated throughout cinema as a means for extending sets, adding dramatic landscapes and vistas, and placing actors in locales that did not exist before the camera. Many iconic cinematic images are matte paintings—the Statue of Liberty buried in the sand at the end of *Planet of the Apes* (1968), the warehouse into which the Arc of the Covenant is secreted

Matte paintings have created numerous iconic images in cinema, such as this twist ending of *Planet of the Apes* (1968, Twentieth Century–Fox). Frame enlargement.

at the conclusion of *Raiders of the Lost Ark* (1981), the mountainside home of Philip Vandamm in *North by Northwest* (1959). The vistas of ancient Rome in *Quo Vadis* (1951), *Ben-Hur* (1959), *Spartacus* (1960), *Gladiator* (2000), and comparable films are matte paintings. Bodega Bay lay several miles from the water, and Hitchcock wanted a bayside location, so Albert Whitlock painted one. Viewers of *The Birds* (1963) hardly suspected that they were looking at a painted town. Sets that viewers may believe are on-camera locations photographed as live action frequently prove to be matte-painted fabrications. The penthouse office of Howard Roarke (Gary Cooper) in *The Fountainhead* (1949) has an elaborate and soaring ceiling that is a matte painting. Much of the Hindley Hall mansion that Gregory Peck walks through in *The Paradine Case* (1947) is rendered as a series of matte paintings, which include staircases, chandeliers, and even banisters that the actors walk behind. Hitchcock was particularly fond of matte paintings and valued Whitlock's contributions to his later films. The shocking image of a farmer with his eyes pecked out in *The Birds* is a matte painting. During a two-minute sequence in *Torn Curtain* (1967), Paul Newman walks through an East Berlin museum that was created as a series of six matte paintings. The sets were extremely minimal, and most of the locale in each shot was painted. The length of the sequence flaunts the trompe l'oeil effect, daring viewers to see through the 2D painted illusion, but few do. The sets today would be called "virtual." Nothing was there for the actor to interact with. A concept artist on the film recalled, "In this shot Newman had nothing real to react to, and being a Method actor, he needed an environment. So he asks, 'Hitch, what's my motivation for walking in on a straight line?' And Hitchcock says, 'If you don't you will disappear under the matte painting.'"[44]

Virtual sets tend to be considered the provenance of the digital era, but in fact they emerged early in cinema history. In *Since You Went Away* (1944), Claudette Colbert leans out of the upstairs window of a house that is entirely rendered as a matte painting. In 1922 Ferdinand Earle, a matte painter, was shooting actors against black velvet for subsequent compositing into matte-painted environments in his production of *The Rubaiyat of Omar Khayam* (1923). As a *Motion Picture Classic* article in the period stated, the actors didn't know whether "they were acting in the palace of a Sultan, in a dingy hut, on a desert waste, or in a grove of cypresses."[45] About the key role that painting supplied in cinema, director Michael Powell stated, "You hardly ever built more of a set than was necessary for the action with the actors. The rest was added in afterwards as a painting."[46] Powell certainly knew. *Black Narcissus* (1948), which he directed, created its Himalayan locations on a London studio set with matte paintings created by Walter Percy Day. George Lucas loved matte paintings and used them as an essential means for creating the alien worlds in the *Star Wars* movies.

The epic canvas of *Gone with the Wind* (1939) was indeed that, with painted vistas complimenting the live-action cinematography. Producer David O. Selznick knew that innovative visual effects would be crucial to his ability to get the film made. "I could not even hope to put the picture on the screen properly without an even more extensive use of special effects than had ever before been attempted in the business."[47] The film's huge landscapes could not be constructed full size; they were manufactured instead through split-screen effects used to double the size of crowds, front and rear projection, miniature projection, and especially matte painting. Clarence Slifer, who worked with Jack Cosgrove, the head of Selznick's special effects department, estimated that approximately 100 matte paintings were used in the film,[48] creating set extensions, filling out landscapes, and adding skies above sets and actors. Most are blended quite subliminally into the scenes. Live action was shot with a matte box obscuring the portion of the frame where the painting would appear. A few frames of test footage from the scene were then projected onto a sheet of gray Masonite, the shot was traced along with the matte line, and the painting was created and color-tested to match the live action and then optically printed into the unexposed area of original negative. The work was complicated, requiring that Cosgrove and his crew calculate varying sizes for the matte lines, depending on a scene's content and shooting characteristics. As Slifer noted, "There are several things that have to be watched carefully when matting on original photography. [Most of the film's matte shots were composited with original camera negative rather than into dupe footage struck from the negative. This was a riskier procedure but produced better-

looking images.] The width of your matte blend is controlled by the focal
length of the lens, the camera stop, and the distance between the lens and the
matte. As you stop your lens down the matte becomes sharper and pulls into
the picture, so you have to watch for people's heads being cut off and also the
danger of overshooting into the unfinished portion of the set."[49] To match
the color and lighting with live-action footage, the paintings had to be filmed
under a variety of light conditions and at varying focal lengths.

Slifer had designed an aerial optical printer that enabled him to achieve
new effects with matte painting. With aerial image printing, an image (such
as a matte painting) is projected to a focal plane in space (rather than onto a
surface) where it can be photographed by the camera in the optical printer.
It may then be combined with a master plate containing live-action footage
and as well as footage of other optical elements. Cosgrove and Slifer used
aerial printing throughout the film to add smoke or fire effects to matte
paintings. The smoke pouring from a locomotive in the sequence establishing
the Atlanta train station is an optical effect created by printing footage of
smoke in front of an aerial image of a matte painting of the station roof. By
photographing the painting behind the footage of smoke (which had been

Clarence Slifer used an aerial image to composite smoke from the locomotive
engine in front of the matte painting representing the station roof. *Gone with the
Wind* (1939, Warner Bros.). Frame enlargement.

filmed against a clear background), the smoke seemed to naturally cover the train station roof as it would in a 3D world.

Aerial imaging also features in the big pull-back of Scarlett and Gerald O'Hara against a dramatic sunset in the scene where he tells her that he will leave Tara to her after his death and that land is the only thing that endures, that is worth fighting and dying for. The location was synthesized in two ways. For much of the scene, Scarlett and her father stand in a two-shot, framed against the dramatic cloud formations of a stormy sky. The background image was culled from footage Slifer had shot in 1938 of the sky around Los Angeles following a huge rainstorm. The studio asked him to shoot this footage with the intention of using it as background plates in the movie, and it appears in this scene and elsewhere. The scene ends with a reverse-angle cut to the famous pull-back showing the characters as silhouettes standing next to a tree with Tara visible in the distance. The sky this time is a matte painting. The shot composites live-action footage of the characters (stand-ins doubling for Vivien Leigh and Thomas Mitchell) with two matte paintings, depicting the sky and a distant view of Tara (projected into the composite as an aerial image). The tree in the foreground is a miniature model. The complexity of the shot is apparent in the less-than-perfect registration—the pull-back (which was created in the optical printer as a visual effect on the paintings) occasions noticeable jiggling among the image elements.

Cosgrove's department had a nodal tripod for their Technicolor cameras, which enabled them to do modest pans and tilts in shots involving miniatures. When Scarlett returns to Twelve Oaks Plantation, now devastated by the war, she stands in the ruined mansion at the foot of the grand staircase. The lower part of the set was constructed in scale, and the upper portion, showing the top of the staircase and second floor of the mansion, was created as a hanging miniature. Like matte paintings, hanging miniatures are among the most enduring of effects techniques. The miniature model hangs in space near the camera and is positioned so that its lines of perspective match exactly those of the more distant set as viewed on the camera axis. Nodal cameras pivot from a point corresponding with the optical center of the lens, facilitating modest pans or tilts on miniatures because no motion perspective is introduced. (If introduced, motion perspective would reveal the disparity in the positioning of the miniature and the set.) As Scarlett looks at the ruined mansion, a pan and tilt follow the implied line of her gaze and reveal more of the set and the hanging miniature and establish a visual bridge connecting the two.

Nodal camera mounts could create pans and tilts when matte paintings were erected on glass panels placed between the camera and the set, but when paintings were created and photographed in the laboratory, the live-action camera would be locked down. In the decade following *Gone with the Wind*, however, the Dupy Duplicator enabled motion control camerawork connecting live-action footage with matte paintings created and filmed in a studio's special effects department. The system debuted with a shot in *Easter Parade* (1948) that tilts down from a matte painting of Manhattan buildings to a studio set depicting Fifth Avenue. The opening and closing of *An American in Paris* (1951) used the system to dynamically conjoin partial sets with matte paintings depicting set extensions. In a shot introducing Jerry (Gene Kelly), the camera pans from a sidewalk café (the real set) up the three-story building where he lives, revealing him looking out a top-story window. Above the second-floor level, the image is a painting, including roof and sky, and the motion control blend of the image elements is perfect. There is no giveaway as "the camera" seems to execute a single, unbroken move from the street to the rooftop. I use quotation marks because the motion control move is executed by the live-action camera on set and by the laboratory camera photographing the matte painting. The only giveaway in the scene is tongue-in-cheek. The image of Gene Kelly looking out his window is a photograph placed onto the matte painting, and it looks more two-dimensional than the painting! In the film's last shot, Jerry and Lise (Leslie Caron) embrace on the outdoor staircase and the camera tilts up to reveal the matte painting of a Paris cityscape. Henceforth in cinema, camera moves would create perceptually convincing linkages between live action and painted environments, although viewers with careful eyes might perceive the absence of motion perspective in the painted elements. (Using a multiplane set-up with miniature models photographed on a camera move with a painting as the furthermost element could provide a convincing pre-digital simulation of motion perspective relative to a 2D painted surface.)

In the pre-digital era, matte paintings remained 2D effects elements, which was part of their charm. As accomplished as *Gone with the Wind*'s effects are, they show some of the limitations of optical compositing. The jitter in the pull-back from Scarlett and her father makes the aerial image of Tara seem to dance in the frame. Because the pull-back is created in the optical printer, it produces no motion perspective, accentuating the appearance of sky and plantation as flat planes rather than producing the effect of recession in space. As this chapter shows below, digital methods have enabled more immersive treatments of matte paintings and miniature models. In this respect, as with cinematography and performance, digital tools have accentuated the sensuousness and spatial depth-rendering capabilities of contemporary cinema. But digital methods are not breaking with past traditions as represented by the image blends in *Gone with the*

Wind or the virtual sets composited with painted environments in *Since You Went Away* or *An American in Paris*. Throughout its history, the medium of cinema has combined different imaging modes, and the elaborate compositing employed in *Citizen Kane, Gone with the Wind*, and countless other films represents the kind of hand-crafted imaging that Manovich identifies as existing only during cinema's pre-history and its digital present. Painted images play such a role in *Gone with the Wind* that Richard Rickitt was moved to describe the film not as live action but as "an often sumptuous blend of painting and live action."[50]

From 2D to 3D

The transition to digital tools has left the role played by miniature models in visual effects relatively unchanged. The lighthouse that plays such a key role in Martin Scorsese's *Shutter Island* is a miniature model. Peter Jackson's *The Lord of the Rings* offered a definitive demonstration that miniatures could coexist happily with digital methods. Moreover, miniatures are not merely holdovers from an analog era. Filmmakers such as Jackson or Christopher Nolan understand that a miniature on set can anchor digital effects with a palpable sense of physical reality. The term "miniature" often belies the size of the models. On the *Rings* films they were affectionately termed "bigatures" because of their imposing dimensions. The Helms Deep model, for example, was twenty feet across and placed in a huge valley thirty feet across and built with forced perspective so that with armies in the foreground of a shot, the fortress would appear small. The physicality provided to the film by the models elicited an honest approach from the designers who did not cheat the spatial layout. "We tend to be very architecturally honest. By that I mean if our miniature was built to a scale we could walk around it, and it would all look very real—we'd get to the rooms we wanted to get to . . . the internal structure of rooms and corridors was all logically laid out. Also, the camber has to be correct, the cobblestones—right down to the guttering. Everything has to be correct."[51] Moreover, many of the film's all-digital characters, such as the Wargs, were modeled first as maquettes for the artist to study before creating them in the computer. The maquettes showed the Warg's girth, weight, and carriage in real 3D terms. One could walk around them and look at them from different angles. This made the task of replicating them in computer space much easier. This procedure holds true as a general principle of digital character design—computer-designed characters frequently begin life as miniature models.

If digital methods didn't much change the role played by miniature models or their design, the same was not true for matte painting. Miniatures remain what they have always been—physical structures built in a shop. No one, however, works any longer with paint and paintbrush. Painting is performed in computer with a mouse and with electronic versions of brushes. Matte artists who transitioned to digital methods often found the process to be less sensual and physically pleasing than in the old days when they could walk around a painting, smell the paint, or concentrate on the feel of the brush in the hand and on glass, canvas, or Masonite. Bob Scifo said, "The worst part of switching from traditional painting to digital was you had no emotional tie to what you were doing. Painters have this sense of an actual emotional tie to the paint."[52] Michelle Moen, whose credits include *Gladiator*, remarked, "I hated painting on a computer because it wasn't physical anymore. The paintings I worked on were large, 6 feet by 3 feet, and on huge easels." She enjoyed the pleasure of creating something big. "With the computer, it lost all that bigness. The computer was antisocial, too. I'd been working with cameramen, other matte painters, other people, and suddenly I'm in a cubicle staring at a monitor."[53]

On the other hand, the digital realm offered a more powerful toolset. The initial exploration of digital painting occurred in *Young Sherlock Holmes* (1985) in a scene where a medieval knight steps out of the church's stained glass window and menaces a priest. The window and the wall of the church were matte paintings that were photographed and scanned into a computer where their colors and textures were blended with the live-action plate and the animated version of the knight (one of cinema's first CG characters). Matte artist Chris Evans found he got better results with the digital tools. "Matching colors between a painting and the live-action plate and hiding the matte lines are always the greatest challenges in a matte painting, but in digital you can pick the exact color you want from the plate and transfer it into the painting."[54] By merging and dissolving pixels, the blend line between live action and painting can be made invisible.

The final shot of *Die Hard 2: Die Harder* (1990) is a painting created traditionally with brush on a thirteen-by-fifteen-foot canvas showing a snowy airport runway covered with airplanes, military vehicles, emergency equipment, and the film's principal characters along with extras. The painting was digitized from four photographs taken at differing distances and composited with six live-action plates showing characters grouped around the vehicles. The four photographs of the painting were treated as keyframes in an animation sequence, with interpolated footage simulating a thirty-five-second pull-back by a camera. The illusion is very good. Few if any viewers watching the film's final shot suspected they were looking at a painting.

Joe Fordham points out, "This painting still hangs on the wall at Industrial Light and Magic. . . . It is still impressive seen up close in person. Huge!"[55]

Trompe l'oeil is the mode of matte painting. The digital realm, however, enabled matte paintings to interact with live-action components and become more three-dimensional. Matte paintings no longer needed to remain flat, stationary elements in a locked-down shot. Steven Spielberg's *Hook* (1991) demonstrated where the future of matte painting in cinema would be found. The film contains what is probably the first instance of a camera-projected matte painting. ILM's artists digitized a painting of Neverland and texture-wrapped it around a geometric computer model of the island for a scene in which Peter Pan (Robin Williams) flies over the island. Because it was mapped to the scene's 3D CG geometry, the matte painting displayed motion perspective as Peter passed by overhead. Rotating the geometry to simulate point-of-view changes in the flyover produced a similar transformation in the painting. The painting became a 2½D object—not fully 3D because the flat surface was a texture wrapping around the wireframe model, and if the model were not properly rotated, the edges of the wrapping would be visible. But this innovation was very influential—matte paintings henceforth could be dynamic elements in a scene, integrated with camera moves and reflecting appropriate changes in 3D perspective. Matte paintings ceased being planar objects marking the rear wall of an effects shot. They became immersive extensions of 3D space.

The invention of Photoshop by John and Thomas Knoll transformed the creation of cinematic paintings. Knoll worked at ILM at the time, and Adobe placed his software on the commercial market in 1990. Photoshop enabled filmmakers to paint over visible matte lines, blending and blurring image elements, changing pixel information to create perfect joins between disparate image types. It also facilitated the integration of matte paintings with dynamic, 3D landscapes because it integrated well with other software in an image production pipeline. Autodesk Maya, for example, is a widely used program for building the geometry onto which a matte painting can be wrapped. Many matte paintings begin as concept sketches, rough drawings of the landscape that subsequently will be painted. By importing a concept sketch into Maya, an artist can build the geometry underlying the buildings, streets, signage, cliffs, bluffs, mountains, and whatever other features might be included in the sketch or be necessary for the scene. These are created as primitive forms from cubes and cylinders and, using tools in Maya to split and divide polygons or extrude their faces, they can be extended across the location depicted in the sketch as its underlying wireframe forms. Using a free transform tool, the polygons can be warped and stretched to fit the edges and contours of the solid objects in the sketch. The geometry is created in rough form and according to the view established in a camera projection. This establishes the perspective through which the scene will be viewed, in terms of lens focal length, camera position, and aspect ratio. Once built, the scene geometry may be lit with a key or directional light to establish shadows and highlights and can also be rendered as an occlusion pass, a specular pass, Z-depth and alpha-channel passes, and texture passes. The wireframe model can be rendered as a separate pass, as can foreground, midground, and background groupings of the scene's objects. If there is to be a camera move on the painting without a live-action plate, this can be keyframed in Maya as an animated move across scene geometry. If the painting will be composited with a live-action plate filmed with a camera move, then the move might be motion-tracked with a matchmoving program and then imported into Maya or a compositing program like Shake or Fusion for final render.

All the renders in Maya can be saved as a PSD file, a format specific to Photoshop that preserves the renders as separate layers which can be manipulated in the matte painting as it is created in Photoshop. Thus, before any painting occurs in Photoshop, the image may already possess considerable depth, texture, and light information. Painting proceeds based on the render layers, the camera projection, and the geometry established in Maya. Light, shadow, and color effects are brushed on the image, layers and masks are used to add density and depth to image elements, and there is much cloning and multiplication of image elements. These often include textures cloned from photographs. In *The Lord of the Rings: The Two Towers* (2002), for example, Sam and Frodo stand above the River Anduin, which cuts across a vast plain, with the mountains and the city of Minas Tirith visible in the distance. The plain and the mountains are matte paintings because, epic as New Zealand's landscape is, no plain this large exists there, nor are there such dramatic snow-capped vistas. Mathieu Raynault created the sky by cloning photographs he had taken near Wellington and adding painted elements to them, and he mixed photographic textures with painted effects for the mountains as well.

Such procedures involve more than cutting and pasting; software does not substitute for artistry. Digital matte painters need to understand what they see from nature in terms of light, texture, and tonal qualities and must be able to reproduce this. As Max Dennison, who created matte paintings for *The Lord of the Rings* films, *The Da Vinci Code* (2006), *Superman Returns* (2006), and *Star Wars: Episode III* (2005), said, "ILM used to ask all their interviewees for their Matte Department to do an oil painting copy of a photograph. This was extremely clever as it allowed them to see instantly if the applicant could accurately reproduce what he/she was seeing." He added, "Copying and pasting photographs, or using a software package to do this for you will not get you a finished matte painting. Only the matte painter and their well-trained skills will do this."[56]

Matte painting has flourished in the digital era. *The Kite Runner* (2008) tells a story about Afghanistan in the 1970s and subsequently under Taliban rule. The film was shot in the Chinese city of Kashgar, a desert city surrounded by a flat landscape, unlike the mountainous region of Kabul where the story is set. An extensive set of matte paintings created the mountains of Kabul, including a 360-degree painting used in all of the film's aerial shots that depict kite flying. Topographic aerial maps were used to create Kabul's terrain using Maya and Photoshop, and digital set extensions transformed Kashgar into Kabul, with snow created as a digital paint effect on building roofs. Since many of these shots involve camera movement, the painting had to be motion-tracked to the live-action plates. Eighty aerial photographs were combined to extend the vista of Kashgar, and a haze of smoke from stoves and dust from chimneys was animated as a 3D fluid dynamic and composited over the set extensions and matte paintings. Many of the shots in which the painted mountains appear are quite epic in scale, contrasting the diminutive size of a vehicle or person with the towering bulk of the mountains. The compositions often are breathtaking, as are the light and color changes in the paintings according to the time of day or night in which the scene appears.

The Road (2008) presents a bleak post-apocalyptic landscape through which a father and son trudge, trying to reach the coast and hoping for deliverance. The film was shot along a rural highway in Pennsylvania and on a few post-Katrina locations in New Orleans that reflected the hurricane's destructive effects. But all these locales were dressed out with matte paintings and digital geometry to extend the vistas or add texture and atmosphere. Living vegetation was digitally removed from many shots, 3D CG billboards were added to the rural Pennsylvania road, and sky replacements from matte painting made the landscapes look somber, wintry, and barren. When the father and son walk through an abandoned city, they pause before a glass-windowed office building that shows extensive fire damage and see the dark outlines of people on the upper stories. The scene was shot using a Pittsburgh office building, which a matte artist transformed by painting in fire damage, broken glass, and exposed steel girders, and with the people added as a traveling matte effect. The building was a real one, but digital painting took it into the imaginary realm necessitated by the story.

As these examples suggest, today it is often difficult to divide matte paintings from miniatures or the live action components in a scene. Matte paintings are not a 2D addition to a live-action scene. Selective paint effects can be applied to real locations, as in *The Road*. Paintings can incorporate photographic detail and texture, as in *Lord of the Rings*, and paintings can be actively integrated with the scenic dimensions onscreen by being texture-projected onto wireframe geometry, as in *Hook*. The geometry can be rotated to simulate camera moves, with accompanying changes of perspective occurring on the texture-wrapped painting. It is, therefore, not easy to find a clear boundary dividing the domain of matte painting from other image creation tools. In this regard, the art of matte painting has changed considerably from earlier periods when a painting was, indeed, a painting and distinct from live action. Craig Barron, cofounder of Matte World Digital and coauthor of *The Invisible Art*, the authoritative history of matte painting, points out, "It is difficult to categorize what a matte painting shot is today. . . . There are no rules. We do what it takes to produce a realistic illusion. Most filmmakers still call what we do matte shots, and we like that because we see our work as an extension of the original craft. But, it's more accurate to say we are involved in environment creation."[57]

The Digital Backlot

If the integration of matte painting with 3D elements of scenic design represents a distinct change from the past, in another respect digital artists are returning to the past by replicating the venerable Hollywood studio tradition of making films on the backlot. The term "digital backlot" designates the practice of building story locations as CG environments that are composited with live action. As Barron notes, "I think filmmakers might be rediscovering the old studio idea of making their films on the backlot again. . . . You don't need to go on location if it's not really there."[58] Throughout the 1930s and 1940s, during the high period of the Hollywood studios, indoor sets doubled as outdoor locations and rear-screen projection suggested that the actors were standing beside an ocean or were driving on a road or highway. By the late 1960s and early 1970s, however, with the collapse of the studio system and the loss of property and long-term labor contracts, films tended to be shot on location rather than on elaborate studio sets, particularly the movies that have come to be known as the New American Cinema. *Easy Rider* (1969), *The French Connection* (1972), and others in that wave of production derived an aura of grit and drama from using real environments. Dennis Hopper took a 16mm camera to Mardi Gras for a sequence in *Easy Rider*, and the harsh, amateurish appearance and raw, unfiltered imagery of the city's festivities amounted to a manifesto against the tradition of fine-crafted imagery that had accompanied the built-environments of the studio system.

The shift to location shooting began in the 1950s in such films as *On the Waterfront* (1954) and then flourished in the 1960s; it also characterized European cinema. François Truffaut's New Wave manifesto in *Cahiers du Cinéma*, an essay entitled "A Certain Tendency in the French Cinema," decried the reliance on studio sets and overly insistent production design and championed the use of real streets and buildings as sets for filmmaking. *The 400 Blows* (1959) and *Cleo from 5 to 7* (1963) made seminal use of Paris locations. Heated battles ensued among filmmakers and among film critics and scholars between what Charles Affron and Mirella Jona Affron called "the advocates of constructed sets and the partisans of real streets and buildings." But despite the differences of opinion among advocates for real place or fabricated locale, the role of cinematic art direction in each remained quite similar: shaping an environment so that it becomes expressive of character and story and the moods, tones, and conflicts associated with them. Whether the location is built or found, this creative task remains. The extensive location shoots in the era that *Easy Rider* helped define led many studios to shut down their matte painting departments, a notable exception being Disney. The New American Cinema persisted until the middle of the 1970s, and while location filming remains an important legacy of this movement, by mid-decade *Star Wars* had revived the tradition of heavily composited effects shots and in particular matte painting as a means for simulating imaginative landscapes, helping to return American cinema to the backlot practices that had heretofore prevailed.

In this respect, today's digital backlot maintains a continuity of style and aesthetics with cinema in the photochemical era. Clint Eastwood's *Changeling* (2009) and David Fincher's *Zodiac* (2007) exemplify this continuity. Each film builds an urban environment from composites of live action, matte paintings, miniatures, and CGI rather than location shooting. In each case, the locations no longer exist because the films are period pieces. *Changeling* takes place in Los Angeles in 1928, and *Zodiac* in San Francisco during the late 1960s and early 1970s. As Craig Barron noted, you needn't go on location when it's not there. But while the environments are not there for in-situ filming, they can be built as convincing replicas. Eastwood's film portrays the conflict between a mother, Christine Collins (Angelina Jolie), whose son has vanished, and a corrupt police department intent on covering up its own culpability in the case. While Eastwood generally is not identified as a director who relies on visual effects, he has used them in subtle and effective ways, particularly in the late stages of his career. Mount Suribachi, for example, in *Flags of Our Fathers* (2006) is a CG object. *Changeling* contains 180 effects shots—set extensions, matte paintings, crowd augmentation using Massive software, CG buildings, vehicles, and trolley cars. Like productions of the classical Hollywood era, many scenes were shot on Universal Studio's main street, a standing set that has appeared in many films and was digitally dressed in this one to look like L.A. in the period. Eastwood and visual effects supervisor Michael Owens studied period photographs of L.A. and simulated the film's environments based on this information. Of their visual effects strategy, Owens said, "We wanted the most dramatic impact we could get, but without the effects being too much in the forefront. We wanted to show that this was the time and place, but we didn't want to be in your face about it. The look of the city, setting that time period, just gave the story a little more credence and helped to involve the audience more. That was the intention."[59]

In the opening establishing shot, the camera pans along a skyline view of Los Angeles and then booms down to the wooded neighborhood where Christine lives. The shot combines a camera-projected matte painting of the city skyline with live-action footage of her neighborhood that was shot in San Dimas, outside the city. The painting is animated with a motion-tracked camera matching the move in the live-action plate. CG animation of foreground trees hides the transition between the painting and live action. As the camera booms down to the San Dimas street, a CG cable car with tracks and telephone lines transforms the location into a period street, and the glimpse of Los Angeles at the end of the street is another matte painting, projected to simulate perspective shifts in accordance with the live-action camera. The film's final shot also combines live action, CGI, and matte painting—audaciously so, with the shot lingering onscreen for two and a half minutes as the end credits scroll. It shows Christine, who has never found her son but who still maintains hope, walking out of the police station and into the city where she vanishes in the distance. The street scene is Universal's backlot set, built out with digital extensions and a matte painting that adds some towering high-rise buildings at midground and extends the city's architecture to the vanishing point. Pedestrians on the street are composed of a few extras filmed separately and replicated using Massive. All the automobiles, trolley cars, trolley tracks, signage (including a theater marquee advertising *It Happened One Night*), and telephone wires are CG elements. The blends are perfectly executed; with its duration, the shot invites and its illusion sustains the viewer's close scrutiny. This emphasis marks a difference from the way that matte paintings were used in the analog era. Although in some cases, such as the concluding shots of *Raiders of the Lost Ark* or *The Birds,* a painting might be held on screen for more than a minute at a time, in general the presentation did not invite close scrutiny from the viewer. Because the painting represented the most distant portions of the set or location, the dramatic center of interest in a scene typically was elsewhere, in the foreground or midground, and shot composition did not stress the incorporation of the painted background in the way that *Changeling* does.

Some of the film's environments are entirely synthetic. Christine takes a taxi to the police station to hear testimony from a witness who may know her son's fate. As her taxi turns the corner in front of the police station and stops there, almost everything that one sees on screen is a CG object or a matte painting. The street is full of pedestrians, heavy traffic, densely spaced buildings, and networks of wires hanging overhead. All this looks real, as if it has been photographed on set with Angelina Jolie, and yet almost nothing was. The virtual set was mostly bluescreen and included only the taxi, a bit of sidewalk, and several parked vehicles. The virtual set was relatively small, and the taxi does not traverse much distance on screen. The short focal length composition, however, exaggerates depth perspective and makes the cab seem to travel more than it does, and the elaborate CG environment built around it expands the urban vista dramatically. But the set's virtual nature does not preclude naturalism. Even small details are true to the environment. As the taxi pulls up in the foreground, its windshield and side windows catch reflections of the surrounding buildings. These are motion-tracked painted elements, and they connect the live-action taxi with the digital world it inhabits. This digital world emulates L.A.'s appearance in the period according to conventions of naturalism rather than eye-catching spectacle. The style is recessive; the production design does not attempt to show off the digital toolbox that was employed. Eastwood has been among the most stylistically conservative of contemporary directors, one beholden to the filmmaking norms of studio

The final shot of *Changeling* (2008, Universal Pictures) augments a digitally enhanced studio backlot location with a matte painting held on screen throughout the film's lengthy closing credits. Frame enlargement.

pictures in the classical era, and his unfussy, highly effective use of digital imagery in *Changeling* shows how compatible these modern tools are with a filmmaking practice inflected by the norms of an earlier period.

As such, the production design exemplifies the level of décor identified by Charles and Mirella Jona Affron as punctuative. In their study *Sets in Motion*, an analysis of production design in films from the silent era to 1960, they classify designs according to degrees of intensity.[60] In the level they refer to as punctuative, sets help to articulate narrative by functioning as more than background; they are stylistically dense and expressive in ways that emphasize time, place, and mood but without insisting upon their own presence as stylistic artifacts. While the Affrons write about sets throughout their book, they acknowledge that in practice what they have designated as a "set" may consist of numerous elements, which include locations, miniatures, and paintings. Thus while the urban environment appearing on screen in the last shot of *Changeling* is not a set in the sense of a single locale, as a built environment that is part of the film's production design it poetically conveys the irresolvable mystery that underlies the narrative: what has happened to Christine's son? In the film's last act, she learns that he was abducted by a child molester and imprisoned with other boys on a ranch, where some were killed. She also learns from a boy who successfully escaped that her son, too, tried to get away but may have been shot and killed by the kidnapper. His fate remains uncertain, and, as Christine leaves the police station, she maintains a hopeful attitude; but an end title informs us that, while she continued to search, she never located him. The urban environment that swallows her up, therefore, at film's end conveys the impenetrability of the circumstances surrounding the boy's fate. Christine walks away from the camera with her burden and disappears, swallowed by an environment that pays her no heed. The spatial density of the city expresses an epistemological opacity, a condition of concealed secrets, hidden fates, and it therefore evokes mood and moral as well as period. It provides the final punctuation in a narrative that ends without resolution.

Zodiac portrays efforts by police and city journalists to discover the identity of the Zodiac killer, who terrorized San Francisco and surrounding areas with a string of serial killings that began in 1968. As discussed in chapter 2, the film uses digital methods to create a naturalistic, almost documentary-like style. Fincher shot the murder scenes on many of the actual sites, but these and other city locations had to be altered significantly in order to show San Francisco as it appeared at the time. An early establishing shot, for example, introduces the city with an aerial view that sweeps from the waters of the bay to the Port Authority terminal and surrounding buildings. The terminal is now a shopping complex. The area today looks more upscale than it did in the period, and many buildings have disappeared or undergone renovation. Thus Fincher could not go on location and shoot what he found, if his goal was to depict San Francisco in historically accurate terms. Although the location exists, it would need to be filmed as a built environment rather than as a found environment. Accordingly, the flyover of the Port Authority terminal is an all-CG sequence, consisting of a geometrical model of the site treated as a 3D matte painting and given animated effects, which include CG cars traveling along a street. The shot was built from architecturally accurate information derived from city blueprints from the period and photographs taken by a U-2 spy plane. Photogrammetric analysis enabled the effects artists to assemble the scene's 3D geometry. Photogrammetry is a method of extracting the 3D structure of a scene from 2D images, in this case photographs of the Port Authority area showing what it looked like at the time. Lines of sight by the cameras in the photographs are triangulated to recover the underlying dimensional structure. Lighting information can be recovered as well, enabling digital modelers to simulate highlights and shadowing on the buildings in ways consistent with how light would be distributed in the actual location. Paul Debevec at the University of California at Berkeley developed algorithms permitting the derivation of a scene's dimensional structure from only a few widely spaced photographs, as well as a method of view-dependent texturing enabling the projection of detailed 2D information from the images onto a scene's 3D geometry.[61] This approach and others like it furnished methods of scene building that have now become quite standard in contemporary film. Chapter 5 discusses more about photogrammetry and Debevec's work with image-based lighting.

The photogrammetric methods, the wireframe geometry built from them, and the digital painting and CG animation laid atop the geometry create a photographically convincing helicopter shot of the port area, one that performs the traditional narrative task of establishing a location. Like the closing shot of *Changeling*, it is an audacious shot because everything in it is CG and because the action takes place in bright sunshine, lighting that would reveal flaws rather than concealing them. But very few of the film's viewers, unless they knew these production details, were aware they were watching a fabricated environment on screen. It is, however, an indexical environment in that the CG imagery was built from archival sources and retains their trace.

Other environments in the film are all-CG, such as a high-angle shot from atop the Golden Gate Bridge or the digital matte painting introducing Vallejo and the Napa River on the Fourth of July. Many others are augmentations of CG and live action, such as the murder scene at Washington and Cherry

The period view of San Francisco shown in a helicopter flyover is an all-digital environment constructed using photogrammetric methods. *Zodiac* (2007, Paramount Pictures). Frame enlargement.

Streets, where Zodiac shoots a taxi driver, and the subsequent police investigation at the site. The intersection no longer looked as it did then, so Fincher re-created much of it as CG with the actors on bluescreen sets. When Mark Ruffalo, as Detective Dave Toschi, walks along the street tracing Zodiac's path, he was filmed with a mobile bluescreen, permitting the actor to be composited into a digital environment. Based on photographs from the period, the buildings appearing in the scene are alternately CG objects and matte paintings. Live-action camera moves were tracked onto the CG environment so that, as the camera travels with Toschi along the street, the corresponding motion perspective is replicated in the surrounding digital environment.

These methods enabled Fincher to visualize San Francisco in historically accurate terms, something that could not be done with this degree of perceptual realism using a traditional photochemical approach. Under that approach, scenes could be dressed with props and period vehicles to suggest the era, but the large-scale flyovers of the port of Vallejo or the exacting visual re-creation of the environments where the killings took place would be beyond these methods. Moreover, *Zodiac*'s approach exemplifies the goals of location shooting; the locales are reproduced reliably, albeit as constructions rather than as found environments. The digital backlot, in this case, permits the filmmaker to replicate historical locations from a now-distant era according to parameters of indexical realism. Far from undermining such realism, *Zodiac*'s digital design establishes a realist aesthetic, measured from and authenticated by the photographic record of place in the period.

Fincher employed built environments more radically on his next film, *The Curious Case of Benjamin Button*. Most of its locations were filmed on partial sets and bluescreen environments. The film's iconic image—the backward-running clock invented by Gateau (Elias Koteas)—is a CG object, and the train station in which it prominently hangs and which appears in twenty-nine shots throughout the film is a 3D digital model lit, painted, and dressed differently according to the time period in which it appears. When Benjamin sits with his dying father at sunset on a lakeside dock, the country house behind them is a CG object, and the beautiful sunset and sky before them is a digital matte painting. The lake was real but its placid surface was digitally altered to add currents of motion appropriate for the scene's dramatic context. The most impressive of the film's built environments appears during the lengthy section portraying young Benjamin's sojourns at sea, working as a hand on the *Chelsea*, a tugboat. These are the first sections in the film where Brad Pitt appears as an actor onscreen with the other players. The tug travels throughout the Mississippi River, up the eastern seaboard, into the Atlantic, and to Russia's Murmansk harbor. Each of these environments—the New Orleans docks, the Mississippi, the New York skyline, Murmansk—is an all-digital creation. The tug was a full-size model shot on a bluescreen set and attached to a gimbal that rocked it to simulate waves, and live-action footage shot with the model was inserted into the synthetic environments. The rivers and oceans through which it sails were rendered according to fluid dynamics, and cities and docks were built as 3D models or matte paintings according to archival records of how these places looked in the period. When World War II begins, the *Chelsea* helps to patrol the Atlantic searching for U-boats, and it goes down in combat with one. The *Chelsea*'s captain defiantly rams the U-boat in a sequence that is all CG when the action is covered in long shot. These are intercut with close views of the actors on the tug's bluescreen set. Benjamin's sojourns on the *Chelsea* represent a major portion of the film, all done on a digital backlot.

Evolution of Backlot Filming

A comparison of two maritime battle epics—*The Sea Hawk* (1940) and *Master and Commander* (2004)—shows the advances that digital tools have brought to backlot filming and also the continuities of style and technique that connect contemporary films with the visual effects methods of classical Hollywood. *The Sea Hawk* was a state-of-the-art Warner Bros. production planned as an immediate follow-up to *Captain Blood* (1935), a swashbuckler whose extraordinary popularity launched the career of Errol Flynn. The production was delayed, but this enabled Warners to develop an innovative maritime studio tank where full-scale models of English and Spanish warships

The sequences showing the *Chelsea* at sea present virtual environments constructed by motion-tracking greenscreen footage into matte-painted environments. *The Curious Case of Benjamin Button* (2009, Warner Bros.). Frame enlargement.

could be filmed in simulated seas. *Master and Commander* was a Twentieth Century–Fox production with more than 700 visual effects shots created by ILM, Weta Workshop, Asylum, and other firms. Both films depict naval warfare involving English ships captained by heroes, played by Errol Flynn and Russell Crowe. In *The Sea Hawk*, Flynn battles Spanish galleons, while *Master and Commander* depicts on ongoing series of confrontations between Crowe's ship *The Surprise* and a deadly French adversary, *The Acheron*. *Master and Commander* is set almost entirely at sea, while *The Sea Hawk* integrates the high-sea adventures with scenes on land.

The key point is that both films were made using simulated maritime environments. Neither was shot on location at sea. Warner Bros.' policy was to avoid the risks inherent in building practical ships and shooting scenes with them live on the ocean, as MGM had done with *Mutiny on the Bounty* (1935). It was far easier to build an environment at the studio and work in its controlled confines. Thus, as Rudy Behlmer writes, "*The Sea Hawk* can be regarded as the high-water mark of epics made on a studio lot."[62] Peter Weir, director of *Master and Commander*, similarly resolved to avoid location work: "I had read all the books about films shot at sea, including *Moby Dick* and *Jaws*, and that had decided me on spending as little time at sea as possible. A film like this could have easily spiraled out of control if we had tried to shoot more of it out on the ocean."[63]

Flynn's naval heroics in *The Sea Hawk* are created from a blend of miniature and full-scale models filmed in the studio's maritime tank and on a backlot lake. The massive tank was big enough to hold a 135-foot English man-of-war and a 165-foot Spanish ship, placed on steel foundations and a track-and-wheel system that enabled the models to be maneuvered in simulations of naval combat. The tank was deep enough that, when filled with water, wounded and dying seamen could be filmed toppling from the ships' rigging and decks and plunging into the water. A painted cyclorama behind the ships contained an image of sky and ocean, and Anton Grot, the film's brilliant art director, employed a wave machine for simulating ocean currents by projecting ripples behind the cyclorama. Complimenting the full-scale model were partial sets, built on a gimbal and rocked to convey the movements of a ship. Miniature ships were filmed on a lake backed by a painted sky. Each miniature had tiny, working cannons and was maneuvered by an operator concealed from the camera's view. In films of the period, miniatures on water were typically photographed by a camera placed just above the waterline using a wide-angle lens to keep water and ships in focus. Shooting at the waterline enhanced the ships' apparent size and bulk. The ships were shot at high speed, about 70 fps, according to Behlmer, in order to scale a miniature's behavior in line with the mass, inertia, and gravity that would properly operate on the full-size object the miniature stood in for. A formula stipulated the frames-per-second necessary for producing this simulation (the square root of the object's true size divided by the miniature's size and multiplied by twenty-four). The miniature ships were dressed with tiny figurines representing the crewmembers.

As ingenious as these methods are, they limited the filmmakers' abilities to depict the story situations. Visual point of view, for example, in the scenes where Flynn and his men are at sea is very restricted. The camera typically views Flynn backed by the ship's set with only a tiny portion of the muslin cyclorama sky being visible; the sky appears flat and without animated detail. Camera views avoid showing Flynn against the sea or sky, and camera movements are not used to connect characters with the maritime environment, as in, for example, a crane shot away from the ship showing it traversing the ocean. As a result of this limited perspective, it never feels true that Flynn and his men are at sea. In the story, they are, but not on screen. The images don't show the characters in their setting in ways that are perceptually convincing. The ocean is mainly an off-camera presence in the maritime scenes except when the miniatures are involved. And as splendid and charming as these models are, they look like miniatures placed on a body of water that lacks the density of the ocean. Photographing miniatures on water was always troublesome and challenging because water never scaled convincingly, even when filmed at high speed.

Like *The Sea Hawk*, *Master and Commander* is a dry-dock film, but its blend of traditional and digital effects enables it to create powerfully convincing images of men at sea, battling the elements and each other. Aubrey's ship,

The camera's line of sight is limited in scenes purporting to show Captain Thorpe (Errol Flynn) at sea. The ocean environment generally is not shown. Instead, characters are placed against the ship's set and a cyclorama representing the sky. *The Sea Hawk* (1941, Warner Bros.). Frame enlargement.

The Surprise, was built as a full-scale, 120-foot model mounted on a gimbal. Weta Workshop built detailed miniatures of *The Surprise* and *The Acheron* and filmed these against bluescreen, and in composited shots they were populated with CG characters whose activity—climbing rigging, engaging in combat—is far different from the nonmoving figurines that dressed *The Sea Hawk*'s miniatures. The ocean environment is a palpable presence in the film, and it is not computer generated. It derived from real location plates—35mm footage shot during a voyage around Cape Horn and composited with the miniature and full-scale ship models. Effects artists built the film's ocean by finding waves that they liked and rotoscoping these or portions of them from the footage. Each was then digitally adjusted as a separate layer for rendering, and the representation of a dense volume of water was constructed by compositing numerous layers of waves atop one another. Because the 2D ocean plates did not include any camera moves, these had to be motion-tracked into the footage, and in many cases camera perspective in the 35mm footage had to be transformed to match the positioning of the ship models. As an effects artist noted, "We weren't able to just take a single plate of water and stick one of our boats in it. We had to pull bits of water and waves from multiple plates and combine them to create a shot, building camera moves into it."[64] These manipulations result in a maritime world in which the camera can execute bold moves around a full-scale model with live actors, or a miniature composited with live and CG performers. In doing so, the process can reveal an adjoining ocean environment that looks dynamic and active. The digital ocean is animated with motion-tracked virtual camera moves to match what was done with the live-action camera. Screen action is blocked with more complex choreography than what can be found in *The Sea Hawk*. Characters and camera move in dynamic ways that unite the various 2D and 3D environments that have been composited together. The choreography creates believable parallax in relation to onscreen objects and the surrounding ocean. These camera moves, executed as live action and as digital animation tracked into the built environment, create perfect blends of 2D surfaces and 3D objects. As a result, characters and sea cohabit dramatic space in perceptually convincing ways, unlike *The Sea Hawk* where this relationship is suggested but not portrayed. Moreover, in the latter film, the changes between effects technologies stand out clearly. The full-scale model of Flynn's ship is distinct from the miniature version, as are the dramatic possibilities afforded by each. Dialogue, character interaction, and close-camera framings occur in the full-scale environment, whereas physical action shot from afar typifies the presentation of the miniatures. *Master and Commander* blends its effects tools imperceptibly. Nathan McGuinness of Asylum, the effects firm that built the film's CG ships and handled shots for the opening battle and the storm at sea, said, "At any point in the finished movie you could be watching a model ship in a CG sea or a CG ship in a real sea or even the cannon of a CG ship firing real fire and smoke at a model ship in a real sea. . . . We can merge the best of the old and new techniques."[65]

McGuinness said that the goal in using visual effects on the film was to "create a sense of complete realism." He added, "I hope not a single viewer even considered that what they were watching was not totally real."[66] David Fincher sought similar goals in *Zodiac* and *The Curious Case of Benjamin Button*, as did Eastwood and his effects artists on *Changeling*. These, in fact, have been the longstanding and traditional goals of production design in cinema. As Beverly Heisner writes, "The illusionistic world seen in films, whatever it recreated, had to look like its authentic counterpart. This was one of the primary goals of art directors in the twenties: How do we make film sets look real? By the late twenties that problem had been solved and art directors could convince an audience that what they were seeing was the real thing, whether Ancient Rome or the pioneer West."[67] Cedric Gibbons, MGM's supervising art director, wrote that a chief challenge for the art department "is to make something look real

The nautical world in *Master and Commander* (2003, Twentieth Century–Fox) is persuasive and convincing, but it is a virtual environment. The digital backlot is today's successor to studio filmmaking in the classical Hollywood era. Frame enlargement.

which is not."[68] At first glance, the credo of filmmakers who prefer to work on actual locations seems to be that, as Heisner summarizes, it has to be real to look real. But if that credo is flipped, "it has to look real to be real" becomes not only the maxim of studio and digital backlot filmmaking but states the broader goal of production design in general. Whether production design is studio-created or location-driven, as the Affrons point out, it aims to present a fictional world as convincingly real: "In that vast majority of films that seek to produce a strong reality effect, which is to say the vast majority of feature films, the dominant narrative intention would have suffered drastically had the set, constructed or not, appeared other than true to life."[69]

This condition holds as well for films whose built environments are intended to evoke a realm of stylization and fantasy. The virtual sets, chiaroscuro lighting, and selective color placement in *Sin City* (2005) evoke a world that remains stylistically consistent and true to its intentions for the duration of the narrative. The creation of visual effects environments is a more encompassing domain than set design or art direction as these traditionally have been understood. Unlike a physical set, the digital set does not exist on camera and is created in the render operations and compositing that follows. *Avatar*'s (2009) lush rainforest world of Pandora was constructed by Weta using a library of 3,000 plants and trees, and while it is precisely detailed in the finished film, it was largely a virtual world for the actors working on greenscreen sets. Nevertheless, the creation of this visual effects environment proceeded in traditional ways, with concept sketches and paintings and physical models pointing the way to the digital designs. Robert Stromberg, one of the film's production designers, stated, "Even though the Pandora environments would be virtual, they went through the same growing pains you'd have with any set design, and we had to follow all the guidelines of traditional production design."[70]

The virtual environments in *Speed Racer* (2008), such as the splendor of the Driver's Club, were sometimes created from high-resolution photographs. For the Driver's Club, digital photos were taken inside a centuries-old Berlin castle using HDRi (high dynamic range imaging) methods. These involve sampling a scene's light range by taking numerous pictures, which include bracketed underexposures at the shoulder of the light curve and bracketed overexposures at the toe. Merging the exposure information in the picture series produces images containing a more extended light curve and greater texture and detail across that curve. The castle photos were tiled together and projected onto a 3D geometry built for the scene. A matte painter erased and blended the fit lines and changed and enhanced colors in accord with the film's overall design concepts. The still photos created a virtual background, filled in post-production with sixty actors playing the scripted scene. As the film's cinematographer noted, "We would never have been able to bring that many people into that room [in the castle], let alone cameras, lighting and everything else that comes with a movie production."[71]

The scene is an amalgamation and synthesis of HDR photography, décor from a real location, live action, CG, camera mapping, and painting. It is a built environment, not a found location, and yet it contains visual information from the real castle, with the HDRi methods extracting more data from the castle than ordinary photography could have achieved. This synthesis of disparate image types represents the digital extension of traditional production design operations with a more immersive outcome. As 2D textures become 3D surfaces and camera moves are projected into virtual space, as photographs furnish textures for painting and painting adds layers to live-action imagery, cinema finds new ways of expressing its fundamentally hybrid nature. The digital and the indexical are not in a relation of opposition but are a dialectical moment in an ongoing process of stylistic continuity. In the next chapter, I examine these issues from the standpoint of HDRi, radiance maps, and stereoscopic filmmaking, and discuss the immersive designs such approaches make possible.

CHAPTER 5

Immersive Aesthetics

Cinema marries a compelling presentation of sound and moving images to the depiction of what often are worlds of the imagination. The more perceptually convincing these imaginary worlds can be made to seem, the more virtual and immersive the spaces of story and image become. As we have seen, digital tools enhance the perceptual realism of effects sequences. They thus help to fulfill one of cinema's historical objectives. Cinema belongs to a long history of illusion spaces that aim for maximum perceptual credibility, and many of its technological innovations can be understood as advances upon this underlying goal, most notably the digital tools that enable filmmakers to composite real and synthetic characters, objects, and spaces in imperceptible ways. Indeed, Robert Neuman, a supervisor of stereoscopic film production for Walt Disney Animation Studios, states that technological development in cinema has taken the medium toward a more immersive aesthetics, providing viewers with greatly intensified sensory experiences relative to earlier generations of filmmaking. Cinema, he writes, "has had a history of innovations that tend toward higher and higher degrees of immersion." These include color, widescreen, and multichannel sound. "Film emulsions and now digital display technologies have advanced in resolution and dynamic range to make the alternate reality being presented by the filmmaker a more compelling illusion. Even non-display related film innovations such as the zoom lens or the steadycam [sic] represent a technology aimed at pulling the viewer deeper into the experience."[1]

Indeed, an ideal of sensory immersion is embedded in cinema and extends beyond it to other media in ways suggesting that there is an enduring human fascination with the experience of virtual spaces and perspectives. Oliver Grau has traced the history of illusion spaces that aim to maximize the viewer's sense of being *in* the picture, and he concludes that these constitute an ongoing feature of Western art. "Virtual reality forms part of the core of the relation-ship of humans to images. . . . In each epoch, extraordinary efforts were made to produce maximum illusion with the technical means at hand."[2] He shows how viewing spaces from the Great Frieze in the Villa dei Misteri at Pompeii, circa 60 B.C., to Gothic cathedral ceilings, nineteenth-century panoramas, and cinema in conventional, stereoscopic, and IMAX formats have aimed to minimize or occlude the observer's awareness of image borders and of being separated from the image. In the seventeenth century, painter and architect Andrea Pozzo created spectacular trompe-l'oeil perspectives on the ceiling of Saint Ignatius's Church. Viewing the flat ceiling from a prescribed point, the observer perceives a deep recession of brightly colored, ornately decorated space that depicts an allegorical narrative of Ignatius's apotheosis. The vista seems to draw the viewer upward toward heaven. Alison Griffiths writes that brightly colored and spatially expansive Gothic cathedrals "were intrinsically multimedia, multisensory spaces" and that "spectacle and a heightened sense of immersion were not only expected but came to define the very nature of the overall religious experience."[3] She defines immersive spaces as eliciting a bodily sense of participation from viewers. "One feels enveloped in immersive spaces and strangely affected by a strong sense of the otherness of the virtual world one has entered, neither fully lost in the experience nor completely in the here and now."[4]

Prior to the invention of cinema, panoramic photographs and paintings offered spectators epic views of cities, rivers, and historical landmarks and became a popular form of visual spectacle. Engulfing panoramas created by Robert Barker, for example, enabled audiences to step into a widescreen vista that activated peripheral vision and concealed the boundaries of the painted image. *Grand Fleet at Spithead* (1794) offered spectators an image measuring 280 feet in diameter. Barker perfected a system and an apparatus for producing the curved geometries of space that, when mounted as a 360-degree panorama, would seem to appear as straight lines. Barker stitched together his series of views in a subtle fashion. As Martin Kemp notes, "Their panoramic images are essentially polygonal views arranged cylindrically, with the junctions between the serial views suitably 'softened.'"[5] As we see below, this is remarkably like contemporary procedures for stitching a panoramic HDR (high dynamic range) photograph from individual images.

Thomas Horner's view of London from atop the dome of Saint Paul's Cathedral offered a dramatically curving view of the city and the Thames, requiring viewers to ascend to viewing galleries at the top of the Regent's Park Colosseum where they emerged from darkness into the brightly lit gallery exhibiting the circular painting. They could walk around the space, immersed in its vistas and not be bound by the limitations of the static eye found in traditional forms of painting. Many panoramas placed a three-dimensional terrain between viewers and painting to accentuate motion parallax as viewers or the viewing station moved across the length of the painting. Of Anton von Werner's 1883 panorama, *The Battle of Sedan*, Grau writes, "The *faux terrain*, the three-dimensional extension of the one-dimensional picture, had the function of integrating the observer, it came up close to the spectators, particularly in the section where hand-to-hand combat was depicted, and this strategy of virtually removing boundaries led, or rather pulled, the observer into the depths of the image space."[6] The procedure bears resemblance to the use of matte paintings in cinema, in that their usual placement is behind live-action elements of the frame, hiding the boundary between a photographed three-dimensional volume of space and the 2D painted rendering. Engulfing the spectator by removing visible edges to the compositions, concealing the framing of the image, the panoramas (or cycloramas, as the circular variants became known) anticipate today's multistory IMAX screens, which surround viewers with dramatic imagery so large that its edges extend beyond the limits of a viewer's peripheral vision, and the popular amusement park rides such as "Back to the Future" or "Spider Man 3D" at Universal Studios. These rides place viewers in motorized vehicles surrounded by 360-degree moving image projections that are augmented by physical stimuli. Walt Disney introduced "A Trip to the Moon" in 1955 at Disneyland (California), seating viewers in a mock-up of a rocketship to experience simulated space travel replete with moving images of stars projected above and below their seats.

The first ride-movie experiences appeared well before these popular attractions, however. Debuting in 1904, *Hale's Tours and Scenes of the World* provided viewers with a virtual rail tour of scenic locations. Viewers seated in a facsimile of a train car watched front- or rear-projected imagery simulating views taken from the cowcatcher on the front of the engine, showing the rails stretching before the train and dramatic scenery passing by. Sound effects and rocking movements in the car helped to intensify the visual illusion. As Raymond Fielding writes, "Auditory, tactile, visual, and ambulatory sensations . . . provide a remarkably convincing illusion of railway travel."[7] As a 1906 promotional catalog proclaimed, "The entire picture is filled with hypnotic views that make the beholder steady himself to catch the motion of the rounding curves. It is impossible not to imagine that you are actually on the train."[8] *Hale's Tours* and its imitators were wildly popular and are the antecedents of today's movie-themed motion simulation rides. Lauren Rabinovitz writes that this category of films works according to a "cinematic rhetoric of hyperrealism. [Such films] do so by appealing to multiple senses through experiences featuring forward movement, wraparound screens, objects or lights flashing in the viewer's peripheral vision, subjective camera angles, semisync realistic sound, seat or floor movement, and narratives that alternate danger and command."[9]

The enduring cultural practice of placing viewers into immersive, virtual spaces came naturally to cinema, with its ability to provide moving images and to combine pictures with sound. Richard Allen writes that cinema's replication of depth perspective and movement made it the perfect medium for inducing what he calls "projective illusion," the experience of "a pictorial or dramatic representation as if it were a fully realized world of experience and not a representation."[10] And cinema's embrace of narrative meant that projective illusions could be sustained across time. Martin Kemp describes the emergence after 1800 of traditions of picture-making that aimed to overcome the limitations of a static linear perspective by providing enhanced, intensified spatial views. Anamorphic images, panoramas, perspective viewing boxes, and the stereoscope attempted to go beyond one-point perspective. "These new forms of illusion sought to replicate the perceptual effects of parallax and motion. The effects of motion involved the turning eye and the mobile subject."[11] Cinema's ability to display parallax through camera movement and a mobile point of view via editing meant that it would be a most powerful participant in this emergent tradition of heightened visual experience. Wheatstone's stereoscope had preceded the invention of photography, but the two were soon conjoined. While photographic stereoscopes proliferated, however, cinema did not establish itself as a stereoscopic medium. The development of optical effects, though, enabled filmmakers to provide glimpses of the strange dimensions that so intrigued Wheatstone when he gazed into his pseudoscope and to embed these with the properties of parallax and mobile perspective, thereby enhancing the perceptible richness of the virtual, 2D viewing space that the medium provided to its viewers. As we will see, though, efforts to develop the medium's stereoscopic potential have been an enduring feature of cinema history and suggest that the evocation of Z-axis space may yet prove to be one of the medium's natural affinities.

If so, it would fall within what André Bazin famously referred to as "the myth of total cinema." This myth, he claimed, was a desire by the inventors of the medium to create "a total and complete representation of reality . . . a perfect illusion of the outside world in sound, color, and relief."[12] It is significant that Bazin refers to this motive as a myth. He calls the objective idealistic and platonic, and he points to the "obstinate resistance of matter to ideas," that is, the failure to make of this myth a reality. The halting efforts during cinema's first century to move toward a stereoscopic display evidence this resistance of matter to idea. An objective of total cinema may also be incongruent with aesthetic expression. As Robert Neuman emphasizes, mastering an aesthetic form entails using it as a filter. "Art is the filtering of reality. It is characterized more by what is left out than what is put in."[13] Working on *Avatar* (2009), James Cameron believed that aesthetic and technical discipline was essential for the film to succeed. Unlimited creative possibility could not be the goal. "Early on, we came up with the principle of denying ourselves infinite possibility—which sounds wrong. You'd think you'd want to embrace the infinite possibility; but you don't, because you'll never get there. Ever."[14]

If by its nature art operates within sets of constraints, and if cinema in many of its forms aims to provide viewers with an immersive virtual space, one that is perceptually enveloping, then this dialectic of limit and possibility may furnish the medium with an essential condition underlying its appeal to filmmakers and audiences. In his study of special effects in cinema, Dan North points to the medium's dualistic nature, noting that "a major aspect of cinema's fascination lay in its synthesis of photographic verisimilitude and fantastic, transformative effects."[15] North rightly observes that while these are often construed as the traditions embodied by Lumière and Méliès, they are not dichotomous modes but interconnected ones. And as such, North argues, the tradition of visual effects appeals to

Aesthetic expression embraces limits. *Avatar* expanded the technological base of cinema by integrating digital imaging practices into filming and production, but director James Cameron understood that artistic design was predicated upon limitations. Frame enlargement.

dualistic motives in the spectator—to enjoy the illusion while seeking out an understanding of how it was done. According to North's historiography, special effects in the movies derive from traditions established in the magic theater of nineteenth-century Europe, where science and entertainment were conjoined. Mirrors, glass screens, lantern projections, and magic acts promoted production techniques emphasizing an overt pictorial theatricality that the movies inherited. The theater presentations also emphasized the scientific principles of perception and physics that underlay the illusions. North suggests that special effects in cinema partake of this tradition of revelation and astonishment that informed the magic theater, where audiences delighted in magical illusions while simultaneously seeking to understand how they were produced. Today's viewer who delights in the fantasy of *Lord of the Rings* while devouring the DVD supplements that explain how the effects were created is exhibiting behavior like that of the nineteenth-century theater patrons, desiring the magic in the act as well as an understanding of its production. Thus North writes that special effects exhibit "a spectacular dialectic" between the profilmic elements (those that were before the camera during principal photography) and the synthetic elements that are created separately. Special effects postulate a relationship between what is real and what is technologically mediated. Special effect techniques "are essentially disruptive—they upset the notion that everything within the frame is evidence of an event occurring before the camera." Watching a special effect, the viewer "is challenged to perceive the joins between composited elements." All special effects, he contends, leave some traces of their composited nature; joins remain visible, and spectators remain hypercritical of visible imperfections even while desiring to surrender to the illusion. "But the illusion is *never* [emphasis in original] perfect. There is always a dynamic friction between the special effect and the filmic space it infiltrates."[16] With these theoretical premises, North critiques accounts of special effects that he deems are teleological in constructing narratives about filmmakers' progressive and improving abilities to project and perform illusion. The self-reflexive nature of special effects (they call attention to themselves) and the viewer's critical awareness of experiencing illusion call into question "a widespread impression that the development of special effects has been driven by a series of incremental improvements and modifications moving towards a capacity for absolute simulation and imperceptible illusion."[17]

My own view is somewhat different. Digital tools have taken filmmaking very close to accomplishing imperceptible illusion. As to whether viewers of necessity notice effects, it all depends on the aesthetic objectives of a particular film. The elaborate transformations of inanimate objects in *Transformers* are deliberately ostentatious and attention-grabbing; the synthetic environments in *Changeling* and *Master and Commander* are not. Visual effects need not exist in a state of dialectical tension with live-action elements, and it is doubtful that the medium includes among its essential characteristics a belief by viewers that everything in the frame evidences an event that occurred before the camera. Editing expands and contracts story time; changing camera positions break the depicted action into constituent elements. Viewers almost never see events depicted holistically; fragmentation of time and space is the normative condition. A viewer who believes that what is visible onscreen, in whole or in part, happened the way it was photographed—or that everything inside the frame is actual and authentic—is poorly schooled in the ways of cinema.

Visual effects at times can be disruptive; they can extend themselves as a spectacular dialectic. Viewers may see them simultaneously as a technological achievement and as an authentic part of the imaginary narrative world, but it depends. Angela Ndalianis writes, "We remain astounded at the effortless magic of the transformations we see before us, yet these very transformations also remind us that they are special effects and ask us to be astounded at the technology that produces such magic. This combination of the irrational with the rational is experienced as the ambivalent tension that tugs at the spectator: the oscillation between emotion and reason—between the sensory and the logical."[18] Again, a film like *Transformers* might elicit this kind of dualistic response, but visual effects can simulate representational worlds and characters in ways that are subtler and less ostentatious. In such cases, the ambivalent tension that Ndalianis describes seems unlikely to arise, at least much beyond the general experience one feels at all movies of being both inside and outside the screen world. The objective common to much feature filmmaking of soliciting belief in a screen world, of sustaining the illusion, disinclines filmmakers from doing things that trigger a viewer's awareness of the medium. Richard Allen's description of projective illusion, in this regard, as a singular condition sustained by cinema, gets at this facet of filmic experience. He writes that projective illusion does *not* involve a condition of medium awareness on the part of the spectator; it is characterized by the loss of this awareness. "In projective illusion I experience a pictorial or dramatic representation as if it were a fully realized world of experience and not a representation."[19] Allen points out that in cinema "special effects greatly increases the scope of projective illusion, allowing for the experience of fully realized fictional worlds that extend far beyond the boundaries of our own."[20] Indeed, the pleasures that movies like *Lord of the*

Rings or *Avatar* provide spectators are those of an immersive illusion that is sustained as an experience and not as a representation. The last thing that effects artists want is for a bad matte line to break the illusion. To the extent that a viewer's experience of visual effects remains self-conscious and self-aware, then it is bad matte lines and their ilk that often are responsible.

Are the joins always visible, as Dan North claims? During the classical era of Hollywood studio filmmaking, the effects department in a studio was housed as a separate operation, supplying optical effects to supplement principal cinematography of the stars and supporting players. This division of labor did reflect prevailing attitudes about the questionable legitimacy of "trick" photography relative to on-set direction of actors. And during this era, the joins in an optically composited shot were visible. Matte lines stood out clearly, parallax and lighting failed to match properly in rear-screen projection, and live-action characters did not interact convincingly with the monsters and fantasy creatures that were composited into a shot. As Noel Carroll remarked about *King Kong* (1933), "The space of many of the shots sporting battling, back-projected behemoths in the background and tiny humans in the foreground seems curiously disjunct. The monsters inhabit tangibly different spatial zones than the humans."[21] Stitching these joins often required ingenuity from filmmakers. As Joe Fordham notes, "Ray Harryhausen went a long way to integrate his stop-motion puppets more dexterously with performers—Jason fighting seven skeletons in 'Jason and the Argonauts' or the cowboys roping the allosaurus in 'Valley of Gwangi.'" Harryhausen found ways of using painting and props to create physical connections between live action and animation, and the brilliance of his work lay in his ability to create an emotional performance in and through the animation. As Fordham rightly points out, "What sells it is performance; you really feel there's emotion in the fantastic creatures."[22]

Digital rendering and compositing have diminished the severity of these limitations to the point that the joins today are no longer always visible. The outlandish creatures in movies like *Clash of the Titans* (2010) are clearly fanciful creations and virtual characters, but viewers drawn to the film will be prepared to believe in them, provided the movie can sustain its projective illusion. A viewer watching *Toy Story* is responding to Woody and Buzz and their cohorts, who are designed not to be effects but characters. And the capability for creating immersive experiences provided by digital tools strengthens those medium characteristics that Allen identifies as projective illusion. I turn now to a discussion of several such capabilities.

Lossless Master Audio

Digital rendering and compositing create more persuasive image blends than were possible in the era of optical printing because they enable effects artists to anchor visual effects with a stronger basis in perceptual realism and to invest the resultant image with significant degrees of indexicality. This latter claim may be surprising given that, as we have seen, one of the orthodox assumptions in the literature on digital images is that CG is incompatible with indexicality. In fact, however, digital media enable new forms of indexicality that were not possible to establish in the analog era. These characterize sound as well as image. Scholars have written about indexicality mainly in relation to images, but the category needn't be restricted to visual information. Cinema is a medium of picture and sound, and sound was one of the medium's first components to go digital. The perceived credibility, impact, and immersiveness of visual effects owe much to sound design. Watching *Master and Commander*, for example, the viewer's sensory impression of being on a nineteenth-century warship at sea is shaped by the superlative virtual environments created digitally but also by the three-dimensional sonic field conveyed by multichannel sound effects depicting a nautical environment. Cinema's sonic component can be far more expressive in a digital mode than it was during the era when movies carried a single-channel optical soundtrack. Optical soundtracks produced very poor sound, with a limited frequency response that turned loud effects, like gunshots or high-volume passages in a film score, into noise because the necessary space to encode them exceeded the area available between the picture frames and the sprocket holes on a strip of celluloid. The introduction of Dolby Stereo in the mid-1970s brought four-channel sound to the movies, but it remained analog and optically encoded. Dolby SR, introduced in 1986, offered a means of noise reduction to overcome one of the inherent limitations of optical sound. Low-volume effects often had been overtaken by the hiss of the optical track, and Dolby's noise reduction scheme facilitated a somewhat wider dynamic range. Digital sound arrived in 1991 with a one-off system developed by Kodak for *Terminator 2—Judgment Day*, but it was Dolby Digital (appearing initially on *Batman Returns* [1992]) and DTS (carried initially on *Jurassic Park* [1992]) that established the enduring formats of digital cinema sound. Each offered six channels including a dedicated channel for bass, making film sound a spatially immersive experience for viewers. (Some widescreen formats in the 1950s, such as Cinerama, offered multichannel sound, but this was an exception to the dominant norm of mono audio.) Henceforth, an aesthetic imbalance prevailed in cinema, with sound being three-dimensional and married to a 2D picture display.

While digital sound in this period provided a greatly enhanced frequency response and enabled complex sound mixes and spatial information unheralded in the optical mono era, its indexical status was limited by high rates of compression. Dolby placed its digitally encoded soundtrack in the small area between the sprocket holes on a strip of celluloid, and DTS used time code to sync with audio playback via CD. Both systems used lossy forms of data compression, with Dolby's compression ratio being approximately 10:1. As a result, audio information that was present in the original studio sound mix dropped out.

While this has remained a problem for films projected on celluloid, the advent of Blu-ray as a viewing medium provided a tremendous increase in data storage capability (50 gigabytes as compared with 8.5 gigabytes on a standard DVD) and new eight-channel audio systems for utilizing it. Dolby TrueHD and DTS-HD Master Audio offer lossless forms of data compression, and many Blu-ray disks also carry uncompressed LPCM (linear pulse code modulation) soundtracks. Each of these formats produces an accurate record of all the information contained in the original studio master recording, with no loss of audio data. Listening to a movie soundtrack on Blu-ray in one of these audio formats provides the indexical experience of hearing the original studio master mix. Analog optical soundtracks never came close to reproducing the dynamic range of the soundtrack as originally recorded and mixed. Chaplin, for example, composed a layered, intricately detailed score for *City Lights* (1931), but the limitations of recording-to-film in the period made mush out of his music. His friend and co-star Henry Bergman said, "It is interesting, the terrible deficiencies of the medium are too apparent. I don't think they will ever overcome them. Thirty-five of the very finest artists played the score for *City Lights* so beautifully on the set. Through the mechanics of the microphone it became something else."[23] Analog audio in cinema offered a low level of indexicality, whereas the lossless audio data formats provide the full range of sound that filmmakers and sound designers have created.

High Dynamic Range Imaging

Despite the important place that live-action-camera reality holds in the theory and aesthetic practice of realistic filmmaking, the camera is a poor instrument compared with the human eye. It is a lossy instrument that fails to capture the full range of luminosity in a scene or environment. The human eye can respond to a dynamic range of 100,000:1 luminance levels; a camera, depending on the speed of the lens, the latitude of the film, and the size of its digital sensor, captures far fewer. Theories of cinema that take the camera as an indexical agent accurately capturing what is before it have neglected to consider the significance of this characteristic—a single analog or digital image created in camera is a low-level facsimile of the lighting environment from which it derives. By contrast, HDR (High Dynamic Range) images can capture the full radiance of an environment. In effect, they provide a comprehensive radiance map of the set or location that they document. An HDRi environment contains a record of all the light values and information present in a scene and can be used to light synthetic 3D objects or digital characters when these must be composited with elements of live action. HDRi provides a widely used toolset in contemporary visual effects.

Working at the Lawrence Berkeley National Laboratory, Greg Ward developed the format of floating point images that would be essential for creating HDRi. When digital effects came to the movies, computers were 8-bit systems and so were image file formats. The 24-bit paint system developed by Alvy Smith in 1977, for example, allocated 8 bits per channel (red, blue, green). The 24-bit designation referred to the number of bits per pixel (8 red, 8 blue, 8 green, yielding a possible 16 million colors), but each channel only had eight bits. An 8-bit format has a maximum of 256 brightness levels per channel, and these values are absolute. Black (designated with RGB values 0,0,0) and white (RGB 255,255,255) represent the ends of an 8-bit format's illumination range, beyond which visual information is clipped or lost. An 8-bit format offers low dynamic range because of this tendency to clip information and because the incremental steps between values—shifting a brightness level in one channel from 50 to 51—is fixed and allows for no discrimination or image definition between those levels. Moreover, an 8-bit format offers only a poor approximation of the range of illumination to which the eye can respond. A floating-point format, by contrast, offers a seemingly infinite amount of brightness values by replacing integers with decimals and enables rendering operations to be performed on HDR images rather than the clipped values inherent in the 8-bit format. Thus in a floating-point system, a pixel could have a value of less than zero, a value of .4529, or one greater than 255. It can be blacker than the black and whiter than the white of an 8-bit system, resulting in a significant expansion of dynamic range. Visual information need not be lost even when an image is converted for output to a lossy format like positive print film or a 24-bit display system. "Tone mapping" designates this process of conversion, and floating-point values enable the artist to manipulate image levels to retain information that the lossy format otherwise would clip.

Ward's floating-point format enabled him to design a new approach to image rendering. Released in 1987, Radiance was the first physically based rendering system, a category of renderers that are now widespread in visual effects lighting. Prior to this, and as explained in chapter 2, lighting a CG environment was a labor-intensive process under which the digital artist would set a key light, then fill and back lights and map shadows and textures according to the way that light ought to react with objects in the environment. This local illumination approach, which worked by specifying source lights, was similar to what a cinematographer might do in lighting a set or location, except that the source lights were all virtual. A physically based render system, by contrast, calculates the behavior of light globally in an environment according to real luminance values and scene geography. It's not necessary to define and position individual light sources; rather than source lighting, the approach aims to create global illumination. An HDRi radiance map can supply the luminance values needed by the rendering software for lighting the digital environment. This approach is called image-based lighting.

Paul Debevec of the University of Southern California performed the pioneering work in image-based lighting that the film industry rapidly adopted for visual effects. In a classic 1998 SIGGRAPH paper, Debevec wrote, "We propose that computer-generated objects be lit by actual recordings of light from the scene, using global illumination" and high dynamic range imaging.[24] An HDRi can be obtained by taking successive exposures of a mirror ball (aka a light probe) placed in the environment for which a radiance map is needed. Debevec placed a mirror ball in a domestic kitchen setting that contained natural, electric, and indirect lighting and photographed it in one-stop increments in a shutter-speed range of one-quarter to one-thousandth of a second. A mirror ball can capture the full 360 degrees of light in the environment. (An alternative to using a mirror ball is photographing with a fish-eye lens. Radiance maps of set lighting used for CG on the Angelina Jolie thriller *Salt* [2010] were obtained by photographing 360 degrees of coverage with a fish-eye lens in a series that went three stops over and three stops under.)[25] Taking numerous photographs with a range of exposure settings permits a photographer to capture the full range of light in the scene. A single photograph, with a fixed shutter setting and f-stop, could not sample the full range of luminance values; clipping of dark and bright areas would occur. As Debevec wrote, "A single low-dynamic range photograph would be unable to record the correct colors and intensities over the entire scene."[26] The HDRi images can then be unwrapped from spherical perspective and used to re-create the original light environment;

real and synthetic objects in the scene that require lighting can be texture-mapped with the radiance values from the HDRi images.

Debevec demonstrated the utility of this approach for cinema with his short film *Fiat Lux*, exhibited at SIGGRAPH 1999. A digital version of Saint Peter's Basilica was created using photogrammetry based on an HDRi radiance map derived from photographs taken inside the cathedral. Only a few images were needed to generate the digital version of the cathedral. The radiance map furnished by the HDRi provided the lighting for the CG building, and Debevec then filled the basilica with CG spheres and monoliths. These were animated, and their surfaces reflected the true lighting characteristics of the cathedral's interior. He wrote, "The key to making the computer generated objects appear to be actually present in the scene was to illuminate the CG objects with the actual illumination from the Basilica."[27] The HDRi radiance map provided an indexical image of the cathedral's illumination, and it furnished the realism necessary for conveying the idea that the CG objects were inside the actual cathedral. Image-based lighting proved very applicable to cinema because filmmakers have an ongoing need to composite actors into real and virtual environments in ways that maintain consistent lighting cues.

Beginning in 2000, Industrial Light and Magic began research on a file format that could incorporate floating-point HDR data. Existing 8-bit formats did not offer sufficient color fidelity for visual effects, and in 2002 ILM released its OpenEXR format publicly so that it might become an industry standard. Now widely used throughout the effects industry, OpenEXR offers high dynamic range (1 billion:1) imaging capabilities, 16-bit and 32-bit floating-point formats, lossless data compression, and the ability to be expanded to as many channels as needed so that separate elements of a render need not be stored as separate files. *Harry Potter and the Sorcerer's Stone* (2001), *Men in Black II* (2002), *Gangs of New York* (2002), and *Signs* (2002) were the first films rendered using OpenEXR. At the time of this writing, all films are viewed on low dynamic range display devices—television screens, celluloid projected upon a wall screen—so these output formats cannot do justice to the amplitude of the visual information present in HDR images. The format, however, offers the great advantage of tone mapping, the ability to recalibrate image information for the output device without suffering the kind of garish clipping that occurs in a low dynamic range image source. Moreover, even after tone mapping for a low range device, the HDR file retains all of its information; nothing is lost.

To provide a pathway connecting HDRi and image-based lighting with filmmakers' needs to composite actors into real and synthetic environments, Debevec designed a series of iterations on a device he entitled Light Stage

Signs (2002, Touchstone Pictures) was among the first generation of feature films to be composited using ILM's OpenEXR image file format. Frame enlargement.

(Light Stage 1 appeared in 2000), which captured photographic records of an actor's face illuminated under all lighting levels and in a range of 360 degrees. This radiance map of the performer's face could be used to facilitate seamless digital compositing of the actor into a scene under any lighting condition. Light Stage 2 (2001) sped up the imaging process so that the actor could model a series of facial expressions captured under all lighting conditions. These then could serve as sources for keyframing the animation of a digital character. On *Spider-Man 2* (2004), Sony Pictures used Light Stage to place Alfred Molina's face on Doc Ock, the villain with octopus tentacles who tries to destroy Spider-Man. Molina was photographed in Light Stage 2 and also photographed in a marker-based facial capture session. The latter generated data needed to build a library of expressions for the digital character. Using a fish-eye lens, an HDRi record was made of the sets in which Doc Ock appeared. These radiance maps furnished the lighting environments for matching the digital character to the live actors who had been filmed on set or in a greenscreen environment. The Light Stage images of Molina's face showed the animators how he looked under the requisite conditions stipulated by the radiance map for a scene. The digital rendering of his face could be composited onto the Doc Ock body with seamless and realistic lighting that was true to the reflectance characteristics of Molina's actual face.

Light Stages 3 (2002) and 5 (2005) surround the performer with a dome of LED lights and use high-speed photography, enabling the actor to move and give a performance while a full-range record is compiled of diffuse and

Light Stage imaging enabled accurate lighting of Alfred Molina's face when seen on the digital character of Doc Ock. *Spider-Man 2* (2004, Columbia Pictures). Frame enlargement.

specular lighting characteristics. Using Light Stage's infrared matte channel, the actor can be composited into a real or synthetic environment and lit with an HDRi radiance map. Debevec has also been able to videograph a performer in a Light Stage with lighting that replicates the radiance map of an HDRi environment and then composite the performer into the environment that generated the map. Thus he composited an actress into a cathedral that had been mapped with HDRi, and reflections of blue light from the stained glass windows and yellow from the candle-lit altar were visible on her face in the composited image. The method furnishes a convincing replication of environmental light and a key means of achieving the ongoing challenge of effects shots that blend real and synthetic elements. "The lighting of the two elements needs to match: the actor should exhibit the same shading, highlights, indirect illumination, and shadows they would have had if they had really been standing within the background environment."[28] *King Kong* (2005), *Superman Returns* (2006), *Spider-Man 3* (2007), *Hancock* (2008), and other films have used Light Stage methods for generating realistic lighting on digital characters in real environments or on real performers in virtual environments. A variation on Light Stage imaging created illumination on the digital head replacements used in *The Social Network* (2010) for a pair of twins, the Winklevoss brothers, who were portrayed by a single actor.

Floating-point image formats and HDRi are now standard in visual effects imaging because of the increased dynamic range, color rendition, and lighting realism that they offer. Many of the urban vistas seen in *Batman Begins* (2005), for example, were created from panoramic HDR images. These were built from tiled photographs taken of city exteriors with a digital still camera.

The RAW exposures (shooting in RAW mode eliminates image processing by the in-camera software) were made at intervals of two stops across a ten-stop range.[29] The images were then combined to supply panoramic views of Gotham City that included fully lit interior windows and décor in the high-rise buildings. HDRi mapping of environmental light furnishes an indexical level of realism in visual effects that relies on placing actors or objects in spaces that they inhabit virtually. It does so by lighting the virtual space according to the luminance values of the actual environment, and the Light Stage methodology provides an indexical connection between the virtual scene and the actual diffuse and reflective characteristics of an actor's face as it is illuminated under varying conditions.

Stereoscopic Cinema

Floating-point image compositing and HDRi radiance maps furnish visual effects with immersive levels of light and color information. They enable filmmakers to seamlessly blend the image of a real actor to that of a synthetic character or to light a digital environment with the actual light that was present on set or on location. Light can be employed as the indexical property of real environments and can be mapped onto synthetic characters to place them in those environments in visibly credible ways. In a similar fashion, performers shot on greenscreen can be lit with a radiance map and given the luminance values of a scene or location that they never inhabited. Rendering in HDRi overcomes the finite luminance range of an 8-bit color system and permits tone mapping operations that take digital imaging closer to the artistry of painting than the brute mechanics of photochemical imaging permitted. Digital imaging tools have increased the persuasiveness of visual effects by eliminating the zones of spatial separation between live action and synthetic characters and environments that prevailed in the era of optical printing. They have transformed formerly 2D elements, such as matte paintings, into representations of locale that exhibit parallax, camera perspective, and motion animation. They have blurred the boundaries between matte paintings and live action. The optical characteristics of camera perspective can be achieved in digital animation, and camera perspective can be simulated doing things that no camera could ever do, such as rack focusing a background element into clarity without altering the focal crispness of elements in a foreground plane. In these and other ways, digital visual effects have achieved levels of plasticity and persuasiveness that eluded the imaging capabilities available to earlier generations of filmmakers. Visual effects thus get closer than did their analog counterparts to the medium's enduring goal of providing an immersive experience, of bringing the viewer closer into the picture or of enhancing its sensory appeals. On the other hand, the medium has not yet integrated as a standard component of its aesthetic and technological identity a key element that belongs to its immersive orientation. That element is stereoscopy. While film sound is now spatialized in three dimensions, cinema's image remains a 2D window onto a world whose third dimension is represented by monocular depth cues, those that are perceivable by one eye only.

Some viewers and critics deride 3D as a gimmick. Roger Ebert wrote a widely read opinion piece for *Newsweek* entitled "Why I Hate 3-D (And You Should Too)" in which he listed nine reasons why he believes 3D is unnecessary, wasteful, or intrusive.[30] These include factors ranging from exploitation (studios charge higher prices for tickets to 3D movies), loss of luminance compared with ordinary movies (3D looks dimmer), and the inducement of nausea and headaches in some viewers. His argument overall is that 3D adds nothing useful to the experience of cinema. The most important component in the argument is Ebert's claim that 3D is the waste of a dimension. "When you look at a 2-D movie, it's already in 3-D as far as your mind is concerned." Adding a third dimension artificially, he writes, "can make the illusion [of dimensional space] less convincing."

Ebert is quite correct in his view that in fundamental ways conventional cinema already is 3D. As observers we perceive spatial layout according to numerous depth cues that act in concert to provide redundant information about the positioning of objects in a volume of space. There is some variation in the number and names of depth cues as given by different scholars, but among the most important are occlusion or overlap (near objects occlude farther objects along a line of sight), relative size (objects appear smaller with increasing distance), height in the visual field or picture plane (farther off looks higher up), aerial perspective (hazing from the atmosphere and a color shift toward blue affect very distant objects), motion parallax (differences in the apparent rate of motion according to distance from the observer), convergence (movement of the eyes toward each other to sight a near object), accommodation (change in the shape of the eye's crystalline lens to focus on a near object), and binocular disparity (differences in the retinal location of an object as found in each eye). James Cutting and Peter Vishton show that the effectiveness of these depth cues varies systematically with viewing distance.[31] They categorize viewing distance in terms of personal space (up to six feet from the observer), action space (up to 100 feet), and vista space (objects beyond 100 feet). In vista space the cues that operate effectively are the monocular depth cues—occlusion, height in the visual field, relative size, and aerial perspective. Action space privileges occlusion, height in the visual field, relative size, binocular disparity, and motion perspective. Within personal space, binocular disparity, convergence, accommodation, occlusion, and relative size operate. Of these depth cues, the only ones relevant to stereo (two-eyed) vision are binocular disparity and convergence, and as Cutting and Vishton show, their efficacy is mainly confined to the zone of personal space. This is a zone that cinematography tends to exclude, favoring instead action space and vista space. As Cutting elsewhere has argued, "I think stereo films fail as an important medium because stereo in the real world enhances noticeable depth differences only [in areas] nearest to the viewer and . . . this is not a region of space that is important to most filmmakers."[32] In this respect, Ebert is correct that traditional cinema is 3D—it exploits the cues for real-world spatial layout that operate effectively at the viewing distances most often established by cinematography (camera to subject distance) and theater seating (moviegoer to screen distance). Neither instance is a viewing zone in which stereo vision provides efficacious cues about depth. Instead, the monocular cues operate there, and these are the ones that are also pictorial cues in that a flat picture surface can fully reproduce them.

Moreover, many of cinema's routine stylistic devices work to accentuate the information provided by these depth cues. A wide-angle lens will exaggerate relative size disparities, making objects near the camera seem especially large in comparison with more distant objects. Traveling shots through a forest, as shown by Kurosawa in *Rashomon* (1950) and *Throne of Blood* (1957) and Oliver Stone in *Platoon* (1986), present robust motion parallax; rates of displacement in the frame vary strikingly between near-and-far-ground foliage and trees. Blocking of action within the frame often introduces dramatic changes in the size and positioning of objects. In *Key Largo* (1948), Bogie gets the drop on Edward G. Robinson, as gangster Johnny Rocco, and Rocco's panic is conveyed by dynamic perspective changes in a single shot. Rocco and one of his hoods are trapped in the cabin of a small fishing boat, and Rocco stands by the door in the background of the frame, trying to spot Bogie on the upper deck. Then, as the frame is held, Rocco walks forward, toward the camera, until his face and shoulders are inches from the lens. He becomes a looming presence filling the frame. He holds that position for a moment and then moves away, to the midground. The perspective changes are emphatic and cue the viewer to concentrate on the changing depth information that the blocking of the shot provides. The information is not gratuitous; it conveys story information about the character's emotional state. It also accentuates the three-dimensional information displayed on screen, inscribing space as a volumetric medium inhabited by characters and making these changes maximally visible to viewers.

Planar, conventional cinema replicates many 3D cues, and filmmakers have used dynamic staging to accentuate these, as in this shot where Edward G. Robinson looms into the camera. *Key Largo* (1948, Warner Bros.). Frame enlargement.

These considerations would seem to suggest that Roger Ebert and other critics of 3D are right, that it adds nothing and fails as a stylistic device because cinema doesn't need it; cinema already is 3D. And they are right up to a point, as I have tried to show. At the same time, the objections are prescriptive, and much the same thing has been said in earlier periods about additions to cinema's technological array—sound, color, widescreen. Like these features, stereoscopy has been an enduring element of cinema since its inception; it is not a marketing gimmick that surfaced in the 1950s and has reappeared today. The historical duration of stereoscopy's connection with cinema suggests that there is a fundamental affinity in the medium for it and that the long dominance of moving images defined by monocular depth cues may have more to do with technological problems that beset the initial stereoscopic systems than with its lack of relevance for the aesthetics of the medium. Wide-angle lenses, moving camera shots, action choreography within the frame—these are methods for managing and accentuating the information about spatial layout relevant to storytelling style and content. If an essential attribute of cinema is direction in depth—the tableau staging of early cinema quickly gave way to analytic editing—then stereoscopy takes this attribute to a new level. As I describe presently, 3D shifts the existing aesthetics of editing and shot composition to accommodate the novel challenges of choreographing the Z-axis as a storytelling device.

Stereoscopy as an Enduring Element of Cinema

Lenny Lipton points out that existing visual culture is one with "a marked planar bias. . . . Photography, rich in depth cues, and cinematography, even richer because of the possibility of motion parallax, nevertheless remain planar, or one-eyed, media."[33] And yet, as Ray Zone notes, "Stereography preceded photography. The impulse to capture life and replicate it with movement, color, sound, and three dimensions was present at the dawn of photography and motion pictures."[34] H. Mark Gosser has provided an estimate of the number of stereoscopic moving picture devices marketed, patented, or described in books from 1852 until nearly a decade after the invention of cinema.[35] In 1852, Jules Duboscq patented the first stereo motion picture device, the stereofantascope, which was a phenakistiscope outfitted with twelve pairs of stereo images. From 1852 to 1894, according to Gosser's figures, forty stereo motion picture devices had been created. From 1895, the year in which the Lumière brothers showed projected motion pictures to an audience, through 1903, an additional fifty-two devices were designed, suggesting that the advent of projected cinema stimulated the search for a 3D application of moving photographic images. And in the thirty years after 1895, nearly 300 patents for stereo film devices were filed in the United States and Europe.

In 1890, William Varley, a London photographer, invented a stereo movie camera that used roll film, and his associate William Friese-Greene used it to shoot footage of pedestrians in Hyde Park. Many of cinema's pioneers were interested in developing 3D applications. Thomas Edison and W.K.L. Dickson included provisions for stereoscopy in their patent applications for the kinetoscope. Dickson continued research into stereo cinema and in 1899 patented a camera that used prisms to split the image into right eye–left eye pairs. The distance between the prisms could be adjusted, enabling manipulations in the amount of depth effect. The Lumière brothers patented a glass plate stereo viewing device in 1900, and, in a 1936 article published in the *Society of Motion Picture Engineers Journal*, Louis Lumière described a stereo camera system he had created that featured a horizontally moving film strip carrying the stereo image pairs as adjacent frames.[36] Edwin S. Porter, who made *The Great Train Robbery* (1903), also made stereo films, and he projected these at New York's Astor Theater in 1915 in an anaglyph system under which the audience used glasses with lenses tinted red and green to see the stereo effect. The first stereo feature film, *The Power of Love*, was released in 1922. Novelty shorts in 3D—*Plastigrams* and *Stereoscopiks*—were released nationally in 1927. Hollywood's 3D boom of the 1950s is well known and is somewhat notorious for exploiting the Z-axis for cheap emergence effects. The boom began with Arch Oboler's *Bwana Devil* (1952). Its box office success led to several years of 3D production that then tailed off quickly.

Why was Hollywood's flirtation with stereoscopy in the 1950s (and in a brief flurry of productions in the early 1980s) so short-lived? The answer most often given is the inconvenience for viewers of having to wear glasses to see 3D effects. And yet, if this is the reason, how does one explain the substantial portion of industry revenues (11 percent) accruing to the 2009 boxoffice from 3D screenings that required the use of glasses? (Higher priced tickets for 3D screenings are partly responsible, but this does not explain the wide appeal of *Avatar* and *Alice in Wonderland*.) Hollywood's 1950s 3D boom capped more than a century of interest and experimentation in stereoscopic moving image displays. Why, then, didn't 3D take hold at that time or before? Numerous problems beset attempts to use celluloid film as a stereoscopic medium, and the answer may lie there rather than in the often-maligned need for glasses. *Bwana Devil* and the other films of that period were screened using two projectors running in an interlocked fashion, which invited a nearly insurmountable host of problems that were inherent with celluloid film. To avoid eyestrain, a viewer needs to see the right-eye and left-eye images in perfect registration and without any ghosting or bleeding of one image channel into another. This outcome could not be reliably achieved using film. Shooting with a dual lens system required that the lenses be perfectly calibrated to minimize optical aberrations introduced by barrel distortion, spherical aberration, bokeh, and other irregularities. Color timing of the left and right prints must be exactly alike. The warp and weave of film in the projector gate (and camera gate if a dual camera shoot is used), arc lamp amperage and lumens, framing of each film strip for the screen, optical characteristics of the projector lenses, phase syncing of each shutter—all these factors needed perfect alignment in a dual projector system, a demanding task that most theaters could not devote their resources to achieving. Lipton references a study conducted in 1953 that found that 25 percent of sampled theaters had errors of synchronization in the stereoscopically projected images.[37] This is a high rate of error, suggesting that a fundamental weakness of Hollywood's 3D boom lay in the technology. The medium of celluloid was inherently unsuitable as a technology for inducing stereoscopy. Film was too unruly, too irregular in its taking and in its projecting to enable viewers to achieve acceptable amounts of stereoscopic fusion. Ed Marsh, the 3D consultant for *Journey to the Center of the Earth* (2008), which was shot on high-definition video, has said, "Film is very fragile for movies that have to be perfect twice. On the projected film image, there's weave, and in a 3-D presentation, both eyes have to track weave independently. . . . It's one of many film-related factors that can contribute to eye-strain during 3-D presentations."[38]

Digital cinema largely has solved these problems. Today 3D is found mainly in films that are projected digitally and are entirely CG or involve a substantial amount of digital visual effects integrated with live-action footage. Stereoscopic cinema now is a digital medium, and at the time of this writing, its robust box office suggests that it may be more than the novelty or gimmick claimed by naysayers. The International 3D Society released a study suggesting that 3D movies are driving the weekend boxoffice of general release movies by a margin of 2 to 1 and accounted for 33 percent of box office revenues in the first quarter of 2010.[39] Revenues for the 2D version of *Alice in Wonderland*, for example, failed to reach $40 million at the time of the study's release in March 2010, while 3D revenues surpassed $80 million. The advent of digital 3D began with Disney's release of *Chicken Little* (2005), continued with *Monster House* (2006) and *Meet the Robinsons* (2007), and spiked in popularity and cultural presence with the huge boxoffice accorded to *Avatar* (2009), *Alice*, and *Toy Story 3D* (2010).

Although the stereoscopic version of *Alice in Wonderland* (2010, Walt Disney Pictures) was created in post-production, cinematographer Dariusz Wolski planned for this by making careful choices about lenses, emphasizing short focal lengths to enhance depth of field. Frame enlargement.

Real D, the most widely used digital 3D projection system, illustrates the advances that digital technology has made over dual-projector systems using celluloid. Real D is a single-projector system ensuring that there is no variation of projected image characteristics in the right-eye and left-eye channels. A field-sequential system, it projects the paired images of the stereo view as alternating fields and flashes each field pair three times to achieve a frame rate of 144 fps. This is well above the fusion threshold that viewers require for perceiving smooth motion. Sequential field methods in the past were prone to parallax errors (strobing effects) because the frame rates were not fast enough to keep the visual field information from breaking apart when an object on screen moved quickly. In Real D, Texas Instruments' Digital Light Processing (DLP) technology drives the field sequential views at this high frame rate. A polarization modulator, called a ZScreen, covers the projector lens and switches at the field rate between the left and right images, encoding them with circular polarization that the viewing glasses decode. Image ghosting is controlled using a "ghostbuster," a method for analyzing and predicting the amount of ghosting that will occur in the stereo views and then compensating for this. Lenny Lipton, who invented the ZScreen and was Real D's chief technical officer and who is one of the pioneering scholars of 3D cinema, writes, "The digital projector is a neutral stereoscopic transmitter, doing no harm to the image."[40] He adds, "The deterrents to the widespread acceptance of the stereoscopic theatrical medium have, in principle, been solved by digital projection."[41]

3D Digital Aesthetics

Conventional (planar) cinema is 3D to the extent that it replicates the monocular depth cues that observers employ when viewing spatial layouts in the world at distances of six feet or more. Stereoscopic cinema works by incorporating all the monocular cues and adding to them those that are involved with stereopsis—specifically binocular (retinal) disparity—and convergence. These are activated when viewing objects near at hand and depend on seeing with two eyes. The separation between our eyes (interocular distance) averages 65mm and, as a result, each eye receives a differently angled view of solid objects; these views are displaced relative to one another on the retinas. Binocular disparity increases as we converge our eyes to view near objects. In addition to binocular disparity and convergence, a third informational source—accommodation—operates at close distances to convey 3D spatial information. Accommodation refers to the changes that occur in the shape of the eye's crystalline lens when focusing on near objects. A widespread assumption in the literature on stereoscopic cinema attributes the eyestrain that can occur when viewing 3D movies to a breakdown of the convergence-accommodation response.[42] Convergence and accommodation are neutrally connected and co-occur—as one converges the eyes, one also accommodates to focus on something close at hand. Many writers suggest that eyestrain when viewing 3D movies is brought on by a disconnection between the two—one converges the eyes for objects placed in 3D space in front of the screen while continuing to focus on the screen plane. Eyestrain is said to result from this unnatural behavior. The problem with this view is that stereo movies do not elicit accommodative responses when viewed in a theatrical environment because the screen is too far away. (Moreover, many adult viewers, as the natural result of aging, lose the ability to accommodate the eyes and need glasses for activities such as reading.) It is unlikely, therefore, that accommodation is relevant to 3D cinema in a theatrical viewing environment. Stereoscopic cinema works by eliciting the cues of binocular disparity and convergence and uses as well the monocular cues that have been a customary feature of conventional cinema.

Marrying these new sources of depth information to the old ones that cinema has employed creates aesthetic challenges and opportunities and makes stereo movies a somewhat different medium than planar cinema has been. Stereoscopic cinema alters conventional approaches to shot composition, depth of field, and editing and brings new collaborators onto the production team, most notably the stereographer, the individual who configures and choreographs the application of depth within stereo screen space. Before examining the aesthetics of stereo cinema, it's necessary first to consider how stereopsis on the screen is created. Planar cinema is monocular—nothing on screen depends on viewing with two eyes. The monocular cues create 3D depth, but it is not a stereoscopic depth produced by two-eyed viewing. Cinema has always been 3D (this term, therefore, is not a good descriptor of stereoscopic film, though I will continue to use it because it is familiar), but a planar display does not produce binocular disparity. This discrepancy led Hugo Münsterberg to describe conventional cinema as involving a perceptual conflict—the viewer sees 3D but without stereopsis. Stereoscopic cinema produces the latter by presenting left-and-right-eye views in distinction to the single-eyed image of planar cinema. Binocular images are produced either at the point of filming or in post-production. If produced during filming, then a dual-camera rig is used; alternatively, the second camera view can be created digitally in post. Stereoscopic space is created by manipulating IO (interocular distance, which corresponds with the distance between the optical axes of the two camera lenses and may also be referred to, therefore, as interaxial distance) and convergence (the angles at which the camera axes cross).

Ideally, IO will replicate the average 65mm separation of the viewer's eyes, but in practice filmmakers will vary this setting depending on the screen action or the focal length of the lens used in a shot. IO settings on *Avatar*, for example, ranged from one-third inch to slightly more than two inches. Wide-angle lenses may require a smaller IO setting because of the manner in which they scale perspective information. Objects close to the camera in a wide-angle view will appear much larger, requiring less stereoscopic volume for effect and therefore a smaller IO setting. A camera move that tracks, cranes, or zooms away from an object in close-up to a wider view should be orchestrated with continuous changes in IO so that the viewer perceives a physically continuous space on screen and does not feel like s/he is growing larger or smaller in relation to that space. This is one of the paradoxes of interocular settings—their variation can induce a sensation in the viewer of growing larger or smaller in relation to the screen world. A camera move in *Coraline* (2009), starting on a face in extreme close-up and pulling out to show a house and yard, was animated with an IO change from 0.5mm to 18mm because spatial volume could be minimized in the extreme close-up and maximized for the wider view. The IO settings were smaller than 65mm, the distance between people's eyes, because of the need to scale space according to the size of the puppets and the sets and models they inhabit. Coraline's puppet eyes were 19mm apart. Using a human IO setting would produce the phenomenon of dwarfism in relation to the 1/6-scale puppets and sets. Dwarfism results in stereoscopic displays from excessive IO distances. It can make the observer feel hundreds of feet tall and make distant vistas look abnormally small. The visual reality of *Coraline*'s puppet world depended on making the viewer feel like an inhabitant there rather than like a giant looking at a miniature world. The smaller IO settings created an appropriately scaled volumetric space for this illusion.

Convergence settings determine the proximity of objects in stereoscopic space in relation to the viewer; they work by producing horizontal parallax or displacement in the right- and left-eye images. Objects positioned in front of the screen (between screen and viewer in what Lenny Lipton refers to as "theater space")[43] have negative parallax. The left-eye image is on the right, and the right is on the left, requiring that viewers converge their eyes to fuse the images. Objects behind the screen surface have positive parallax; the right- and left-eye images are not crossed. The maximum positive parallax occurs when left- and right-eye axes are parallel and set for infinite distance. (Movies filmed for IMAX 3D are shot with lenses on parallel axes.) The screen surface is a zero parallax area; no displacement of right- and left-eye images exists there. Filmmakers, therefore, can position objects in front of the screen or behind it by setting negative or positive parallax values. One of the biggest differences between the gimmicky use of 3D in the 1950s and today is the conservative use of parallax. Unlike the garish fly-out effects of the 1950s, excessive parallax is minimized or avoided today so that viewers will not be presented with discomforting image fusion tasks. Convergence values for *Journey to the Center of the Earth*, for example, aimed to keep the main area of interest in a shot close to the screen surface, rather than far out in front or behind, except for key moments where a dramatic effect was needed.

The ability to control convergence settings so as to position objects in stereo space changes the planar screen of conventional cinema to a window in depth through which and out of which objects and characters may travel. (In IMAX 3D the screen is not a window at all, since it is so large that viewers do not see its edges. They are completely inside of it.) Moreover, filmmakers can change the apparent position of the screen, moving it forward or backward and changing its angle as needed. A common situation in which this occurs involves conditions under which a floating window is needed. A floating window is a forward positioning of the screen; it moves nearer in virtual space to the viewer when its edges are repositioned. This is done to avoid or to minimize contradictory spatial cues that can arise when an object or character that is partially off-camera is thrown forward into theater space but is occluded by the edge of the screen. Occlusion is an extremely powerful depth cue and, in such a situation, it contradicts and undercuts the stereo effect. The problem is resolved by repositioning the virtual location of the screen, creating a floating window in front of the character in theater space. The edges of the floating window make the occlusion information noncontradictory. In practice, window violations are common in stereoscopic cinema, because partially framed objects and characters have a dynamic expressive value that filmmakers prize and because it would look artificial to keep everything in theater space inside of the screen borders. While egregious window violations can be addressed with a floating window or avoided entirely with careful compositions, small ones need not be a problem if viewers typically are looking elsewhere. *Toy Story 3*, for example, contains numerous window violations that arise when a character in the foreground of a shot and in theater space is bisected by the frame line. But in all these instances, the area of interest on screen is not at the frame line. Only if viewers look there does a spatial contradiction arise.

These considerations suggest that filmmakers working in 3D need to be acutely aware of where viewers will be looking on screen because stereoscopic depth cues, if not properly controlled, can conflict with the monocular cues in a shot. Lenny Lipton maintains that monocular perspective scales stereopsis in 3D cinema, that the latter is always entwined with the former.[44] Therefore, 3D filmmaking must aim to avoid conflicts such as window violations or excessive IO and convergence settings relative to shot content. Complicating this task is the virtual nature of stereoscopic screen space and the way that it varies depending on where the viewer is sitting. Objects positioned in front of or behind the screen will have different virtual locations as seen by viewers seated in different areas of a theater, and depth information will vary as well. Vergence (converging and diverging eye movements) will be more challenging for viewers seated nearest the screen, and the impression of depth will seem greatest for viewers seated in the rear of the auditorium. This is because a negative horizontal parallax of the two images that is equal to the interocular distance will place an object in theater space midway between screen and viewer. The farther back from the screen the viewer sits, therefore, the greater the apparent magnitude of the depth effect produced by these settings. (Smart viewers at 3D screenings will sit in the center rear of the auditorium.) Excessive parallax will produce a failure of stereoscopy by requiring too much convergence (eventually causing a double image that cannot be fused) or an outward rotation of the eyes (divergence) that does not occur when viewing in the world. Stereoscopic cinema, therefore, elicits physiological responses that planar cinema does not, and its aesthetic challenges lie in calibrating these in ways that are expressive and that facilitate stereoscopic image fusion.

The aesthetics of digital stereoscopic cinema depend on making creative use of the depth effect as a means for expressing narrative, thematic, and emotional meaning and of choreographing Z-axis perspective so that it does not conflict with other image elements. Accomplishing this latter function often entails modifying shooting and editing procedures that are customary in planar cinema. Depth of field, for example, is often quite shallow in contemporary films, and focal planes are used to direct the viewer's attention to salient details necessary for understanding story and character. Shallow-focus compositions do not work as well in stereo 3D because the viewer's eyes tend to explore stereo images more actively than planar ones. The authors of a study comparing 2D and 3D viewing note that in 3D, "the eye movements are more widely spread. The viewers' eye movements show them exploring the details of interesting three-dimensional structures in the shots, and the initial preference to look at actors is slightly diminished."[45] As a result, shallow-focus compositions, especially if blurred areas are large and in the foreground, can pose obstacles to a viewer's desire to explore the Z-axis. Over-the-shoulder shots used in 2D cinema for dialogue scenes are not well configured for 3D screen space because they can elicit window violations and because the foreground character is customarily out of focus. The camera operator on *Journey to the Center of the Earth* pointed out that the cinematography team set focus and convergence at the same point to avoid viewer eyestrain. "You really don't want to have your foreground element, like a shoulder, as out-of-focus as you would in 2-D."[46] A poorly filmed stereoscopic movie, such as *Cats and Dogs: The Revenge of Kitty Galore 3D* (2010), uses the conventional framing and editing techniques of planar cinema and adds stereoscopy to them. The resulting hash fails to make use of what stereoscopy offers—the display of volumetric depth information that is antithetical to shallow-focus framing. Shallow focus reduces depth of field and can make stereoscopic objects look unnaturally flat and planar.

Tron: Legacy (2010) was shot with a stereoscopic camera rig and uses 3D effectively as a narrative tool, although not as effectively for Z-depth information. The story follows Sam Flynn (Garrett Hedlund), who enters the computerized Tron world searching for his father, Kevin (Jeff Bridges). Most of the film takes place inside Tron and was shot in 3D. The film opens and closes, however, with scenes taking place in the normal world, and these are shot as planar, 2D compositions. The narrative technique recalls the distinction in *The Wizard of Oz* (1939) between reality and fantasy as drawn by color. Here, 3D distinguishes the fantasy world of Tron from everyday life, which appears flat in contrast. The clever design also, therefore, draws a distinction between 2D and 3D cinema, with the former being allocated to the depiction of ordinary and banal reality. Once inside Tron, however, many scenes in 3D are shot with shallow-focus compositions and over-the-shoulder shot-reaction-shot cutting. Rather than aggressively using negative parallax, depth is treated as a recessionary variable, with objects and characters placed behind the screen in the positive parallax zone. As a result, the film uses 3D very conservatively and suggests that contemporary patterns of composition and editing may absorb stereoscopy rather than being imaginatively recalibrated to showcase the kind of volumetric world that 3D is best suited to defining.

Selective focus and limited depth of field are problematic in 3D, whereas in 2D filmmaking they are used as effective storytelling tools. *Avatar* cinematographer Mauro Fiore states, "Shallow depth-of-field is an interesting dilemma in 3-D, because you need to see the depth to lend objects a dimensionality."[47] Disney stereoscopic supervisor Robert Neuman writes that "foreground depth of field effects are more of an issue for 3D than background effects. A rack focus will only work in 3D when it is mirroring what our eyes seek to do. If a new subject enters frame and the camera's focus is pulled to that subject with timing that approximates our own physiological response time, the effect will work. If we are watching a two-shot and the camera shifts focus from one subject to another in order to force a shift in our attention, our eyes will tend to rebel."[48] Robert Zemeckis's *Beowulf* (2007) was shot as a 2D film and given a stereographic finish in post-production so that it could be released as both an IMAX 3D picture and in digital 3D formats. Seventy-five percent of the depth-of-field effects in the 2D images were removed for the stereoscopic version. These were shots in which selective focus was employed to emphasize objects in the frame and direct a viewer's attention to salient details. Removing shallow focus resulted in sharpening the image overall to create deep-focus compositions. Rob Engle, the stereographer at Sony Pictures who supervised *Beowulf 3D*, notes, "In 3D filmmaking, a narrow depth of field can be distracting and inhibit the viewer from a truly immersive experience." So after the selective focus compositions of the 2D version became deep-focus images, other means beyond focal plane definition were used to shape the viewer's attention. "Since there are many other tools in filmmaking [besides selective focus] to direct the eye, we would sometimes employ another technique (for example, brighten the subject a bit) if the subject of the shot was no longer clear."[49] Fiore used similar tactics on *Avatar*, relying on contrast and lighting instead of selective focus to direct the viewer's attention.

Creating depth in a stereoscopic film challenges filmmakers to find ways of incorporating planar tools like matte paintings. When viewed in stereoscopic depth, matte paintings can be seen as flat constructions more clearly than is the case in conventional cinema where the entire display is two-dimensional. A 3D matte painting does not face this problem, but 2D and 2½D paintings can be exposed as such in stereoscopic space. Digital tools, however, provide

3D processing of *Beowulf* (2007, Paramount Pictures) enhanced stereoscopic depth by removing focal plane information from the 2D version, such as the defocused foreground in this shot. Frame enlargement.

ways of finessing the problem. Matte paintings used in *Beowulf* were selectively warped; areas that were supposed to be nearer to the camera were given a larger amount of horizontal parallax, lending an impression of depth to the painting as a whole. A related 2D issue in stereoscopy is cardboarding, when the viewer sees a series of stacked planes on screen rather than a gradual recession in depth. The cardboard effect occurs when characters or objects appear unnaturally flat in 3D space, and one contributory cause is lens focal length. Longer lenses are often used in contemporary film to create selective focus (and to beautify the actors), but telephoto perspectives are problematic in stereoscopic space because they tend to stack space as a series of planes. To mitigate cardboarding, shorter lenses often work better for 3D films. Dariusz Wolski shot Tim Burton's *Alice in Wonderland* with short-range lenses to accommodate 3D compositions, with no lens longer than 75mm and the maximum range used only for close-ups.[50] To counter cardboarding, stereographers find that one of their chief tasks is creating roundness for characters, ensuring that they have an appropriate volume on screen and do not appear as cardboard figures. Interaxial spacing and convergence were adjusted throughout *Beowulf* on a per character basis to achieve roundness. Rob Engle writes, "Choice of focal length of the shot camera can also have a very strong effect on the perception of roundness of a character. While a wide-angle lens can exaggerate the roundness of a foreground character, a narrow lens will tend to flatten objects out." Engle's team used Autodesk Maya to recompose the 2D shots and sometimes to alter lens perspective in order to optimize stereographic roundness.

Stereoscopic aesthetics hinge on the effective management of depth, and stereographers compose a "depth score" to organize Z-axis design over time and in ways that express the style and substance of a film's narrative. Filmmakers think in terms of what the Z-axis might express in given scenes and at key points in a narrative. On *Beowulf*, for example, character roundness became a means for expressing power. More powerful characters, such as Beowulf, were given slightly more rounded volumes within shots than were weaker characters. Inter-axial spacing provided a means for achieving this. Larger inter-axial distances enhanced the volumetric depth on screen, and placing a character in the foreground of this enhanced space made that figure visually pronounced in ways that served the narrative and drew on the unique expressive tools and properties of stereoscopic cinema. Robert Neuman's depth score on *Bolt 3D* (2008) was based on two premises. "The first was that the emotional impact of the film's content was proportional to the stereoscopic depth being presented." Opening up the volume of space on screen, either through IO settings or changes in convergence, could achieve emotional appeals in a visual language unique to 3D cinema. Neuman's second premise was that emotional distance from a character or situation is proportional to the viewer's separation from these in 3D space. Neuman reasoned that characters and events playing in negative parallax space (in front of the screen) would convey greater emotional connection and involvement than when these were located at the screen plane or behind the screen. To orchestrate this emotional language of stereoscopic space, Neuman used floating windows to invisibly alter the position and angle of the screen. Using the four corners of the window as independent depth controllers, the virtual screen could be moved forward and backward and have its axis shifted so that it was no longer parallel with the actual screen. "Following these two rules provided the framework for a consistent 3D style for the film. These rules may or may not have unassailable psychological validity, but it is my belief that the audience will unconsciously learn to ascribe associated meanings to the particular stylistic choices made throughout the course of a film, provided that they are presented in consistent fashion."

Stereoscopic cinema privileges deep focus, and in this respect—as well as its associated need for longer shot rhythms—it approximates a Bazinian ideal. Patrick Ogle and H. Mark Gosser both detected a relationship between deep focus as an aesthetic style and 3D cinema. Ogle wrote that "the three dimensional picture would seem to be the next logical step beyond deep focus cinematography."[51] In his history of early stereographic filmmaking,

Stereoscopic cinema privileges deep focus and longer shot lengths. Woody, Buzz, and the gang inhabit a deep-focus space that 3D makes normative. *Toy Story 3* (2010, Pixar). Frame enlargement.

Gosser, in contrast, speculated that deep-focus cinematography might have supplanted stereographic cinema.[52] Deep focus was planar, but in light of the problems with projecting film stereoscopically, it offered an approximation of 3D's enhanced depth effects. Whether deep focus was a substitute for 3D or the latter a next logical step from deep focus, the digital era has harmonized the two. By making stereographic cinema viable, digital modes have encouraged filmmakers to strive for composition in depth as an alternative to the shallow-focus filming and fast cutting that predominates in contemporary planar cinema. By privileging deep focus, stereoscopic cinema necessarily emphasizes longer shot durations. A major reason for this is the need to choreograph parallax so that viewers are not given difficult perceptual tasks, as when rapid cuts might change Z-axis information, abruptly moving objects from in front of the screen to behind it. Cinematographer Russell Carpenter shot James Cameron's *Terminator 2 3-D: Battle Across Time* (1996) and had to rethink the compositional and cutting strategies that were normative in 2D filmmaking. Conventional editing applied to 3D could easily give the viewer what he called "visual whiplash." Carpenter said if you have a shot where something is in front of the screen "and you make a cut, that thing just disappears as if it's vaporizing in front of your eyes! If you then cut to something that's way off in the distance, it's as if somebody's just snapped a rubber-band on your eyeball—it's quite jarring. So a lot of thought had to be given as to where potential cuts would be."[53] Managing transitions in depth occupies a large area of stereoscopic aesthetics. As Tara Handy Turner, Disney's stereoscopic supervisor on *Beauty and the Beast 3D* (2011), writes, "If one shot is very shallow with a focal point behind the screen, and the next shot is extremely deep with a focal point far in front of the screen, the viewer's eyes must quickly re-converge and re-focus for these differing depth budgets. This will likely cause some discomfort, especially if occurring often, and so, for best composition, shot transitions should instead move fluidly from one point of convergence and depth budget to the next."[54] Turner's term—depth budget—refers to the perceptual resources that parallax choreography in a film draws from the viewer, and a key premise of this concept is that these resources are limited. Skillful stereographic filmmaking stays within budget. An effective depth score is budget-driven, orchestrating negative and positive parallax across the narrative arc of the film in ways that creatively engage (and don't exhaust) the viewer's attention and image-fusion capabilities and that also embody important attributes of narrative and dramatic meaning.

The stereographic design of *Coraline* exemplifies these principles. Stereo space and color distinguish Coraline's two worlds. The drab reality she inhabits with her parents is pale, lacking vibrant hues, and is staged at or near a zero parallax region so that stereoscopy is reduced. The exciting and sinister world of Other Mother is rich in highly saturated color and lighting that alternates between warmth and threat. Stereo values in Other Mother's domain are robust, conveying at first Coraline's desire to belong to this world and then conveying the danger posed by Other Mother who turns out to be a spidery nemesis. Camera moves through stereo space in Other World accentuate the Z-axis and make this domain more perceptually enveloping than Coraline's real world. These moves visually convey the irony of Coraline's situation. She at first believes that this might be a better place for her than living with her real parents and the daily frustrations that life with them incurs. Her desire to be in Other Mother's world is stereoscopically portrayed using this emphatic Z-axis information. The narrative reaches its climax when Coraline is brought to realize that Other Mother seeks to entrap and destroy her, at which point the design of stereoscopic space becomes more aggressive yet, with greater use of theater space as sinister objects come at Coraline and at the viewer.

Other than this stylistic change, the film's choreography of stereo space adheres to a conservative use of depth budget. Emergence effects are rarely employed, and the stereo window is treated most often as a recession into depth rather than by having objects enter theater space. This minimized the

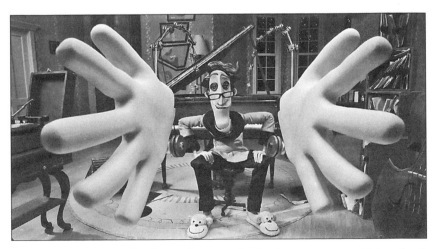

Contemporary 3D production orchestrates its depth score to stay within a depth budget determined by the viewer's physiological limits. Accordingly, it reserves aggressive emergence effects for key dramatic moments. *Coraline* (2009, Focus Features). Frame enlargement.

level of difficulty in the convergence tasks that the viewer must perform. Within the stereo window, cinematographer Pete Kozachik and director Henry Selick skillfully use focal planes and editing in ways that success-fully conjoin these conventional elements of planar cinema with 3D style. Foreground objects often appear in soft focus, but the story context and shot composition direct the viewer's attention away from these areas. Rack focusing is shown to be compatible with stereoscopic depth, used in dialogue scenes to shift between speakers and to follow a character's gaze. The direction in which the viewer is to look is clearly marked in these contexts, and the rack focus anticipates and directs the viewer's necessary shift of attention. Over-the-shoulder compositions are used in dialogue scenes as they are in planar cinema, but because much of the film plays in positive parallax space, no window violations arise. Matte paintings used in the background of shots to establish the mountainous Oregon setting were exposed as 2D constructions in the filming of stereo space, but an acceptable solution to the problem was found. By moving the paintings much farther back from the set, an acceptable amount of motion parallax could be established, which diminished the viewer's sense of the painting as a flat backdrop. *Coraline* demonstrates that customary compositional and editing strategies of planar cinema can be compatible with stereo cinema if used skillfully and with intelligence. Korzachik said, "With very few excep-tions, we did not compromise lighting and camerawork for 3-D constraints. Contrast and depth of field remained useful creative tools."[55]

Cinematographer Vince Pace collaborated with James Cameron to develop a video high-definition, dual-camera rig that Cameron used to shoot his 3D IMAX documentaries, *Ghosts of the Abyss* (2003) and *Aliens of the Deep* (2005). With modifications and improvements, The Reality Camera System was then used to film *Avatar*. The name Pace gave to his camera system expresses his view that stereographic filmmaking approximates natural vision more closely than does planar cinema. Pace said, "What we're trying to do is put the viewer right there and mimic human vision. If we do that, I think we'll feel like we've done our jobs and brought a whole new medium—human eyesight—to the screen."[56] How accurate is the claim that stereographic cinema comes closer to natural vision? As we have seen, stereo cinema incorporates a more complete set of perceptual depth cues than does conventional cinema, and, as a result, it can present spatial layouts in more vivid terms. Moviegoers can look into the stereo window, whereas they cannot look into the cinema frame projected upon a flat screen. They can look *at* the frame but not into it. Gazing into the stereo window affords uniquely visceral pleasures that conventional cinema does not provide, and the need to scale space in stereo terms challenges filmmakers to rethink their application of cinematic tools of composition and cutting. When this is done successfully, as in *Avatar*, *Toy Story 3*, or *Coraline*, the result is an aesthetic expansion of the plastic and narrative powers of cinema. But stereo space does not mimic human vision in the naturalistic way that Pace proposes. The cues of stereopsis have been added to cinema's array of expressive devices, but in ways and under conditions that are stylized and not true to the way that we experience space in daily life. Stereopsis in 3D cinema is more insistent and emphatic than our encounter with it in life. Partly this is a matter of its symbolic and emotional encoding within film narrative. Negative parallax is used for dramatically heightened effects. A character or object that moves forward from the screen into theater space carries an emotional charge that is contextualized by narrative sequence. Robert Neuman's encoding of stereo space in *Bolt 3D* according to an emotional register assigned to specific parallax values is one example. But cinematic stereopsis is insistent as well because it occurs in ways that are spatially untrue to our experience of the world. One of the challenges faced by stereographers is the need to scale 3D for viewing distances, and these vary considerably depending on whether one sees a movie in the theater (and varies there, too, depending on where one sits) or at home, where seating distances are closer to the screen. Interaxial and convergence values have to be set based on an ideal viewing range.

A survey by Sony Pictures in 2010 of digital-ready 3D theaters found screen sizes varying from 17 to 50 feet and projection throw distances of 50 to 180 feet.[57] A mid-row seat in these theaters yielded viewing angles of 35–75 degrees, and the studio decided to compose its 3D images for a viewing angle of 60–75 degrees, aiming for a mid-range. Viewing the film at home on smaller screens and with closer seating would yield diminished 3D effects. The key point in this is that efforts to scale stereopsis in cinema for an ideal viewing distance typically involve calculations of projection throw in a theatrical environment. These distances are well beyond the thresholds for which stereoptic cues work in real life. The efficacy of convergence and binocular disparity both decline linearly with distance, with the falloff more severe for convergence. For objects viewed beyond six feet, convergence and binocular disparity provide little information about spatial layout, and we rely on other information sources to determine where things are located in space. Stereographic cinema invokes these cues under viewing distances for which they do not operate in actual life and in this respect cannot be said to mimic natural vision. When stereopsis configures distant viewing environments in a film, the results look distinctly different than the normal manner in which the world appears to us. We do not have to converge our eyes to see distant objects, nor do these produce much retinal disparity. As a result, stereoscopic space may work best in cinema when used to render environments that are stylized, as in *Toy Story 3* and *Coraline,* and that are governed by irregular perspectives, as in *Alice in Wonderland.* When used to render environments that are meant to look photographically real, the contradiction inherent in stereoptically defined remote objects works against the appearance of naturalism and pulls one out of photographically rendered reality. Moreover, cinematic transitions between scenes and shots with different stereo configurations—cutting from a shot with a character in negative parallax space to a shot where the character is at the screen plane—present the viewer with an experience that has no counterpart in life. 3D cinema is a stylistic mode of viewing that approximates our real-life use of stereo depth cues but invokes them at spatial distances under which we do not encounter them in the world. Accordingly, they acquire greater weight, presence, and vividness on the screen, especially when correlated with dramatic and narrative symbolism. In this respect, stereo cinema is a visual effect and, potentially, one of the most significant, since its deployment reconfigures the stylistic shape of the medium, altering preferred compositional and editing patterns.

The digital revolution in moving image capabilities that has been underway in Hollywood since the 1980s has led inexorably to 3D cinema. As the authors of a study on digital workflow issues in stereo moviemaking write, "Modern stereoscopic 3D (S3D) cinematic production relies heavily on digital tools and pipelines. Although technically possible, avoiding digital processing of the images is not only unlikely, but will probably yield worse results, since digital tools and pipelines inherently solve many of the issues found in traditional S3D film production and present the opportunity to correct for many others."[58] As we have seen, digital projection of stereoscopic movies offers inherent benefits over that of film, and in important ways the production of many digital images finds them already configured for stereoscopic applications. Characters and settings created in computer space in films such as *Toy Story 3* and *Up* (2009) are already in 3D. The Z-axis in computer space is very real. In conventional cinema, it exists at the point of filming but then, when encoded as a 2D display, it vanishes except for the ways that monocular depth cues point to it. Encoding characters and settings created in computer space for stereoscopic display maximizes the perceptual information that has already been built into them, rather than discarding that information as happens when porting the film or sequence to a 2D display mode. Moreover, digital imaging applications like Autodesk Maya offer numerous tools that permit digital stereoscopy to attain levels of sophistication that eluded moviemakers in the celluloid era. Maya permits the creation of one or more virtual cameras and will calculate the desired horizontal parallax for stereoscopic viewing based on the way that the user sets values for interaxial distance and the zero parallax plane. Maya stores this information as metadata, enabling artists to go back and revise the stereo values of a shot as needed. It offers a parameter on the CG camera called "film offset" that produces a horizontal shift in perspective to the camera's predefined area of view. This enables the user to create parallax effects in post-production without the need to toe-in cameras during a shoot, which can create trapezoidal image distortions detrimental to a viewer's ability to fuse left and right image channels. Maya permits the creation of multiple stereo camera pairs and the ability to assign different pairs to objects and characters in a scene. This optimizes the configuration of stereo values, allowing characters to be treated independently in terms of their volumetric attributes or a midground area to be defined with stereo values different than the foreground and background. In *Beowulf*, this approach was used to delineate characters emotionally and symbolically in terms of their perceived roundness. Multipass rendering enables parallax values to be adjusted in the render and allows for different image layers, offering filmmakers an ability to fine-tune stereo values as needed. A digital workflow configures parallax and interaxial values as fine-grained and flexible units of expression, articulating character and narrative alongside cinema's traditional elements of style.

The production of *Pirates of the Caribbean: On Stranger Tides* (2011) illustrates these features. The film was shot using the 3D camera rig developed by Vince Pace and James Cameron and with Red One cameras shooting RAW files at 4K resolution. The camera lenses were set on parallel axes, and convergence and interaxial settings were defined and manipulated in post-production. The choreography of stereoscopic space can be achieved very effectively as a matter of post-production processing.

The technological issues that hampered the development of stereoscopic cinema throughout the medium's history have largely been solved. As a result, stereoscopy has become a currently quite profitable visual effects modality. And its potential for narrative art and visual design has drawn Steven Spielberg (*Tintin* [2011]), Martin Scorsese (*The Invention of Hugo Cabret* [2011]), and Werner Herzog (*Cave of Forgotten Dreams* [2010]) to stereoscopic work. Like Wheatstone's pseudoscope, stereoscopic cinema gives us a glimpse into a world whose volumetric properties exceed our own in terms of their dynamic range, their vividness, and their infinite scalability. Rather than mimicking natural sight, it offers a heightening of vision, a glimpse through the looking glass into an immersive domain that all visual effects, in one way or another, have proffered so beguilingly to viewers. How long 3D in its present form—dependent on displaced dual-eye images and requiring glasses for decoding—will persist remains an open question. But in one format or another, 3D is part of cinema's future, just as it has been an indelible feature of its past.

Conclusion
The Pleasures of Illusion

Visual effects were developed at cinema's inception, building upon traditions for representing visual illusions that already existed in photography, theater, and other arts. Dan North has demonstrated how the practices of Victorian magic theater were incorporated into cinema's early development, as trick films and as filmic records of performances by stage magicians. Cinema has never existed without visual effects, and yet they have been relatively neglected by our theories of the medium. This is partly because, as Richard Allen points out, "the idea of illusion has played a central role in sustaining the negative characterization of mass culture against high art," a conflict that film theory has often recast as "an opposition between an ideological mass culture and an emancipatory modernism."[1] Visual effects create illusions, and cinema's provision of illusion has been seen as being ideologically suspect.

Yet, without visual effects, we have no cinema. Edison's *The Execution of Mary, Queen of Scots* (1895) used an in-camera edit to substitute a dummy for the actress and show Mary's decapitation. The work of Georges Méliès is taken as the progenitor of this kind of filmmaking, but others joined him. G. A. Smith used double exposures to show ghosts in *The Corsican Brothers* (1898), and Robert W. Paul used stop-motion animation to portray an automobile on a trip through outer space in *The '?' Motorist* (1906). Cecil Hepworth's simulated camera effects showed *The Explosion of a Motor Car* (1900) and *How It Feels to Be Run Over* (1900). Fantasy and trick films, however, did not furnish the sole provenance where visual effects flourished. Effects also proved compatible with realistic subject matter. Miniature models of buildings, landscapes, and ships provided filmmakers with a means for dramatizing noteworthy events, as in *The Battle of Santiago Bay* (1898), *Windsor Hotel Fire* (1899), and *Eruption of Vesuvius* (1906). Filmmakers used every mechanical device they could devise to overcome the constraints of time, space, and budget governing what might be filmed. Glass shots, hanging miniatures, and matte-and-counter-matte systems proliferated throughout silent-era filmmaking. Optical printing and rear-screen projection proved viable in the early 1930s and became staples of studio filmmaking. Filmmakers used visual effects to create imaginary worlds for the camera and to embellish and augment the realities of place when filming in the actual world.

The Lumière brothers made actualities, but they also made trick films. On the 1895 Cinematograph program, *Workers Toppling a Wall* was shown normally to audiences and then run backward, intriguing viewers with images of time in reverse and the wall reconstituting itself as whole. As Dan North has written, "Early cinema has been dichotomized to imagine a distinction between the fantastic capabilities of the earliest films and documentary-based, non-narrative observational filming."[2] As he points out, this is a false dichotomy, and yet our thinking about cinema often incorporates such dichotomies. Realism and fantasy are taken as oppositional modes, each with its own forefather, Lumière and Méliès. Spectacle is taken as being antithetical to narrative. The digital counters the analog and the indexical. Humanly crafted visual images contrast with computer-generated images. These dichotomies have impeded our ability to see visual effects as a core modality of cinema rather than as a peripheral one that supplements the filming of live action.

As we have seen, digital visual effects are as compatible with a naturalistic style as they are with more overt forms of fantasy. Clint Eastwood's *Changeling* (2008) and David Fincher's *Zodiac* (2007) are low-key, naturalistic films that anchor their period dramas in a strongly evoked depiction of historical place and time. Neither film is what one might call effects-driven, and yet visual effects provided each filmmaker with a crucial means for achieving a desired patina of realism. The seafaring adventures depicted in *Master and Commander* (2003) take place in a virtual world that looks quite real but never existed before the cameras. Digital methods for achieving perceptual realism have given filmmakers widely expanded abilities to make the screen world credible and convincing, whether it be the nineteenth-century naval warfare depicted in *Master and Commander* or the gods and monsters in *Clash of the Titans* (2010). These are composited screen worlds, created from layered image elements, a methodology that is no different from practices of narrative filmmaking prevalent throughout screen history. As visual effects supervisor Ken Ralston (*Forrest Gump, The Polar Express*) points out, "Synthetic sets have always existed—look at a matte painting from a movie in 1930. Okay, that's not a 'digital backlot,' but it's an 'analog backlot.' It's the same trick."[3] The presence or absence of visual effects does not determine the degree of fantasy or realism that a film possesses. This is largely a matter of narrative and genre and the constructions of style. Shilo T. McClean points out that when critics discuss what they call "effects movies," they are usually talking about science fiction or action-adventure films. "As soon as one moves into the wider field of filmmaking, the nonspectacular uses of effects become more apparent and the nonspectacular uses of effects within the traditional genres also become obvious."[4]

Movies that might fairly be criticized as effects-driven represent a tiny fraction of the filmmaking that incorporates visual effects. Digital tools now enable filmmakers to craft seamless virtual worlds, to achieve convincing blends of live action and computer animation. Filmmakers can make effects insistent, overwhelming, and, indeed, overbearing, but industry consensus tends to view a disregard for narrative as a sign of poor filmmaking. Given the tensions between narrative and "attractions" that are historically embedded at a deep level in cinema, it is worth remarking upon the continuing relevance of narrative as the organizing framework for popular cinema and for the deployment of visual effects. If a story is poorly constructed and egregiously bad in its presentation, no amount of visual effects will save it, and poor effects do not compromise a well-told tale. Effects artists themselves agree on these points. Visual effects supervisor Bill Taylor (*The Fast and the Furious*, *Star Trek Nemesis*) said, "One of the best movies ever made, *North by Northwest*, has some matte paintings in it that are real pokes in the eye, frankly. But it doesn't matter, because the audience is always with the movie."[5] Gollum became an important, ground-breaking CG character, according to animation supervisor Randall Cook (*The Lord of the Rings* trilogy), in large part because he was well written. "He was written as a star turn, a scene stealer . . . [but] without his being written as an interesting character in the first place, Gollum wouldn't have been that successful. It was really the first great part to come along for a CG character."[6] Creature effects creator Alec Gillis (*Aliens*, *Spider-Man*) complained, "In the last *Matrix* movie, there were hundreds of Agent Smiths fighting with Neo. Interesting concept. But then they fight and they fight, and pretty soon it is clear that Neo is indestructible and the Agent Smiths are unstoppable—so why are we watching this?"[7] If a narrative suspends the rules of reality by making a character indestructible or possessed of special powers, there ought to be a reason for doing so that works at the level of story. Visual effects cannot be total substitutes for narrative craft. As Stan Winston said, "*Jurassic Park* wasn't successful because of the effects. *Terminator* wasn't successful because of its effects. *Lord of the Rings* wasn't successful because of its effects. They were all great stories."[8] Bad effects films, such as *Van Helsing* (2004), demonstrate poor production decisions by studio executives and filmmakers rather than anything about the nature of visual effects. Miniature effects supervisor Matthew Gratzner (*Godzilla*, *The Aviator*) says, "Blame the studios because they're putting scripts into production that are terrible. If a high percentage of these films *didn't* have effects in them, they'd be unwatchable."[9] Viewers at the movies do not often seek spectacle for its own sake. They may want visual effects to show them things they haven't seen before, but they also want the effects to be integrated into a story that is well told. The most common complaint lodged against *Avatar* (2009) by viewers who didn't like the movie was not that the effects were poor or were insufficiently spectacular but that the story was too conventional and familiar, like *Pocahontas* or *Dances with Wolves* in outer space.

André Bazin, whose shadow has loomed large in these pages, distinguished between filmmakers who put their faith in reality and those who put their faith in the image. This can be a useful distinction between cinematic modes and styles, but, as I hope to have shown, aesthetic and social objectives and context often trump technology. Filmmakers who put their faith in reality may find that digital tools enable them to work faster and lighter when on location and that there is no necessary disjunction between a desire to use the camera as a recording mechanism and storing data on memory cards. While I have questioned the degree to which cinema usefully can be understood as a photographic medium, the indexical value of the image—when relevant to a given production's aesthetic or social objectives—is not of necessity threatened by digital modalities. Digital imaging not only sustains indexical values but offers filmmakers new tools and new modes for creating such value. These include methods for re-creating locations in a virtual environment, for capturing the entire range of light in a scene, for nesting reality-based perceptual cues into scenes regardless of their referential content, and for building the performance of a live actor into a digital character. By preserving indexical values, these methods provide expanded modes of creative expression, offering actors, for example, opportunities to perform types of characters that hitherto they could not play so convincingly.

A corollary of the notion that digital images lack indexical value is the idea that they belong to a different register and category of picture-making from photographic images. Deborah Tudor points to a perceived relationship "between analog and digital that situates 'film' as an emotional register and 'digital' as a sterile image capture process."[10] She continues, "The breakdown runs roughly along lines of 'emotional, warm, live, and organic' for analog footage, including analog effects (post production). 'Sterile, cold, perfect, and artificial' feature in descriptions of digital effects."[11] As I noted in the introduction, CGI has proven to be a most unfortunate term, bringing to critical discussion of digital effects a kind of inherent biasing toward the emotional register that Tudor describes. The idea that computers generate pictures makes the resulting images seem soulless and inhuman in comparison with analog modes that are crafted by human hands. On the contrary, however, the algorithms that permit wrapping a computer object with photographically derived textures or creating terrain procedurally from elevation maps were designed to facilitate creative expression. And these images indeed are crafted by human hands.

Digital images have different properties from filmic ones—an absence of grain and motion blur, for example—which gives rise to a practice that Tudor calls "technostalgia," the use of new technologies to imitate older ones. The emulation of anamorphic 'scope cinematography in *WALL-E* (2008) is an example of this. As John Dykstra points out about film, "We revere it as our prime surrogate for reality."[12] But film doesn't capture reality or duplicate its appearance except at a low level. Its exposure latitude, for one thing, is too narrow to reproduce the range of light that a human observer can see in a location. In time the look of film will yield to the look of digital, and at some point should digital be replaced after furnishing the norm, it will provide a new source of technostalgia. Cinema, indeed, is changing, but these changes can be found mainly in the new distribution channels that digital delivery modes make possible, moving the popular experience of cinema away from big screens and public gatherings and toward small displays, intimate, private, and mobile settings. As a corollary of this, cinema has lost a commanding place in popular culture. It now coexists with other media on a cluttered communication landscape. Movies remain popular, but cinema can no longer be said to be our most important art form. Although cinema's institutional framework and the mechanisms by which it reaches viewers have changed, less so have the narrative formulas and aesthetic practices that filmmakers use to draw viewers to the screen. The digital toolbox furnishes new capabilities and new aesthetics while maintaining continuity with the past.

Oliver Grau writes that the search for immersive forms of illusion is strongly anchored in the history of Western art. Immersive illusions blur and erase distinctions between viewer and image, and the quest for increasingly thorough and persuasive illusory spaces is ongoing. "Panorama, film, and computer image displays are aggregates of continually changing machines, forms of organization and materials; in spite of all efforts at standardization, they are seldom stable but always driven by the fascination of increasing the illusion."[13] The history of cinema shows a continuing movement within the medium toward providing viewers with greater perceptual immersion, achieved by stylistic accretions in the areas of framing, lighting, editing, color, sound, large-format film gauges, stereoscopic space, and high-definition video. Visual effects have played key roles in this history by freeing filmmakers from the constraints of available locales and the story situations that would support these. Visual effects enabled filmmakers to travel anywhere in the imagination and to create images of fanciful domains on the other side of the looking glass, but also to simulate reality in ways that otherwise eluded travel budgets and production resources. Using visual effects, filmmakers achieved increasingly persuasive illusions, from the earliest mattes and glass shots to today's multipass digital compositing, motion tracking, and stereoscopically rendered space. When Edwin S. Porter used mattes in *The Great Train Robbery* (1903) to join views inside a telegraph office and rail car with outdoor action visible through their windows, he knew that screen spaces need not be adjacent or have any natural connection in terms of real-world geography. Screen space is composited and constructed rather than photographed—this principle furnishes the basis for cinema to operate as a narrative art. Unable to film the White House for key scenes in the Angelina Jolie thriller *Salt* (2010), the filmmakers took photographs from which they pulled textures to dress a computer-built White House and its environs. With visual effects, filmmakers composite and construct narrative worlds that cannot, for reasons of time, space, or budget, be filmed directly. Our theoretical understanding of cinema often has underestimated the extent to which the screen realities constructed by the medium are composites, amalgamations of image types and filming methods. Visual effects are fundamental components of cinema, essential to its ability to communicate as a narrative medium.

As James Cameron pointed out, visual effects do seduce reality. They emulate objects and locales and imbue these with the photographic appearance of connection and causation, and they replicate the perceptual cues that viewers rely on in making sense of the visible and audible world. As such they stand in for this world and even can counterfeit it, and by offering immersive image spaces, they beckon audiences in a beguiling fashion, promising to raise the curtain on domains of the imagination. This quest for visualizing the imagination drove the first generations of engineers and scientists who developed raster and vector graphics, pixel paint systems, and texturing and lighting algorithms. Transitioning away from photochemical methods of image generation opened new domains of pictorial expression and made novel cinematic modes possible. Live and digital characters interact naturalistically, screen space can be configured as monocular or stereoscopic, and film's unique mode of perception need not be abandoned in a digital domain. Logarithmic exposure values, lens distortion, grain, and the color space of individual film stocks and of systems like three-strip Technicolor can be emulated digitally. Audiences have taken great delight in these changes.

The history of cinema and the history of visual effects are inseparable. Both came into being from the nineteenth-century juncture of art and science that gave us optical toys and a popular desire for more vivid, machine-hosted illusion spaces. Craig Barron has suggested that cinema originated as a visual effect. This perception stands our familiar understanding of cinema on its head. Instead of organic images, ones reflecting a minimal amount of post-production processing, what if cinema's essence, indeed, is composed of visual effects? Editing is a visual effect. So is lighting and deep-focus cinematography. These are normative indexes of film style, and yet they are constructions upon profilmic reality in ways no less artificial than the use of matte paintings or hanging miniatures. The costumes worn by actors are visual effects, and, in light of cinema's composited nature, it makes no sense to differ with the logic that motion capture provides actors with the means of wearing digital costuming and makeup. Here is the most fundamental conceptual challenge that the digital toolbox presents to us—it compels us to reconsider the medium-constituting implications of narrative cinema's amalgamated nature.

It's tempting at this closing stage to speculate on the future, but prognostications always court disaster. Events turn out otherwise. I have written about cinema as a screen-based medium. Whether that screen is 2D or stereoscopic with floating windows or a hologram, it defines an area to which viewers direct their attention while remaining relatively immobile. This mode remains resistant to change. Storytelling is an ancient art that has never lost favor. Nevertheless, gaming modes, where the virtual camera instantiates the player as a first-person participant in the action, will exert a continuing influence over cinematic design. And screen-based modes of cinema viewing will yield cultural space to virtual reality systems in which images are projected directly upon the retina. The computational rendition of pictorial design will maintain its place as cinema's new horizon, and audiences will continue to embrace the manner in which numbers invigorate pictures. Cinema will retain its documentary value and functions in a digital realm. An aesthetic of realism invested in filming events before the camera with minimal processing and manipulation will continue to flourish in a digital world—more so, even, to the extent that digital modalities make everyone with a camera into a potential documentary filmmaker. But as a medium of popular storytelling, cinema rests upon the foundation provided by its visual effects. The hidden cuts, trapdoors, and painted backdrops of Méliès have yielded to the algorithmic simulation of organic processes that George Lucas unintentionally brought into the filmic fold when he recruited the NYIT computer scientists to work on the *Star Wars* series. That opened cinema to a mode of pictorial design whose boundaries seem limitless. If Craig Barron is right that cinema originates as a visual effect, then he may be right as well that the history of cinema finds its juncture at these two events. As he said, "Perhaps Méliès and Lucas will be the two Georges that become the bookends of cinema."[14]

NOTES

INTRODUCTION

1. Dan North, *Performing Illusions: Cinema, Special Effects and the Virtual Actor* (New York: Wallflower Press, 2008), 6.

2. Ibid., 10.

3. Sigmund Freud, "The Uncanny," in *Sigmund Freud: Collected Papers*, vol. 4, trans. Joan Riviere (New York: Basic Books, 1959), 368–407.

4. Kristen Whissel, "The Digital Multitude," *Cinema Journal* 49:4 (Summer 2010): 90–110.

5. Jody Duncan, "The Seduction of Reality," *Cinefex* 120 (January 2010): 146.

1. THROUGH THE LOOKING GLASS

1. Barbara Maria Stafford and Frances Terpak, *Devices of Wonder: From the World in a Box to Images on a Screen* (Los Angeles: Getty Publications, 2001), 112.

2. Scott Bukatman, *Matters of Gravity: Special Effects and Supermen in the 20th Century* (Durham, N.C.: Duke University Press, 2003), 91.

3. Michele Pierson, *Special Effects: Still in Search of Wonder* (New York: Columbia University Press, 2002), 93–136.

4. Charles Csuri, "Panel: The Stimulation of Natural Phenomena," *Computer Graphics* 17:3 (July 1983): 137.

5. Herbert Freeman, *Interactive Computer Graphics* (Los Alamitos, Calif.: IEEE Computer Society Press, 1980).

6. Charles Csuri and James Shaffer, "Art, Computers and Mathematics," *AFIPS Conference Proceedings*, vol. 33 (Washington, D.C.: Thompson Book Company, 1968), 1293.

7. Wayne Carlson, *A Critical History of Computer Graphics and Animation* (2003), http://design.osu.edu/carlson/history/lessons.html.

8. John Whitney, *Digital Harmony: On the Complementarity of Music and Visual Art* (Peterborough, N.H.: Byte Books, 1980), 123.

9. Michael Noll, "The Digital Computer as a Creative Medium," *IEEE Spectrum* 4:10 (October 1967): 90.

10. Ibid., 95.

11. Ivan Sutherland, "Sketchpad: A Man-Machine Graphical Communication System," AFIPS Spring Joint Computer Conference, Detroit, Michigan, May 21–23, 1963, 329.

12. Alvy Ray Smith, "Digital Paint Systems: Historical Overview," Microsoft Technical Memo 14, May 30, 1997, 2.

13. Steven Coons, "Surfaces for Computer-Aided Design of Space Forms," MIT/LCS/TR-41 (June 1967), http://publications.csail.mit.edu/lcs/pubs/pdf/MIT-LCS-TR-041.pdf.

14. Lawrence Roberts, "Machine Perception of Three-Dimensional Solids" (1963), http://www.packet.cc/files/mach-per-3D-solids.html.

15. Robert Rivlin, *The Algorithmic Image: Graphic Visions of the Computer Age* (Redmond, Wash.: Microsoft Press, 1986), 30.

16. Estelle Shay, "Company File: Pixar," *Cinefex* 55 (August 1993): 23–24.

17. I thank Joe Fordham for pointing this out to me.

18. Smith, "Digital Paint Systems," 5.

19. William T. Reeves, "Particle Systems—A Technique for Modeling a Class of Fuzzy Objects," *Computer Graphics* 17:3 (July 1983): 359.

20. Ibid., 367.

21. Loren C. Carpenter, "Computer Rendering of Fractal Curves and Surfaces," *Computer Graphics* 14:3 (July 1980): 109.

22. Personal communication to the author, December 14, 2010.

23. Alan Fournier, Don Fussell, and Loren Carpenter, "Computer Rendering of Stochastic Models," *Computer Graphics* 25:6 (June 1982): 383.

24. Pierson, *Special Effects*, 136.

25. Ibid., 155.

26. For details, see Joe Fordham, "In Dreams," *Cinefex* 123 (October 2010): 38–69.

27. Personal communication to the author, December 14, 2010.

28. Jody Duncan provides a comprehensive portrait of the film's effects techniques in "The Beauty in the Beasts," *Cinefex* 55 (August 1993): 42–95.

29. Personal communication to the author, December 14, 2010.

30. Duncan, "Beauty in the Beasts," 91.

31. Jody Duncan, "On the Shoulders of Giants," *Cinefex* 70 (June 1997): 81.

32. Mark Cotta Vaz, *Industrial Light and Magic: Into the Digital Realm* (London: Virgin Publishing, 1996), 123.

33. Warren Buckland, "Between Science Fact and Science Fiction: Spielberg's Digital Dinosaurs, Possible Worlds, and the New Aesthetic Realism," *Screen* 40:2 (Summer 1999): 185.

34. Tom Gunning, "Gollum and Golem: Special Effects and the Technology of Artificial Bodies," in *From Hobbits to Hollywood: Essays on Peter Jackson's Lord of the Rings*, ed. Ernest Mathijs and Murray Pomerance (New York: Rodopi, 2006), 347.

35. Bukatman, *Matters of Gravity*, 90.

36. Stephen Prince, "True Lies: Perceptual Realism, Digital Images and Film Theory," *Film Quarterly* 49:2 (2006): 27–37.

37. Personal communication to the author, December 14, 2010.

38. Richard Rickitt, *Special Effects: The History and Technique* (New York: Billboard Books, 2007), 188–190.

39. Quoted in Duncan, "Beauty in the Beasts," 92.

40. Ibid., 66.

41. Ibid., 64.

42. Personal communication to the author, December 14, 2010.

43. Pierson, *Special Effects*, 120.

44. Ibid., 124.

45. Geoff King, *Spectacular Narratives: Hollywood in the Age of the Blockbuster* (New York: I. B. Tauris, 2000), 48.

46. Aylish Wood, "Timespaces in Spectacular Cinema: Crossing the Great Divide of Spectacle versus Narrative," *Screen* 43:4 (Winter 2002): 370–386.

47. Bukatman, *Matters of Gravity*, 113.

48. Annette Kuhn, ed., *Alien Zone II: The Spaces of Science Fiction Cinema* (London: Verso, 1999), 5.

49. Andrew Darley, *Visual Digital Culture: Surface Play and Spectacle in New Media Games* (London: Routledge, 2000), 104.

50. Viva Paci, "The Attraction of the Intelligent Eye: Obsessions with the Vision Machine in Early Film Theories," in *The Cinema of Attractions Reloaded*, ed. Wanda Strauven (Amsterdam: Amsterdam University Press, 2006), 122.

51. Shilo T. McClean, *Digital Storytelling: The Narrative Power of Visual Effects in Film* (Cambridge, Mass.: MIT Press, 2007).

52. Wood, "Timespaces in Spectacular Cinema," 373.

53. Tom Gunning, "The Cinema of Attraction: Early Film, Its Spectator, and the Avant-Garde,"in *Film and Theory: An Anthology*, ed. Robert Stam and Toby Miller (Malden, Mass.: Blackwell, 2000), 230.

54. Tom Gunning, "An Aesthetic of Astonishment: Early Film and the (In)Credulous Spectator," *Art and Text* 34 (Spring 1989): 119.

55. Ibid., 121.

56. Gunning, "The Cinema of Attraction," 234.

57. Charles Musser, "A Cinema of Contemplation, A Cinema of Discernment: Spectatorship, Intertextuality and Attractions in the 1890s," in Strauven, *The Cinema of Attractions Reloaded*, 176.

58. Malcolm Turvey, *Doubting Vision: Film and the Revelationist Tradition* (New York: Oxford University Press, 2008), 99, 101.

59. Jonathan Crary, *Techniques of the Observer: On Vision and Modernity in the Nineteenth Century* (Cambridge, Mass.: MIT Press, 1992), 6.

60. Mary Ann Doane, *The Emergence of Cinematic Time* (Cambridge, Mass.: Harvard University Press, 2002), 72.

61. Scott Curtis, "Still/Moving: Digital Imaging and Medical Hermeneutics," in *Memory Bytes: History, Technology, and Digital Culture*, ed. Lauren Rabinovitz and Abraham Geil (Durham, N.C.: Duke University Press, 2004), 218–254.

62. John Durham Peters, "Helmholtz, Edison, and Sound History," in Rabinovitz and Geil, *Memory Bytes*, 177–198.

63. Lauren Rabinovitz and Abraham Geil, "Introduction," in Rabinovitz and Geil, *Memory Bytes*, 13.

64. Lisa Cartwright, *Screening the Body: Tracing Medicine's Visual Culture* (Minneapolis: University of Minnesota Press, 1995), 3.

65. Hermann von Helmholtz, "The Recent Progress of the Theory of Vision," in *Popular Scientific Lectures*, selected and introduced by Morris Kline (New York: Dover, 1962), 97.

66. See Robert J. Silverman, "The Stereoscope and Photographic Depiction in the 19th Century," *Technology and Culture* 34:4 (October 1993): 729–756.

67. Ibid., 110.

68. Nicholas J. Wade and Stanley Finger, "The Eye as an Optical Instrument: From Camera Obscura to Helmholtz's Perspective," *Perception* 30 (2001): 1158.

69. Martin Kemp, *The Science of Art: Optical Themes in Western Art from Brunelleschi to Seurat* (New Haven, Conn.: Yale University Press, 1990), 13.

70. Philip Steadman, *Vermeer's Camera: Uncovering the Truth Behind the Masterpieces* (New York: Oxford University Press, 2002).

71. David Hockney, *Secret Knowledge: Rediscovering the Lost Techniques of the Old Masters* (London: Thames and Hudson, 2001), 12.

72. Nicholas J. Wade, "Philosophical Instruments and Toys: Optical Devices Extending the Art of Seeing," *Journal of the History of the Neurosciences* 13:1 (2004): 105.

73. David A. Cook, *A History of Narrative Film*, 4th ed. (New York: Norton, 2004), 1.

74. Keith Griffiths, "The Manipulated Image," *Convergence* 9:4 (2003): 16.

75. Wade, "Philosophical Instruments," 102.

76. Sir Charles Wheatstone, "Description of the Kaleidophone, or Phonic Kaleidoscope," in *Brewster and Wheatstone on Vision*, ed. Nicholas Wade (New York: Academic Press, 1983), 205.

77. Ibid., 108.

78. David Brewster, "Circumstances Which Led to the Invention of the Kaleidoscope," in Wade, *Brewster and Wheatstone on Vision*, 202.

79. Wheatstone, "Description of the Kaleidophone, or Phonic Kaleidoscope," 206.

80. Wheatstone, "Contribution to the Physiology of Vision—Part the First," in Wade, *Brewster and Wheatstone on Vision*, 67.

81. Anne Friedberg, *The Virtual Window* (Cambridge, Mass.: MIT Press, 2006), 60.

82. Ibid., 116.

83. Quoted in Wade and Finger, "The Eye as an Optical Instrument," 1172.

84. Hemholtz, "Recent Progress of the Theory of Vision," 173.

85. Marta Braun, *Picturing Time: The Work of Etienne-Jules Marey (1830–1904)* (Chicago: University of Chicago Press, 1992), 52.

86. Cartwright, *Screening the Body*, 3.

87. Lev Manovich, *The Language of New Media* (Cambridge, Mass.: MIT Press, 2001), 104.

88. David E. Meyer and Sylvan Kornblum, "Speed and Accuracy of Saccadic Eye Movements: Characteristics of Impulse Variability in the Oculomotor System," *Journal of Experimental Psychology* 15:3 (1989): 543.

89. M. H. Pirenne, *Optics, Painting, and Photography* (Cambridge: Cambridge University Press, 1970), 183.

90. Ibid.

91. David Rodowick, *The Virtual Life of Film* (Cambridge, Mass.: Harvard University Press, 2007), 9.

92. Quoted in Peter Wollen, *Signs and Meanings in the Cinema* (Bloomington: Indiana University Press, 1976), 123–124.

93. Roland Barthes, *Camera Lucida: Reflections on Photography*, trans. Richard Howard (New York: Hill and Wang, 1981), 5.

94. Ibid., 76.

95. Ibid., 87.

96. Andre Bazin, *What is Cinema?*, vol. 1, ed. and trans. Hugh Gray (Berkeley: University of California Press, 1967), 14.

97. Manovich, *Language of New Media*, 294–295.

98. Crary, *Techniques of the Observer*, 2.

99. Sean Cubitt, *The Cinema Effect* (Cambridge, Mass.: MIT Press, 2004), 250.

100. Bazin, *What Is Cinema?*, 46.

101. Manovich, *Language of New Media*, 146.

102. Ibid., 198.

103. Helmholtz, "On the Relation of Optics to Painting," 285.

104. Steadman, *Vermeer's Camera*, 159.

105. Ibid., 1.

106. Whitney, *Digital Harmony*, 126.

107. Michael Rubin, *Droidmaker: George Lucas and the Digital Revolution* (Gainesville, Fla.: Triad Publishing Company), 107.

108. Ibid., 175.

2. PAINTING WITH DIGITAL LIGHT

1. Leon Shamroy, "The Future of Cinematography," reprinted in *American Cinematographer* (March 1999): 128.

2. Ibid., 28.

3. "Wielding the Double-Edged Sword: Digital Post and Effects," *American Cinematographer* (May 1995): 30.

4. Ibid., 27.

5. Ibid.

6. Ron Magid, "ILM Breaks New Digital Ground for *Gump*," *American Cinematographer* (October 1994): 45, 46.

7. Mark Cotta Vaz and Patricia Rose Duignan, *Industrial Light and Magic: Into the Digital Domain* (New York: Ballantine Books, 1996), 138.

8. Paul Harrill pointed this out to me.

9. Linwood G. Dunn, "Optical Printing and Technique," in *The ASC Treasury of Visual Effects*, ed. Linwood G. Dunn and George Turner (Hollywood, Calif.: ASC Holding Company, 1983), 92.

10. Dunn, "The Cinemagic of the Optical Printer," in Dunn and Turner, *The ASC Treasury of Visual Effects*, 240.

11. Dunn, quoted in Richard Rickitt, *Special Effects: The History and Technique* (London: Aurum Press, 2007), 74.

12. Edlund, quoted in Rickitt, *Special Effects*, 78.

13. Knoll, quoted in Vaz and Duignan, *Industrial Light and Magic*, 160.

14. Dunn, "Cinemagic," 240.

15. Ron Brinkman, *The Art and Science of Digital Compositing*, 2nd ed. (New York: Morgan Kaufmann, 2008), 547–553.

16. Ibid., 514–520.

17. Jody Duncan, "The Seduction of Reality," *Cinefex* 120 (January 2010): 130.

18. Paul Debevec, "Rendering Synthetic Objects into Real Scenes: Bridging Traditional and Image-based Graphics with Global Illumination and High Dynamic Range Photography," *SIGGRAPH '98: Proceedings of the 25th Annual Conference on Computer Graphics and Interactive Techniques* (New York: ACM, 1998), 189.

19. Per H. Christensen, Julian Fong, David M. Laur, and Dana Batali, *Ray Tracing for the Movie 'Cars,'* http://graphics.pixar.com/library/RayTracingCars/paper.pdf.

20. Hayden Landis, "Production-Ready Global Illumination," SIGGRAPH Course Notes #16 (2002).

21. Ibid., 97.

22. Philipp S. Gerasimov, "Omnidirectional Shadow Mapping," in *GPU Gems*, ed. Randima Fernando (New York: Addison-Wesley, 2004), 193–203.

23. William Donnelly and Joe Demers, "Generating Soft Shadows Using Occlusion Interval Maps," in *GPU Gems*, 205–215.

24. William T. Reeves, David H. Salesin, and Robert L. Cook, "Rendering Antialiased Shadows with Depth Maps," *Computer Graphics* 21:4 (July 1987): 283–291.

25. Athena Xenakis and Erin Tomson, "Shading Food: Making It Tasty for *Ratatouille*," in *Anyone Can Cook—Inside Ratatouille's Kitchen*, SIGGRAPH Course Notes #30 (2007), http://graphics.pixar.com/library/AnyoneCanCook/paper.pdf.

26. Stefan Gronsky, "Lighting Food," in *Anyone Can Cook*, 34.

27. Xenakis and Tomson, "Shading Food," 27.

28. Gronsky, "Lighting Food," 34.

29. Quoted in Douglas Bankston, "The Color-Space Conundrum Part Two: Digital Workflow," *American Cinematographer* (April 2005): 82.

30. Ibid., 78.

31. Bob Fisher, "Black-and-White in Color," *American Cinematographer* (November 1998): 60.

32. Bob Fisher, "Escaping from Chains," *American Cinematographer* (October 2000): 40.

33. Ibid., 47.

34. David Wiener, "Chasing the Wind," *American Cinematographer* (May 1996): 38.

35. David E. Williams, "Symbolic Victory," *American Cinematographer* (November 2006): 84.

36. Stephen Pizzello, "Darkest Noir," *American Cinematographer* (September 2006): 45, 48.

37. John Bailey, "The DI Dilemma, or: Why I Still Love Celluloid," *American Cinematographer* (June 2008): 93.

38. Roger Deakins, "The DI, Luddites and Other Musings," *American Cinematographer* (October 2008): 82.

39. Jon Silberg and Stephen Pizzello, "Cinematographers, Colorists and the DI," *American Cinematographer* (June 2009): 81.

40. Mark Hope-Jones, "Portrait of a Lady," *American Cinematographer* (September 2008): 43.

41. Bailey, "The DI Dilemma," 97.

42. Personal communication to the author, January 2011.

43. John Belton, "Painting by the Numbers: The Digital Intermediate," *Film Quarterly* 61:3 (Spring 2008): 61, 62.

44. Ibid., 59.

45. Ibid., 62.

46. Robert L. Carringer, *The Making of Citizen Kane* (Berkeley: University of California Press, 1996), 82.

47. Fred W. Sersen, "Making Matte Shots," in Dunn and Turner, *The ASC Treasury of Visual Effects*, 87.

48. Rochelle Winters, "Love on the Rocks," *American Cinematographer* (July 2001): 60.

49. Jay Holben, "Hell on Wheels," *American Cinematographer* (August 2004): 48.

50. Patricia Thomson, "Horror in Hi-Def," *American Cinematographer* (April 2001): 66.

51. Bill Desowitz, "Fincher Talks *Benjamin Button* and VFX," http://www.awn.com/articles/production/fincher-talks-ibenjamin-buttoni-and-vfx.

52. Holben, "Hell on Wheels," 48.

53. Michael Goldman, "With Friends Like These . . . ," *American Cinematographer* (October 2010): 29.

54. David E. Williams, "Cold Case File," *American Cinematographer* (April 2007): 41.

55. Ibid., 48.

56. Vittorio Baroncini, Hank Mahler, Mattieu Sintas, and Thierry Delpit, "Image Resolution of 35mm Film in Theatrical Presentation," http://www.cst.fr/IMG/pdf/35mm_resolution_english.pdf.

57. Jay Holben, "A Need for Speed," *American Cinematographer* (May 2008): 44.

58. Ibid., 47.

59. Belton, "Painting by the Numbers," 61.

60. Julie Turnock, "Before Industrial Light and Magic: The Independent Hollywood Special Effects Business, 1968–75," *New Review of Film and Television Studies* 7:2 (June 2009): 135.

61. Joe Fordham, "A Beautiful Death," *Cinefex* 109 (April 2007): 78.

62. Joe Fordham, "The Human Project," *Cinefex* 110 (July 2007): 33–44.

63. André Bazin, "The Virtues and Limitations of Montage," in *What Is Cinema?*, vol. 1, trans. Hugh Gray (Berkeley: University of California Press, 1967), 45.

64. Bazin, "The Evolution of the Language of Cinema," in *What Is Cinema?*, 34.

65. Bill Desowitz, "Hello *WALL-E!*: Pixar Reaches for the Stars," *Animation World Network*, http://www.awn.com/articles/production/hello-iWALL-Ei-pixar-reaches-stars.

66. For a summary, see Joe Demers, "Depth of Field: A Survey of Techniques," *GPU Gems*(New York: Addison-Wesley, 2004), 375–390.

67. Iain A. Neil provides a good comparison of spherical and anamorphic lens perspectives in "Lenses in Cinematography," *Optics and Photonics News* (January 2004): 26–33.

68. Iain Stasukevich, "Expert Eyes Enhance *WALL-E*," *American Cinematographer* (July 2008): 26.

69. Berys Gaut, *A Philosophy of Cinematic Art* (New York: Cambridge University Press, 2010), 19.

3. ACTORS AND ALGORITHMS

1. Remington Scott, "Sparking Life: Notes on the Performance Capture Sessions for *The Lord of the Rings: The Two Towers*," *Computer Graphics* (November 2003): 17.

2. Pamela Robertson Wojcik, "The Sound of Film Acting," *Journal of Film and Video* 58 (Spring/Summer 2006): 71.

3. James Naremore, *Acting in the Cinema* (Berkeley: University of California Press, 1988), 96.

4. I thank Patty Raun for emphasizing this point.

5. Cynthia Baron and Sharon Marie Carnicke, *Reframing Screen Performance* (Ann Arbor: University of Michigan Press, 2008), 4.

6. Michael Caine, *Acting in Film* (New York: Applause Theatre Book Publishers, 1990), 66–67.

7. Jay Leyda, *Film Makers Speak* (New York: Da Capo Press, 1977), 441.

8. Mark J. P. Wolf, "The Technological Construction of Performance," *Convergence* 9:4 (2003): 48.

9. Wojcik, "The Sound of Film Acting," 80.

10. Ibid.

11. Bill Desowitz, "Fincher Talks 'Benjamin Button' and VFX," *Animation World Network*, January 9, 2009, http://www.awn.com/articles/production/fincher-talks-ibenjamin-buttoni-and-vfx.

12. Lisa Bode, "No Longer Themselves? Framing Digitally Enabled Posthumous 'Performance,'" *Cinema Journal* 49:4 (Summer 2010): 69.

13. Tom Gunning, "Moving Away from the Index: Cinema and the Impression of Reality," *differences* 18:1 (2007): 38.

14. Personal communication to the author, February 8, 2011.

15. Richard Rickitt, *Special Effects: The History and Technique* (New York: Billboard Books, 2007), 190.

16. Brad Bird, "Foreword," in Ed Hooks, *Acting for Animators* (Portsmouth, N.H.: Heinemann, 2003), vi.

17. Hooks, "Introduction," in *Acting for Animators*, xiv.

18. Frank Thomas and Ollie Johnston, *The Illusion of Life: Disney Animation* (New York: Disney Editions, 1981), 66, 177.

19. Ibid., 474, 475.

20. Jody Duncan, "The Tippett Touch," *Cinefex* 121 (April 2010): 78.

21. Pascal Pinteau, *Special Effects: An Oral History*, trans. Laurel Hirsch (New York: Harry N. Abrams, 2004), 320.

22. Lucilla Potter Hoshor, John W. Finnegan, and Larry Lauria, "Acting and Drawing for Animation," SIGGRAPH Course Notes #07 (2004), http://portal.acm.org/citation.cfm?id=1103912&CFID=21634578&CFTOKEN=85758684.

23. John Kundert-Gibbs and Kristin Kundert-Gibbs, *Action! Acting Lessons for CG Animators* (Indianapolis: Wiley Publishing, 2009), 15.

24. Ibid., 71.

25. Ibid., 68.

26. John Lasseter, "Principles of Traditional Animation Applied to 3D Computer Animation," *Computer Graphics* 21:4 (July 1987): 43.

27. Ibid., 42.

28. Ibid., 35.

29. Pinteau, *Special Effects*, 260.

30. R. D. Walk and C. P. Homan, "Emotion and Dance in Dynamic Light Displays," *Bulletin of the Psychonomic Society* 22 (1984): 437–440; W. H. Dittrich, T. Troscianko, S. Lea, and D. Morgan, "Perception of Emotion from Dynamic Point-Light Displays Represented in Dance," *Perception* 25 (1996): 727–738.

31. Frank E. Pollick, Harold Hill, Andrew Calder, and Helena Paterson, "Recognising Facial Expression from Spatially and Temporally Modified Movements," *Perception* 32 (2003): 813–826.

32. Frank E. Pollick, Helena M. Paterson, Armin Bruderlin, and Anthony J. Sanford, "Perceiving Affect from Arm Movement," *Cognition* 82 (2001): B51–B61.

33. Tim Hauser, *The Art of WALL-E* (San Francisco: Chronicle Books, 2008), 49.

34. Sonoko Konishi and Michael Venturini, "Articulating the Appeal," Pixar Technical Memo #07–12, http://graphics.pixar.com/library/ArticulatingAppeal/paper.pdf.

35. Gordon Cameron, Robert Russ, and Adam Woodbury, "Acting with Contact in *Ratatouille*—Cartoon Collision and Response," Pixar Technical Memo #07–10, http://graphics.pixar.com/library/CartoonCollision/paper.pdf.

36. Personal communication to the author, January 2011.

37. Ron Magid, "Reanimating a Familiar Foe," *American Cinematographer* (November 1997): 52.

38. Ibid.

39. Ibid.

40. Vivian Sobchack, "At the Still Point of the Turning World," in *Meta-Morphing: Visual Transformation and the Culture of Quick-Change*, ed. Vivian Sobchack (Minneapolis: University of Minnesota Press, 2000), 133.

41. Wolf, "Technological Construction of Performance," 49.

42. Thomas and Johnston, *The Illusion of Life*, 326.

43. Pinteau, *Special Effects*, 261.

44. Mark Cotta Vaz, *The Art of The Incredibles* (San Francisco: Chronicle Books, 2004), 28.

45. Ibid., 59.

46. Ibid., 66.

47. Pinteau, *Special* Effects, 265–266.

48. John Edgar Park, "Behind the Scenes on *Final Fantasy*," *Animation World Network*, http://www.awn.com/articles/production/behind-scenes-ifinal-fantasy-spirits-withini.

49. Jody Duncan, "Flesh for Fantasy," *Cinefex* 86 (July 2001): 43.

50. Ibid.

51. Peter Plantec, "Crossing the Great Uncanny Valley," *Animation World Network*, http://www.awn.com/articles/production/crossing-great-uncanny-valley.

52. Masahiro Mori, "The Uncanny Valley," *Energy* 7:4 (1970): 33.

53. Elizabeth A. Rega and Stuart S. Sumida, "Anatomical Considerations in Facial Motion Capture," *Computer Graphics* 43:2 (May 2009):http://portal.acm.org/citation .cfm?id=1629216.1629220&coll=DL&dl=GUIDE&CFID=21634578&CFTOKEN=85758 684.

54. Plantec, "Crossing the Great Uncanny Valley."

55. Rega and Sumida, "Anatomical Considerations in Facial Motion Capture."

56. "Beowulf: Breaking Ground with Mocap," *fxguide*, November 27, 2007, http:// www.fxguide.com/modules.php?name=News&file=article&sid=455.

57. Plantec, "Crossing the Great Uncanny Valley."

58. Bill Desowitz, "Beowulf: A New Hybrid for an Old Tale," *Animation World Network*, http://www.awn.com/print/articles/production/ibeowulfi-new-hybrid-old-tale.

59. Rick DeMott, "*A Christmas Carol*: The Performance Capture Experience," *Animation World Network*, http://www.awn.com/articles/feature/christmas-carol-performance-capture-experience.

60. Ibid.

61. Rickitt, *Special Effects*, 222.

62. Joe Fordham, "Middle-earth Strikes Back," *Cinefex* 92 (January 2003): 74.

63. Ibid.

64. Personal communication to the author, January 2011.

65. Henrik Wann Jensen, Stephen R. Marschner, Marc Levoy, and Pat Hanrahan, "A Practical Model for Subsurface Light Transport," *SIGGRAPH '01: Proceedings of the 28th Annual Conference on Computer Graphics and Interactive Techniques* (New York: ACM, 2001), 511–518.

66. Ibid., 85.

67. Andy Serkis, *The Lord of the Rings: Gollum: How We Made Movie Magic* (New York: Houghton Mifflin, 2003), 83, 84.

68. Personal communication to the author, January 2011.

69. Serkis, *The Lord of the Rings: Gollum*, 48, 49.

70. Ibid., 97.

71. Ibid., 108.

72. Roger Ebert, "Lord of the Rings: The Return of the King," *Chicago Sun-Times*, December 17, 2003, http://rogerebert.suntimes.com/apps/pbcs.dll/article?AID=/20031217/REVIEWS/312170301/1023.

73. Don Shay, Joe Fordham, and Jody Duncan, "State of the Art: A Cinefex 25th Anniversary Forum," *Cinefex* 100 (January 2005): 66.

74. Jody Duncan, "The Seduction of Reality," *Cinefex* 120 (January 2010): 91–92.

75. Ibid., 119.

76. Ibid., 72.

77. Jody Duncan, "The Unusual Birth of Benjamin Button," *Cinefex* 116 (January 2009): 72.

78. Ibid., 88.

79. Ibid.

80. Ibid., 74.

81. Ibid., 72.

82. Rachel Abramowitz, "*Avatar*'s Animated Acting," *Los Angeles Times*, February 18, 2010, http://articles.latimes.com/2010/feb/18/entertainment/la-et-avatar-actors18-2010feb18.

83. Ibid.

84. Mark Harris, "Mark Harris on the 'Acting' in 'Avatar,'" *Entertainment Weekly*, January 22, 2010, http://www.ew.com/ew/article/0,,20339177,00.html#.

85. Ibid.

86. Kristin Thompson, "Motion Capturing an Oscar," *Observations on Film Art*, February 23, 2010, http://www.davidbordwell.net/blog/?p=7126.

87. Abramowitz, "Avatar's Animated Acting."

88. Kirsten Moana Thompson, "Space, Spectacle, and Movement: Massive Software and Digital Special Effects in *The Lord of the Rings*," in *From Hobbits to Hollywood: Essays on Peter Jackson's Lord of the Rings*, ed. Ernest Mathijs and Murray Pomerance (New York: Rodopi, 2006), 299.

89. Don Shay, Joe Fordham, and Jody Duncan, "State of the Art: A Cinefex 25th Anniversary Forum," *Cinefex* 100 (January 2005): 76.

90. Abramowitz, "*Avatar*'s Animated Acting."

91. Serkis, *The Lord of the Rings:Gollum*, 117.

4. DIGITAL ENVIRONMENT CREATION

1. Barbara Robertson, "Painting the Town," *Computer Graphics World* 26:9 (September 2003).

2. Joe Fordham, "Into the Maelstrom," *Cinefex* 110 (July 2007): 62.

3. Ibid., 63–64.

4. Personal communication to the author, January 24, 2011.

5. Jody Duncan, "Iron Clad," *Cinefex* 122 (July 2010): 43.

6. André Bazin, "The Ontology of the Photographic Image," in *What Is Cinema?*, vol. 1, ed. and trans. Hugh Gray (Berkeley: University of California Press, 1967), 13.

7. Ibid., 14.

8. Roland Barthes, *Camera Lucida: Reflections on Photography*, trans. Richard Howard (New York: Hill and Wang, 1981), 5, 87.

9. Rudolph Arnheim, "On the Nature of Photography," *Critical Inquiry* 1 (September, 1974): 155.

10. Ibid., 157.

11. Barbara E. Savedoff, "Escaping Reality: Digital Imagery and the Resources of Photography," *Journal of Aesthetics and Art Criticism* 55:2 (Spring 1997): 203.

12. Sergei Eisenstein, "Through Theater to Cinema," *Film Form*, ed. and trans. Jay Leyda (New York: Harvest Books, 1949), 5.

13. Philip Rosen, *Change Mummified: Cinema, Historicity, Theory* (Minneapolis: University of Minnesota Press, 2001), 303.

14. Savedoff, "Escaping Reality," 210.

15. Steven Shaviro, "Emotion Capture: Affect in Digital Film," *Projections* 1:2 (Winter 2007): 39.

16. Keith Griffiths, "The Manipulated Image," *Convergence* 9:4 (2003): 24.

17. Berys Gaut, *A Philosophy of Cinematic Art* (New York: Cambridge University Press, 2010), 71.

18. Rosen, *Change Mummified*, 314.

19. Braxton Soderman, "The Index and the Algorithm," *differences* 18:1 (2007): 156.

20. Lev Manovich, *The Language of New Media* (Cambridge, Mass.: MIT Press, 2001), 295.

21. Shaviro, "Emotion Capture," 39, 40.

22. Tom Gunning, "Moving Away from the Index: Cinema and the Impression of Reality," *differences* 18:1 (2007): 30, 31.

23. Tom Gunning, "Gollum and Golem: Special Effects and the Technology of Artificial Bodies," in *From Hobbits to Hollywood: Essays on Peter Jackson's Lord of the Rings*, ed. Ernest Mathijs and Murray Pomerance (New York: Rodopi, 2006), 347.

24. Soderman, "The Index and the Algorithm," 156.

25. Mark Wolf, *Abstracting Reality: Art, Communication, and Cognition in the Digital Age* (Lanham, Md.: University Press of America, 2000), 262.

26. Rosen, *Change Mummified*, 314.

27. I discuss the Abu Ghraib images in more detail in *Firestorm: American Film in the Age of Terrorism* (New York: Columbia University Press, 2009).

28. Markus H. Gross, "Computer Graphics in Medicine: From Visualization to Surgery Simulation," *Computer Graphics* (February 1998): 53.

29. Scott Curtis, "Still/Moving: Digital Imaging and Medical Hermeneutics," in *Memory Bytes: History, Technology, and Digital Culture*, ed. Lauren Rabinovitz and Abraham Geil (Durham, N.C.: Duke University Press, 2004), 246.

30. Ibid., 219.

31. Timothy Binkley, "The Vitality of Digital Creation," *Journal of Aesthetics and Art Criticism* 55:2 (Spring 1997): 108, 112.

32. Personal communication to the author, January 14, 2011.

33. Philip Gourevitch and Errol Morris, *Standard Operating Procedure* (New York: Penguin, 2008).

34. Joel Snyder, "Picturing Vision," *Critical Inquiry* 6:3 (Spring 1980): 526.

35. Joel Snyder, "Photography, Vision, and Representation," *Critical Inquiry* 2:1 (Autumn 1975): 152.

36. Noel Carroll, *Engaging the Moving Image* (New Haven, Conn.: Yale University Press, 2003), 8.

37. Ibid., 262–263.

38. Mark Cotta Vaz and Craig Barron, *The Invisible Art: The Legends of Movie Matte Painting* (San Francisco: Chronicle Books, 2002), 42.

39. Rudy Behlmer, "*The Sea Hawk* Sets Sail," *American Cinematographer* (July 1996): 88.

40. Vincent LoBrutto, *By Design: Interviews with Film Production Designers* (Westport, Conn.: Praeger, 1992), 5.

41. Ibid., 8.

42. Richard Rickitt, *Special Effects: The History and Technique* (New York: Billboard Books, 2007), 115.

43. Vaz and Barron, *The Invisible Art*, 181.

44. Ibid., 177.

45. Quoted in ibid., 57.

46. Ibid., 72.

47. Ronald Haver, *David O. Selznick's Hollywood* (New York: Alfred A. Knopf, 1980), 249.

48. Clarence W. D. Slifer, "Creating Visual Effects for *GWTW*," in *The ASC Treasury of Visual Effects*, ed. George Turner (Hollywood, Calif.: ASC Holding Company, 1983), 133.

49. Ibid., 130.

50. Rickitt, *Special Effects*, 26.

51. Gary Russell, *The Lord of the Rings: The Art of "The Two Towers"* (New York: Houghton Mifflin, 2003), 11.

52. Vaz and Barron, *The Invisible Art*, 267.

53. Ibid., 262, 263.

54. Mark Cotta Vaz, *Industrial Light and Magic: Into the Digital Realm* (New York: Ballantine Books, 1996), 96.

55. Personal communication to the author, January 14, 2011.

56. *Matte Painting 2: d'artiste Digital Artists Master Class* (Adelaide, Australia: Ballistic Publishing, 2008), 69.

57. Barbara Robertson, "Painting the Town," *Computer Graphics World* 26:9 (September 2003).

58. Charles Affron and Mirella Jona Affron, *Sets in Motion: Art Direction and Film Narrative* (New Brunswick, N.J.: Rutgers University Press, 1995), 24.

59. Jody Duncan, "Urban Renewal," *Cinefex* 117 (April 2009): 12.

60. Affron and Affron, *Sets in Motion*, 37.

61. Paul E. Debevec, Camillo J. Taylor, and Jitendra Malik, "Modeling and Rendering Architecture from Photographs: A Hybrid Geometry-and-Image-Based Approach," http://ict.debevec.org/~debevec/Research/debevec-siggraph96-paper.pdf./

62. Behlmer, "*The Sea Hawk* Sets Sail," 86.

63. Jody Duncan, "Victory at Sea," *Cinefex* 96 (January 2004): 16.

64. Ibid., 26.

65. Quoted in Rickitt, *Special Effects*, 137.

66. Ibid.

67. Beverly Heisner, *Hollywood Art: Art Direction in the Days of the Great Studios* (Jefferson, N.C.: McFarland, 1990), 4.

68. Ibid.

69. Affron and Affron, *Sets in Motion*, 41.

70. Jody Duncan, "The Seduction of Reality," *Cinefex* 120 (January 2010): 94.

71. David Tattersall, "A Need for Speed," *American Cinematographer* (May 2008): 49.

5. IMMERSIVE AESTHETICS

1. Robert Neuman, "*Bolt 3D:* A Case Study," *Proceedings of SPIE* 7237, 72370F (2009), http://spiedigitallibrary.org/proceedings/resource/2/psisdg/7237/1/72370F_1?isAuthorized=no.

2. Oliver Grau, *Virtual Art: From Illusion to Immersion*, trans. Gloria Custance (Cambridge, Mass.: MIT Press, 2003), 5.

3. Alison Griffiths, *Shivers Down Your Spine: Cinema, Museums, and the Immersive View* (New York: Columbia University Press, 2008), 18, 19.

4. Ibid., 3.

5. Martin Kemp, *The Science of Art: Optical Themes in Western Art from Brunelleschi to Seurat* (New Haven, Conn.: Yale University Press, 1990), 214.

6. Grau, *Virtual Art*, 106.

7. Raymond Fielding, "Hale's Tours: Ultrarealism in the Pre-1910 Motion Picture," in *Film Before Griffith*, ed. John L. Fell (Berkeley: University of California Press, 1983), 117.

8. Quoted in ibid., 127.

9. Lauren Rabinovitz, "More than the Movies," in *Memory Bytes: History, Technology, and Digital Culture* (Durham, N.C.: Duke University Press, 2004), 102.

10. Richard Allen, *Projecting Illusion: Film Spectatorship and the Impression of Reality* (New York: Cambridge University Press, 1995), 82.

11. Kemp, *Science of Art*, 212.

12. André Bazin, "The Myth of Total Cinema," in *What Is Cinema?*, vol. 1, trans. Hugh Gray (Berkeley: University of California Press, 1967), 20.

13. Neuman, "*Bolt 3D*."

14. Jody Duncan, "The Seduction of Reality," *Cinefex* 120 (January 2010): 146.

15. Dan North, *Performing Illusions: Cinema, Special Effects and the Virtual Actor* (New York: Wallflower Press, 2008), 50.

16. Ibid., 2, 4.

17. Ibid., 2.

18. Angela Ndalianis, "Special Effects, Morphing Magic, and the 1990s Cinema of Attractions," in *Meta-Morphing: Visual Transformation and the Culture of Quick-Change*, ed. Vivian Sobchack (Minneapolis: University of Minnesota Press, 2000), 260.

19. Allen, *Projecting Illusion*, 82.

20. Ibid., 109.

21. Noel Carrol, *Philosophical Problems of Classical Film Theory* (Princeton, N.J.: Princeton University Press, 1998), 135.

22. Personal communication to the author, January 14, 2011.

23. Quoted in Jeffrey Vance, *Chaplin: Genius of the Cinema* (New York: Abrams, 2003), 206.

24. Paul Debevec, "Rendering Synthetic Objects into Real Scenes: Bridging Traditional and Image-Based Graphics with Global Illumination and High Dynamic Range Photography," *SIGGRAPH '98: Proceedings of the 25th Annual Conference on Computer Graphics and Interactive Techniques* (New York: ACM, 1998).

25. Iain Stasukevich, "Cat and Mouse," *American Cinematographer* (August 2010): 39.

26. Debevec, "Rendering Synthetic Objects," 3.

27. Paul Debevec, "Computer Graphics with Real Light," 191.

28. Paul Debevec, Andreas Wenger, Chris Tchou, Andrew Gardner, Jamie Waese, and Tim Hawkins, "A Lighting Reproduction Approach to Live-Action Compositing," *SIGGRAPH '02: Proceedings of the 29th Annual Conference on Computer Graphics and Interactive Techniques* (New York: ACM, 2002).

29. "Double Negative Breaks Down *Batman Begins*," *fxguide*, July 18, 2005, http://www.fxguide.com/modules.php?name=News&file=print&sid=262.

30. http://www.newsweek.com/2010/04/30/why-i-hate-3-d-and-you-should-too.html.

31. James E. Cutting and Peter M. Vishton, "Perceiving Layout and Knowing Distances: The Integration, Relative Potency, and Contextual Use of Different Information about Depth," in *Perception of Space and Motion*, ed. William Epstein and Sheena Rogers (New York: Academic Press, 1995), 69–117.

32. James E. Cutting, "Perceiving Scenes in Film and in the World," in *Moving Image Theory: Ecological Considerations*, ed. Joseph D. Anderson and Barbara Fisher Anderson (Carbondale: Southern Illinois University Press, 2005), 14.

33. Lenny Lipton, *Foundations of the Stereoscopic Cinema: A Study in Depth* (New York: Van Nostrand Reinhold, 1982), 16.

34. Ray Zone, *Stereoscopic Cinema and the Origins of 3-D Film, 1838–1952* (Lexington: University Press of Kentucky, 2007), 4.

35. H. Mark Gosser, *Selected Attempts at Stereoscopic Moving Pictures and Their Relationship to the Development of Motion Picture Technology, 1852–1903* (New York: Arno Press, 1977), 321.

36. Zone, *Stereoscopic Cinema*, 142–143.

37. Lipton, *Foundations of the Stereoscopic Cinema*, 44.

38. Stephanie Argy, "An Eye-Popping Adventure," *American Cinematographer* (August 2008): 60, 61.

39. "3D Movie Fans Expand Box Office Says International 3D Society Study," http://www.international3dsociety.com/research.html.

40. Lenny Lipton, "The Stereoscopic Cinema: From Film to Digital Projection," *SMPTE Journal* (September 2001): 590.

41. Ibid., 592–593.

42. See, for example, Marc T.M. Lambooij, Wijnand A. IJsselsteijn, and Ingrid Heynderickx, "Visual Discomfort in Stereoscopic Displays: A Review," *Proceedings of SPIE* 6490, 64900I (2007), http://spiedigitallibrary.org/proceedings/resource/2/psisdg/6490/1/64900I_1?isAuthorized=no.

43. Lipton, *Foundations of the Stereoscopic Cinema*, 238–239.

44. Ibid., 224–225.

45. Jukka Häkkinen, Takashi Kawai, Jari Takatalo, Reiko Mitsuya, and Göte Nyman, "What Do People Look at When They Watch Stereoscopic Movies?," *Proceedings of SPIE* 7524, 75240E (2010), http://spiedigitallibrary.org/proceedings/resource/2/psisdg/7524/1/75240E_1?isAuthorized=no.

46. Argy, "An Eye-Popping Adventure," 67.

47. Jay Holben, "Conquering New Worlds," *American Cinematographer* (January 2010): 45.

48. Neuman, "*Bolt 3D*."

49. Rob Engle, "*Beowulf 3D*: A Case Study," *Proceedings of SPIE* 6803, 68030R (2008), http://spiedigitallibrary.org/proceedings/resource/2/psisdg/6803/1/68030R_1?isAuthorized=no.

50. Michael Goldman, "Down the Rabbit Hole," *American Cinematographer* (April 2010): 38.

51. Patrick L. Ogle, "Technological and Aesthetic Influences upon the Development of Deep Focus Cinematography in the United States," *Screen* 13 (Spring 1972): 65.

52. Gosser, *Selected Attempts at Stereoscopic Moving Pictures*, 302.

53. Christopher Probst, "Future Shock," *American Cinematographer* (August 1996): 41.

54. Tara Handy Turner, "Case Study—*Beauty and the Beast 3D*: Benefits of 3D Viewing for 2D to 3D Conversion," *Proceedings of SPIE* 7524, 75240B (2010), http://spiedigitallibrary.org/proceedings/resource/2/psisdg/7524/1/75240B_1?isAuthorized=no.

55. Pete Kozachik, "2 Worlds in 3 Dimensions," *American Cinematographer* (February 2009): 31.

56. John Calhoun, "Voyage to the Bottom of the Sea," *American Cinematographer* (March 2005): 69.

57. Engle, "*Beowulf 3D*."

58. Sebastian Sylwan, David MacDonald, and Jason Walter, "Stereoscopic CG Camera Rigs and Associated Metadata for Cinematic Production," *Proceedings of SPIE* 7237, 72370C (2009), http://spiedigitallibrary.org/proceedings/resource/2/psisdg/7237/1/72370C_1?isAuthorized=no.

CONCLUSION

1. Richard Allen, *Projecting Illusion: Film Spectatorship and the Impression of Reality* (New York: Cambridge University Press, 1995), 81.

2. Dan North, *Performing Illusions: Cinema, Special Effects and the Virtual Actor* (New York: Wallflower Press, 2008), 50.

3. Don Shay, Joe Fordham, and Jody Duncan, "State of the Art: A Cinefex 25th Anniversary Forum," *Cinefex* 100 (January 2005): 58.

4. Shilo T. McClean, *Digital Storytelling: The Narrative Power of Visual Effects in Film* (Cambridge, Mass.: MIT Press, 2007), 72.

5. Shay, Fordham, and Duncan, "State of the Art," 65.

6. Ibid., 67.

7. Ibid., 54.

8. Ibid., 103.

9. Ibid., 106. Emphasis in original.

10. Deborah Tudor, "Light Bouncing: Digital Processes Illuminate the Cultural Past," *Jump Cut*, http://www.ejumpcut.org/currentissue/deeDigitalCinematog/index.html.

11. Ibid.

12. Shay, Fordham, and Duncan, "State of the Art," 94.

13. Oliver Grau, *Virtual Art: From Illusion to Immersion* (Cambridge, Mass.: MIT Press, 2003), 343.

14. Ibid., 107.

INDEX

ABOUT THE AUTHOR

Stephen Prince is a professor of cinema at Virginia Tech and the author of *Firestorm: American Film in the Age of Terrorism* and *Classical Film Violence*, among many publications in film and media studies.